wh

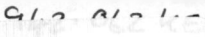

D0191435

RIDGE DANYERS - CHEADLE SITE

Bri P
 je ge *danyers*

HED T ES   BUCK

Rodne *Politics, Peoples and Government*
C. J. Bartlett   *Foreign Policy in the Twentieth Cen*
            Egenio Biagini   *Gladstone*
Jeremy Black   *Robert Walpole and the Nature of Politics in Early
                Eighteenth-Century Britain*
D. G. Boyce   *The Irish Question and British Politics, 1868–1996 (2nd edn)*
Keith M. Brown   *Kingdom or Province? Scotland and the Regal
                Union, 1603–1715*
A. D. Carr   *Medieval Wales*
Eveline Cruickshanks   *The Glorious Revolution*
Anne Curry   *The Hundred Years War*
John W. Derry   *British Politics in the Age of Fox, Pitt and Liverpool*
Susan Doran   *England and Europe in the Sixteenth Century*
Seán Duffy   *Ireland in the Middle Ages*
William Gibson   *Church, State and Society, 1760–1850*
David Gladstone   *The Twentieth-Century Welfare State*
Brian Golding   *Conquest and Colonisation: the Normans in Britain, 1066–1100*
Sean Greenwood   *Britain and the Cold War 1945–91*
S. J. Gunn   *Early Tudor Government, 1485–1558*
J. Gwynfor Jones   *Early Modern Wales, c.1525–1640*
Richard Harding   *The Evolution of the Sailing Navy, 1509–1815*
David Harkness   *Ireland in the Twentieth Century: Divided Island*
Ann Hughes   *The Causes of the English Civil War (2nd edn)*
Ronald Hutton   *The British Republic, 1649–1660*
Kevin Jefferys   *The Labour Party since 1945*
T. A. Jenkins   *Disraeli and Victorian Conservatism*
T. A. Jenkins   *Sir Robert Peel*
H. S. Jones   *Victorian Political Thought*
D. E. Kennedy   *The English Revolution 1642–1649*
D. M. Loades   *The Mid-Tudor Crisis, 1545–1565*
John F. McCaffrey   *Scotland in the Nineteenth Century*
Diarmaid MacCulloch   *The Later Reformation in England, 1547–1603*
W. David McIntyre   *British Decolonization, 1946–1997:
    When, Why and How did the British Empire Fall?*
A. P. Martinich   *Thomas Hobbes*
Roger Middleton   *The British Economy since 1945*
W. M. Ormrod   *Political Life in Medieval England, 1300–1450*
Richie Ovendale   *Anglo-American Relations in the Twentieth Century*
Ian Packer   *Lloyd George*
Keith Perry   *British Politics and the American Revolution*
Murray G. H. Pittock   *Jacobitism*
A. J. Pollard   *The Wars of the Roses*
David Powell   *British Politics and the Labour Question, 1868–1990*
David Powell   *The Edwardian Crisis*
Richard Rex   *Henry VIII and the English Reformation*
G. R. Searle   *The Liberal Party: Triumph and Disintegration, 1886–1929*

8

RIDGE DANYERS - CHEADLE SITE

* 0 0 0 2 1 3 6 8 *

John Stuart Shaw *The Political History of Eighteenth-Century Scotland*
W. M. Spellman *John Locke*
William Stafford *John Stuart Mill*
Robert Stewart *Party and Politics, 1830–1852*
Bruce Webster *Medieval Scotland*
Ann Williams *Kingship and Government in Pre-Conquest England*
John W. Young *Britain and European Unity, 1945–92*
Michael B. Young *Charles I*

Please note that a sister series, *Social History in Perspective*, is now available. It covers the key topics in social, cultural and religious history.

British History in Perspective
Series Standing Order
ISBN 0–333–71356–7 hardcover
ISBN 0–333–69331–0 paperback
(outside North America only)

You can receive future titles in this series as they are published by placing a standing order. Please contact your bookseller or, in case of difficulty, write to us at the address below with your name and address, the title of the series and the ISBN quoted above.

Customer Services Department, Macmillan Distribution Ltd
Houndmills, Basingstoke, Hampshire RG21 6XS, England

THE ENGLISH
REVOLUTION 1642–1649

D. E. KENNEDY

First Published in Great Britain 2000 by
MACMILLAN PRESS LTD
Houndmills, Basingstoke, Hampshire RG21 6XS
and London
Companies and representatives throughout the world

A catalogue record for this book is available from the British Library
ISBN: 0-333-63180-3

 First Published in the United States of America 2000 by
ST MARTIN'S PRESS, INC.,
Scholarly and Reference Division,
175 Fifth Avenue,
New York, N.Y. 10010
ISBN: 0-312-23063-X

Library of Congress Cataloging-in-Publication Data

Kennedy, D.E., 1928–
The English Revolution, 1642–1649/D.E. Kennedy.
    p.   cm. — (British history in perspective)
Includes bibliographical references and index.
ISBN 0-312-23063-X
1. Great Britain—History—Civil War, 1642–1649.   I. Title.   II. Series.

DA415.K+
942.06′2—dc21   99-055928

© D.E. Kennedy 2000

All rights reserved. No reproduction, copy or transmission of this publication may
be made without written permission.

No paragraph of this publication may be reproduced, copied or transmitted save
with written permission or in accordance with the provisions of the Copyright,
Designs and Patents Act 1988, or under the terms of any licence permitting
limited copying issued by the Copyright Licensing Agency, 90 Tottenham Court
Road, London W1P 0LP.

Any person who does any unauthorised act in relation to this publication may be
liable to criminal prosecution and civil claims for damages.

The author has asserted his right to be identified as the author of this work in
accordance with the Copyright, Designs and Patents Act 1988.

This book is printed on paper suitable for recycling and made from fully managed
and sustained forest sources.

10   9   8   7   6   5   4   3   2   1
09   08   07   06   05   04   03   02   01   00

Printed in Hong Kong

For my family

CONTENTS

ACKNOWLEDGEMENTS

I am grateful to the Publishers for the opportunity to write this book, and in particular to the General Series Editor, Jeremy Black, for his kindness and constructive suggestions. My thanks are also due to the University of Melbourne, for providing the context for me to teach and work in Tudor and Stuart history for many years. Among my colleagues and friends I wish particularly to acknowledge Laurie Gardiner, with whom I taught and fought over three decades during which seventeenth-century studies occupied a vital place in the arts faculty at the University of Melbourne. I am grateful to my students, who brought their own intellectual passion to the period and several of whom, like John Adamson, Patricia Crawford, Wilfrid Prest, John Reeve and Alexandra Walsham, have made distinguished contributions to scholarship in this field. Finally, my thanks are due to my daughters, Sarah, Liza and Susannah and my son Roderick and to my wife Bev who has supported me and my work beyond all deserving.

INTRODUCTION

January 30, 1999 marked the 350th anniversary of the execution of King Charles I. Although the execution and the events leading up to it are far distant, they continue to capture the political and historical imaginations of people in England and abroad. Every year, individuals and amateur societies, such as the Society of King Charles the Martyr, lay wreaths at the base of the equestrian statue of King Charles I in London on the anniversary of his execution. Similar floral tributes to the Puritan regiments can be found at the base of the memorial plinth at Edgehill, on the anniversary of the battle in 1642. For a third group, Burford Church in Oxfordshire, where the Leveller mutineers were shot in 1649, is the place of pilgrimage. The victor of course needs no memorial. Parliament's place in the governance of England and its permanency as an institution of government are the lasting legacy of the Civil War. While this commands little commemorative emotion, our sense of Parliament being somewhat jaded from long association, the Civil War was a battle against autocracy by a coalition of parties determined to entrench the Parliamentary system and in some cases to affirm its democratic basis.

The variety of parties and interests gives a unique flavour to these years. Early in the 1640s, paper battle-lines were drawn between King and Parliament. Between 1629 and 1640 the King had exercised his prerogative not to summon a Parliament and had ruled in his own person, on the advice of a Privy Council of his own appointees. This period of 'personal rule', which the Whig tradition of liberal historiography has styled the 'eleven years' tyranny', commenced with the dissolution of Parliament in 1629 and the imprisonment of its leaders. Between 1625 and 1629 the King had precipitately dissolved three parliaments – summoning them when in fiscal need and dissolving them when they became

1

defiant in matters of policy. In 1628 Parliament enacted the *Petition of Right*, setting out what it saw as the rights and privileges of Parliament as against the Crown, particularly in fiscal matters. The *Petition* was a response to the King's attempt to raise 'forced loans' from local gentry, to free himself from dependency on Parliamentary appropriations. In 1625, the Commons had voted to grant the King 'tonnage and poundage' (the proceeds of taxes on trade) on an annual basis rather than for his lifetime, according to custom. When, early in 1629, the King sent an order to the House dissolving the Parliament, the Commons resisted, and two men held the Speaker in his seat to prevent him rising to acknowledge the end of the term while three emergency resolutions were rushed through. These resolutions proclaimed as enemies of the Kingdom and Commonwealth, first, any person promoting popery or Arminianism (neo-Catholicism) in the English Church; second, any person collaborating in the collection of tonnage and poundage which was not authorized by Parliament; and third, any merchant or person paying such tonnage and poundage when not authorized by Parliament.[1] They represent the core items of Parliament's dispute with the King: the religious question, the authority of Parliament in fiscal matters and the King's accountability to Parliament, which was to be achieved through fiscal dependency. For his part, the King in his *Declaration to all his Loving Subjects of the Causes which moved him to dissolve the last Parliament* (10 March 1629) referred to the Parliament's 'innovations (which we will never permit again)' which were designed 'to erect an universal over-swaying power to themselves, which belongs only to us and not to them'. He went on to allege the existence of 'secret designs . . . which were only to cast our affairs into a desperate condition, to abate the powers of our Crown, and to bring our government into obloquy, that in the end all things may be overwhelmed with anarchy and confusion'.[2]

Sir John Eliot, one of the imprisoned leaders, became the martyr of the 1629 Parliament when he died in the Tower of London in 1632. John Hampden continued its fight by mounting a legal challenge in 1637 to the King's levy of 'ship money', a peacetime tax imposed in lieu of the obligations of ports and maritime counties to provide the King with ships in times of national emergency. During the personal rule, Charles enlarged the levy and applied it universally to the point where ship money was costing the kingdom nearly £200 000 a year. This challenge exposed divisions among the judiciary, who only narrowly (7:5) held the King to possess the necessary authority to levy the tax. As the judgment of each judge was delivered over a space of time, the King's authority in the matter was publicly seen to be held in the balance.

However, the major challenge to the personal rule came in 1637 when Charles and Archbishop Laud together tried to impose a prayer book, and a liturgy, upon the Scottish Church (or kirk). The Scots reacted in February 1638 by taking a national oath – the Scottish National Covenant – to preserve the 'true Christian faith' of Presbyterianism against attack and by taking to the streets in widespread rioting. When his attempts to quell the Scottish riots failed, and Scotland raised an army, the King lacked money to support his own army and was forced to sign a truce (the Treaty of Berwick). Charles then summoned Parliament in order to demand supply for a renewed war. He wanted money, not words. But after a decade without a voice, and in an environment of grievance at the burden of the King's taxes, Parliament was more interested in settling grievances than obliging the King's purse. The Parliament which met on 13 April 1640 was dissolved at the King's pleasure on 5 May of the same year and has become known as the Short Parliament.

The Earl of Strafford, the King's Lord Deputy of Ireland, advocated a resumption of the war against Scotland, if necessary using the Irish army. But before the Irish army could be brought to England, the Scots invaded, leaving Charles again in a position of having to sue for peace. Under the Treaty of Ripon the King incurred a daily fee to be paid to the Scots until such time as a permanent peace settlement was reached. As security for payment, the Scots continued to occupy the northern counties of Durham and Northumberland. The King was again under pressure to summon a Parliament to raise money to meet this predicament. He tried to avoid it by calling a Great Council of Peers, 70 or 80 of whom responded, but only to resolve upon an interim settlement until a Parliament could be called. Calling a Parliament was inescapable.

The Long Parliament, as it became known, met from 3 November 1640 until the execution of the King in 1649 and beyond. It secured its position by passing the Act Against Dissolving the Long Parliament Without Its Own Consent, on 10 May 1641. On 12 May, the Earl of Strafford was executed for high treason pursuant to an Act of Attainder, which condemned him for trying to 'introduce an arbitrary and tyrannical government', exercising an 'exorbitant power' and allegedly being prepared to use his Irish army against the King's other subjects. Over the months of June and July Parliament passed a series of Acts designed to abolish the instruments of the King's personal rule. It did away with the Star Chamber and the Court of High Commission, and made it virtually impossible for the King to raise money through taxes without Parliament's consent.

Being financially powerless, Charles could do little but accept these statutory revisions, which cost him political power. His resentment of the process was epitomized in his attempt (in early January 1642) to arrest five leading members of his Parliamentary opposition on charges of high treason. By the time Charles arrived at the House of Commons, the five had disappeared. Parliament subsequently adjourned its sittings to the Guildhall, before returning to sit at Westminster under the guardianship of the London citizen militia (known as the Trained Bands). The King fled London on 10 January for Hampton Court and Windsor, where he began preparations for the military recovery of his kingdom. The geographical separation of King and Parliament manifested and dramatized the extent of their political alienation.

Before the King's departure, news of the Irish rebellion, which had broken out on 23 October 1641, reached London and caused enormous fear among English Protestants and a call for the rebellion to be put down. But Parliament was apprehensive about raising an army in the name of the King when the King was at loggerheads with Parliament. An army would not only increase the King's power, but might be directed against Parliament itself. Thus, from the start, the possibility that an army might become a third force in a hitherto two-party conflict was recognized and caused hesitation about summoning it.

Until the New Model Army came into being in 1645, troops in England were mustered by local gentry or sheriffs as need required. They were organized much like a home guard that could be pressed or levied into service, generally on the basis of personal and regional loyalties.[3] One did not join *the* Army: after 1643 one was likely to be conscripted into one of many local militias whose soldiers were without a standard uniform and perhaps without settled loyalties. Initially, therefore, the Royalist and Parliamentarian forces were patchwork armies, without strong cohesion and often lacking a developed sense of identity outside their county identities. But insofar as the Royalists and Parliamentarians concentrated their recruitment in areas thought to be politically sympathetic, their armies had an ideological core. Repeated battles where the issue was King against Parliament entrenched these ideologies and on the Parliamentarian side transformed the army ethos, as Puritans who were well-represented among the leadership brought their particular logic and spiritual passion to the business of warfare.

With its Royalist members absent in arms for the King, Parliament in 1643 purchased Scottish military assistance by accepting a Presbyterian model for the English Church: mirror-imaging Charles's earlier attempt to impose episcopacy upon Scotland. The vehicle for this agreement was the Solemn League and Covenant, which bound soldiers in the Parliamentarian Army to solidarity with the Presbyterian cause. In 1644, a cleric produced a pamphlet called *The Souldiers' Catechisme* to indoctrinate the ordinary soldiers. In the question-and-answer format of the traditional Christian catechism, it asked 'Is it not a lamentable thing that Christians of the same nation should imbrue [stain] their hands in one another's blood?' and answers:

> I confess it is, but as the case now stands there is an inevitable and absolute necessity of fighting laid upon the good people of the land. . . . We are not now to look at our enemies as countrymen or kinsmen or fellow-Protestants, but rather as enemies of God and our religion and siders with Anti-Christ, and so our eye is not to pity them nor our sword to spare them.[4]

The last sentence is a quotation from the Book of Jeremiah, 48:10. The Puritan Bible, the Geneva Bible, had a gloss on that text which said 'Cursed be he that doeth the work of the Lord with negligence and cursed be he who keepeth his sword from blood'. It was all too easy for radical Protestantism to convert the Christian duty of constant spiritual vigilance and warfare against evil into a duty to engage in physical and political violence. To Puritans, the Civil War became not so much a war fought against the King's temporal power, but a struggle against 'Popish malignants, atheists [and] siders with Antichrist', easily identified as the King's allies, given the King's support for bishops who hindered reformation and upheld popish ceremonies, his Catholic queen, his assault on Scotland's 'true church' and his negotiations with the Irish Catholic rebels.

Herein lies the strangeness of the war to the modern sensibility (although militant Islamic fundamentalism has made 'holy warfare' more familiar than it used to be). The New Model Army held prayer meetings before going into action and mercilessly scrutinized its deeds, motives and outcomes in an attempt to distinguish its mortal and carnal desires for success and glory and its own political ambitions from the 'higher purpose' of which it believed it was the appointed instrument. For soldiers who had '[p]ut on the whole armour of God . . . to stand against the wiles of the devil',[5] the devil was certain to be visible, but he was also known to be deceptive.

A second curiosity of the early years of the Civil War is the claim by all parties to stand for conservative values. The seventeenth century did not share our nineteenth-century legacy of a linear model of social progress.

Its understanding of social patterns was based on an Aristotelian cycle of gold, silver and iron ages, where the values of the past were both restored and enriched by recurrence. 'Revolution' had a meaning conditioned by that context – what we call 'revolution' was 'rebellion' and was regarded as 'the first and greatest and very root of all other sins'.[6] Its archetype was Satan's rebellion against God. Both King and Parliament took up arms to maintain what each believed to be the ancient English constitution and a political system derived from scripture. To the Royalists, the Crown was the fountain of the law and the King was the agent and embodiment of divine authority. It was he whom God had appointed to rule and protect his subjects and his will must prevail. The Puritans adopted rival scriptural authority, casting the King as a tyrant and later as traitor and 'man of blood'. They did not deny the sanctity of the office of King; but this King – Charles Stuart – must be purged as unworthy of the office. Along with the Levellers, although with a different emphasis, they sought a 'return' to laws, institutions and codes of behaviour which they imputed to the past. Again with parallels to Islamic militants, they were in their own eyes revolutionary conservatives.

The growth of Puritan and Leveller sentiment within the Army and its transformation into a standing army capable of resisting the order to disband are among the key developments traced in this book. The period with which it deals ends with the Army in control of Parliament to ensure the execution of the King. This was an extraordinary step for people who in 1642 still asserted that they were fighting for both King and Parliament. The book traces how this extraordinary step came to be taken. It also examines the paradoxical impact of army militancy in liberalizing discourse, even as the Army's increasingly radical platform was implemented at the point of the sword. To its civilian Leveller allies, this meant wrestling with the age-old paradoxes of whether to support a violent means to a peace and whether to entrust a democratic dream to military might. For the other distinctive feature of these years is the emergence of a political language which surfaces from an oral culture in which an idealized version of pre-Conquest England stood for lost constitutional rights and ancient egalitarianism. This is the language of the 'poorest he', laying claim to political rights. It was a language to which elements in both Parliament and the Army were attracted, partly because of its usefulness in imputing sovereignty to 'the people', but it also threatened those institutions by requiring that they become democratic.

In our post-colonial age, with its preoccupation with self-determination and human rights, renewed interest in the voices for radical constitutional change is to be expected. We tune our ears somewhat differently from the historians of the past and hear familiar music made strange by distance. We look at factions and interplay rather than those great opposites starkly displayed in Victorian narrative painting: Cavalier and Roundhead, aristocrat and non-aristocrat, tradition and change, vulnerability and destructiveness, silk and steel. Civil War subjects no longer adorn the walls of the Royal Academy as they did in profusion between 1820 and 1900, when the contrasting persons of Charles I and Cromwell conveyed the Victorians' fear of convulsive change and their sentimentalization of monarchy and family.[7] At the same time, we are not as unreservedly sure as a post-revolutionary French writer that the Roundheads 'struggled for liberty against absolute power, for equality against privilege, for progressive and general interests'.[8] The end of the Cold War has made us sceptical of strong, simplistic contrasts. But in examining the Civil War it is impossible entirely to avoid the great political divide demonstrated by the rival declarations of the Rump Parliament, which abolished the monarchy and dismissed the Lords, and the Convention Parliament of 1660 which reinstated them.

The Rump Parliament 'found by experience that the office of a King in this nation and Ireland, and to have the power thereof in any single person, is unnecessary, burdensome and dangerous to the liberty, safety and public interest of the people'.[9] The Convention Parliament, after little more than a decade, declared that 'according to the ancient and fundamental laws of this Kingdom, the Government is, and ought to be, by King, Lords and Commons'.[10] These are irreconcilable interpretations of the same mass of political and historical evidence. A similar opposition in vantage-point and perception appears in the rival accounts of King Charles in the *Eikon Basilike. The Povrtraictvre of his Sacred Majestie in His Solitudes and Sufferings* – which, as the title suggests, casts Charles iconographically as a Christ-figure, laying down his life for England – and in John Milton's *Eikonoklastes* (idol-breaking) desanctifying the would-be martyr and saint.[11]

The official version of English history encourages a more unitary view. At the Restoration the commencement of Charles II's reign was back-dated to Charles I's death in 1649 to create a fiction of continuous royalist history. The official volumes of the Statutes of the Realm excluded all of the legislation passed by the Commonwealth in its 11-year history. The 'Glorious Revolution' of 1688–9 – which was neither glorious nor a revolution – was pasted over the earlier, bloodier and more revolutionary episode to make England's copy-book look clean. But a study of the period exposes the rift of the great divide within this comfortable pretence to unity.

It is not only the protagonists and their causes who fall to one or other side of the divide, but also students and historians in giving an account of the period. It is impossible to tell the story with complete impartiality. The King cannot be both a martyr and a man of blood. Both perspectives can be respected in those who own them. But the subject matter demands a third-party expression of allegiance, conscious or otherwise, in the professional historical witness. Allegiances are undoubtedly qualified by historical distance and the demands of professionalism, enabling the historian to recognize both the King's duplicity and disguised intransigence and the Puritans' harshness and violence in prosecuting what they convinced themselves was God's cause. But one cannot be engaged with the period and adopt a fully neutral stance because the issues it raises remain fundamental to our political selfhood: whether we are monarchists or republicans, conservatives, progressives or radical activists; whether we respond most to Charles I's mournful face, epitomizing the plight of monarchy, aristocracy and the traditional order or to the commoners' somewhat forced cry of joy at the 'first year of freedom, by God's blessing restored'.[12]

Generally speaking, the Royalists appear to have emerged victorious.[13] In the general culture, the 'Puritan Revolution' is associated with pious cant, religious oppression, sexual repression and English liberty under military rule. Charles I appears as the Renaissance chevalier, patron of the Arts, family man and kingly martyr. Even the significance of the Civil War and regicide has been cast into shadow, with conservative historians labelling the episode merely 'the Great Rebellion' and left-wing historians regarding it as a revolution that remained incomplete. To the Marxist historian Christopher Hill,[14] the Civil War and regicide was a political revolution that bypassed the social revolution that should have accompanied it. It shifted political power from the Crown and the court aristocracy to the Parliamentary gentry claiming to speak on behalf of 'the people'. Like the later French and Russian revolutions, it was an assault upon an *ancien régime* which was standing in the path of progress. But it was what Marxists call a 'bourgeois revolution' in that it merely transferred power between factions of the ruling class without significantly altering the social fabric. Human rights, the voice and role of the disfranchised underclass, even the hegemony of the *ancien régime*, hardly began to be articulated as compared with later revolutionary movements which focused on the proletariat.

But the events of 1642–9 nevertheless wrought what Ronald Hutton has described as 'the most drastic changes to have occurred in the English state since its appearance': so as 'amply [to] deserve the name of the "English Revolution", in the sense that the landmarks of national politics had been almost completely altered'.[15] While the experiment of the Commonwealth lasted only 11 years and must be considered a failure, the Civil War opened a door which can never be closed quite shut, and through which we see fascinating glimpses of a nation reshaping itself, reinterpreting its pre-Norman past and debating its future and the fate of its King. It is a world whose characters speak a dialect of our own language, both familiar and strange, and whose actions are part of a drama of extraordinary moral import and emotional (and spiritual) intensity. Once encountered, the speeches, proclamations, declarations and admonitions of this period reverberate in the mind, as do the rival images from Milton and Marvell: Milton's Fairfax, whose 'firm unshaken Valour ever brings/Victory home, while new Rebellions raise',[16] and Marvell's Charles I, 'the Royal Actor born/The Tragic Scaffold might adorn' who 'nothing common did or mean/Upon that memorable Scene'.[17]

But, as there is nothing so moving or compelling that it cannot be seen more detachedly, so the last word here is given to Sir Edward Nicholas, the King's Principal Secretary and one of the commissioners at Uxbridge, who encapsulated the social disorder preceding the regicide in the following words:

> The King raised a Parliament he could not rule, and the Parliament raised an Army it cannot rule, and the Army has raised Agitators they cannot rule, and the Agitators are setting up the People whom they will be unable to rule.[18]

In fact, 1649 brought military control rather than chaos. But the contemporary perception of what had occurred was that the world had been 'turned upside down'. The King was executed in 1649 and in 1653 Cromwell became the 'Lord Protector'. It is to the process of that inversion that we now turn.

1

THE WAR FOR KING AND PARLIAMENT, 1642–6

The Threshold of War

The King's war against the Scots, conducted during his period of personal rule without Parliament, did not receive the support of the Short Parliament when finally summoned. One of the grievances that lay behind the Long Parliament's Act of Attainder against Strafford was that the King had been induced to wage war on Scotland on the promise of support from the Irish (and Catholic) Army. The Long Parliament called the Scots their 'brethren' and described the war against Scotland disparagingly as the 'Bishops' War': a war fought on behalf of episcopacy, with its echoes of popery, against the Scottish Church to which most Puritan Parliamentarians looked as the model reformed church. When combined with the Irish rebellion, the Bishops' War triggered Puritan paranoia about popish conspiracies to overwhelm Protestantism in the three kingdoms. It was not difficult to feel paranoid when Europe was already experiencing the convulsions of a thirty years' war between Catholics and Protestants. As time went by, Puritans began to suspect that the King himself might be implicated in the conspiracy – if not by design, at least through the influence of 'evil counsel'.

By the end of December 1641 the atmosphere in London was extremely tense, thanks in part to exaggerated rumours of massacres of Protestants in Ireland and of a plot for a general Catholic uprising. This coincided with the Long Parliament's counter-offensive to the Bishops' War, which took the form of a proposal to remodel the English Church along Scottish lines and replace episcopacy with a Presbyterian form of church government. As part of this offensive, and to highlight its considerable concern over the direction Charles I appeared to be taking, on 1 December 1641 Parliament presented the King with a lengthy 'declaration of the state of the kingdom' known as the Grand Remonstrance. This was delivered 'without the least intention to lay any blemish upon [the King's] royal person, but only to represent how [his] royal authority and trust have been abused, to the great prejudice and danger of [his] Majesty, and of all [his] good subjects'.[1] This abuse of trust was attributed to 'malignant parties, whose proceedings evidently appear to be mainly for the advantage and increase of Popery'. These were enumerated as '1. The Jesuited Papists . . . 2. The Bishops and the corrupt part of the Clergy . . . 3. Such Councillors and Courtiers as . . . have engaged themselves to further the interests of some foreign princes or states'.[2] The result was

a most dangerous division and chargeable preparation for war betwixt your kingdoms of England and Scotland, the increase of jealousies betwixt your Majesty and your most obedient subjects, the violent distraction and interruption of this Parliament, the insurrection of the Papists in your Kingdom of Ireland, and bloody massacre of your people.[3]

To quell this danger, the King was invited to concur with Parliament in three matters: reducing the power and influence of the bishops and removing 'oppressive and unnecessary ceremonies' from the Church; appointing to positions of high office and private trust only those in whom Parliament expressed confidence; and retaining for the public benefit any lands forfeited to the Crown as a result of the Irish rebellion to defray the costs to the kingdom of England. Not content to leave it there, the document then gave a protracted account of the 'root and growth' of the alleged conspiracy by imputing to it the 'continual differences and discontents between the King and the people, upon questions of prerogative and liberty', the King's disaffection from Parliament in turning to other sources of supply and the suppression of 'the purity and power of religion'. It then narrated the history of the King's reign (then some 16 years) in more than 200 numbered paragraphs, highlighting instances where Parliament considered the King to have misgoverned the kingdoms as a result of this malign influence. The catalogue included: the dissolution of various Parliaments and the imprisoning of MPs; 'unjust and pernicious' attempts to extort great sums from his subjects through taxes and excises and imposts such as the infamous 'ship money'; assumption of lands and enlargement of the King's forests (contrary to statute); permitting officialdom (including the Courts) to act grossly in excess of jurisdiction; attempting to press new canons and a new liturgy upon Scotland to reduce the Scots to 'such Popish superstitions and innovations as might make them apt to join with England in that great change which was intended'; going to war with the Scots and seeking to engage the whole kingdom in a quarrel of Archbishop Laud's and the Earl of Strafford's making; and attempting to involve the King's army against the Parliament. Some of the King's actions were applauded as having temporarily thwarted the papists' designs, and a defence and justification of Parliament's ordinances (for example, the Act preventing its dissolution without its consent) was included for good measure.

It was not a document likely to please the King, especially when Parliament took the liberty of publishing it before the King had opportunity to reply. In answer (on 23 December), the King commented on the 'desires of great moment' contained in the petition and the 'declaration of a very unusual nature annexed thereto'.[4] He also pronounced himself 'very sensible of the disrespect' shown by Parliament's having sent the document 'abroad in print, by directions from your House as appears from the printed copy'. He clearly saw that resolution for what it was: the start of a propaganda war, in which the communications between King and Parliament were produced more in the hope of enlisting public support than of eliciting a response from the addressee. Labelling the declaration 'unparliamentary', he chose to address only the opening petition and gave an answer both circumspect and politic. Not acknowledging the alleged 'malignant party' and being certain of the integrity of his advisers, he was nevertheless happy to consider specific evidence of abuse of trust in a particular case. With respect to church ceremonies he would call a national synod to examine 'such ceremonies as give just cause for offence', but he believed that no church on earth professed the 'true religion with more purity of doctrine than the Church of England'. As to the appointment of persons, it was 'the undoubted right of the Crown of England' to make appointments without interference, but he would take care to appoint those against whom there could be 'no just cause of exception'. With regard to the Irish lands, it was premature to consider their disposition when the rebellion had not yet run its course. More subtle than his adversaries, the barb was set in the middle of his reply, where he promised to defend the Church not only against all invasions of Popery, but also from the irreverence of those many schismatics and separatists, wherewith of late this kingdom and this city abounds, to the great dishonour and hazard both of Church and State, for the suppression of whom we require your timely aid and active assistance.[5]

The King's seeming restraint, his regal and reasonable manner, barely conceal his intense mistrust of and scorn for the Parliament. In fact, he was adopting what was to be a characteristic course of action: weaving words of loose reassurance and clever reservation while preparing for action. On the same day as he made reply, he appointed Sir Thomas Lunsford Lieutenant of the Tower – a sign of his intention to proceed against the Parliamentary leaders. On 3 January 1642, officers acting in accordance with a King's warrant attended Parliament and demanded that it deliver to them five named members of the House of Commons and one from the Lords to face charges of high treason: a request which Parliament refused as unconstitutional, being a direct breach of privilege. The King attended personally on the following day with an armed force estimated at 500 to apprehend the members and if necessary suppress Parliamentary resistance. While the forewarned members had absented themselves with Parliament's blessing and a violent confrontation was averted, this episode clearly demonstrated the King's preparedness to proceed violently against Parliament, both individually and collectively. It was the point of real rupture in the relations between King and Parliament. Parliament denounced the invasion of its premises and privileges as a 'traitorous design' and declared any person who arrested the five members pursuant to the King's warrant a 'public enemy of the commonwealth' and any person who protected or harboured them as entitled to the privileges and protection of Parliament.

On 10 January 1642, the King left London, which had become unsafe for him, with mixed intentions to raise a militia for his own protection and to increase his might and therefore his hand in dealing with Parliament. Thomas May noted that the Grand Remonstrance had been a watershed in the events leading directly towards war:

At this time began that fatal breach between King and Parliament to appear visibly, and wax daily wider, never to be closed, until the whole Kingdom was, by sad degrees, brought into a ruinous War . . . those Paper-contestations became a fatal Prologue to that bloody and unnatural War which afterward ensued.[6]

Preparations for War

After the King left London, there was still communication between King and Parliament. On 13 February Charles I gave his assent to what proved to be the last two Acts of his reign, passed with the full imprimatur of King, Lords and Commons. These were the Act taking away the right of the bishops to vote in the House of Lords and removing them from secular office (in accordance with the first of the Remonstrance petitions) and the Impressment Act to conscript troops for service against the rebels in Ireland. The Impressment Act raised the inevitable question of who was to command the Army and in particular who was to appoint the commanders, and thereby command its loyalty. To gain control, Parliament claimed the right to appoint the Lords Lieutenant of the counties, who headed the local militia in peacetime. When the King refused, Parliament passed the Militia Ordinance on 5 March, making the appointments and issuing the necessary commissions without him.

Parliament justified this radical decision as an initiative to ensure the security of the King's person and of Parliament and the kingdom following a 'desperate design upon the House of Commons, which we have just cause to believe to be an effect of the bloody counsels of papists and other ill-affected persons'.[7] From York on 27 May the King issued a proclamation condemning the Militia Ordinance as contrary to precedent and 'against the peace of this our kingdom'.[8] His delayed rejoinder offered Parliament a considerable advantage in its recruiting drive. It was not until June that Charles issued his Commissions of Array, mustering the trained and freehold bands of the towns and counties and authorizing his commissioners to suppress any opposition they encountered. Parliament was quick to reject the proclamation and enlarged its claims dramatically by declaring itself to be a High Court of law and council, able to exercise the King's supreme and royal pleasure in a 'more eminent and obligatory manner than it can be by personal act or resolution of his own', even under the Great Seal.[9] This last provision was a significant and necessary claim, since in May 1642 Lord Keeper Littleton had surreptitiously dispatched the Great Seal to the King and shortly after followed it himself to Oxford.

The summary removal of the Great Seal from London to Oxford threw Parliament's administration of justice and conduct of its executive responsibilities into disarray at a critical time. No writs could be issued for the election of members, no commissions for the assizes could be completed, without the formal affixing of the Great Seal. The 'mysterious efficacy' of the Great Seal in the minds of English lawyers made it (in Henry Hallam's words) 'the depository of the royal authority in a higher degree than the person of the king'. As Clarendon wrote of this legal *coup*, the loss of the Great Seal caused the Parliament 'much trouble' and 'the confusion in both Houses was very great'. A Parliamentary warrant was issued for the apprehension of the Lord Keeper 'as had been in the case of the foulest felon or murderer'. It was 'dispersed by expresses over all the Kingdom with great haste'.[10]

It was necessary, therefore, for the Parliament after May 1642 to enunciate very firmly indeed the high principles of its executive authority, to counterbalance the loss of the Great Seal, and to contemplate in due course the need to produce its own Great Seal. By mid-1643, Parliament, after some months of hesitation from the Lords, produced its own symbol of sovereign authority. The King in turn issued a proclamation in November 1643 condemning the 'Counterfeit Great Seale' which had been 'traiterously made . . . by the two pretended Houses of Parliament'.[11] The problems arising from the existence of two competing great seals, each laying a claim to sovereignty, were manifest in the peace proposals put forward during the Civil War. The rival claims to sovereignty – that is, to supreme and exclusive power – made political compromise by either party virtually impossible. Had the political dichotomy not been conceptualized in this way, it might have been possible for the warring camps to have achieved some form of power-sharing arrangement.

The Nineteen Propositions which it sent to the King at York shortly after losing custody of the Great Seal show Parliament's determination to exercise its control over the key matters and resources of government. The King condemned the Propositions as 'too much in the style, not only of equals, but of conquerors'. He thought they proposed a 'total subversion of the fundamental laws' which in the event would enable the common people to 'set up for themselves, call parity and independence liberty'.

Looking along the path that Parliament had mapped out for him in the Nineteen Propositions, Charles foresaw England's 'splendid' frame of government ending in a 'dark, equal chaos of confusion, and the long line of our many noble ancestors in a Jack Cade or a Wat Tyler' (Cade and Tyler had led peasant revolts in 1450 and 1381 respectively).[12] This royal nightmare of revolution was matched in Parliamentarians by a premonition of apocalyptic catastrophe. 'In the way we are', Sir Benjamin Rudyard told the Commons in early July, 'we have gone as far as words can carry Us: We have voted our own Rights and the King's Duty', while the Kingdom stands amazed 'in fearful Expectation of dismal Calamities to fall upon it'.[13] The anxieties and confusions of the summer of 1642 are paradoxical. The civil war in prospect was being widely denounced in our modern sense of being 'condemned', while simultaneously being denounced in the seventeenth-century sense of being promulgated.

The Essex clergyman and Parliamentary supporter, Ralph Josselin, narrates that in midsummer of 1642, before any official declaration of war, 'we began to raise private arms . . . and the King was beginning to raise an army'. Having 'encouraged others to go forth', he was disconcerted when 'poor people in tumults arose and plundered divers houses, papists' and others, and threatened to go farther', whereupon he endeavoured to suppress their zeal 'by private and public means'.[14] Like his King, he had no desire to see the common people 'set up for themselves'. Similarly, Thomas May – Parliament's official chronicler of these events – reports with dismay the first sparks of civil unrest. He writes of the Militia Ordinance and the Commissions of Array 'justling together almost in every County':

> . . . the greatest of the English Nobility on both sides appearing personally, to seize upon those places which were deputed to them either by the King or by the Parliament. No Ordinances from the One, or Proclamations from the Other, could now give any further stop to this general and spreading Mischief. God was not pleased that one Chimney should contain this Civil fire; but small sparks of it were daily kindling in every part of the Land.[15]

May's description uncannily foreshadows Samuel Pepys's later record of the physical catastrophe of the Great Fire, area upon area igniting at random and a whole civil fabric coming to grief.

May also pinpoints the disjunction between the protracted and portentous paper warfare between King and Parliament and the sporadic and contingent nature of the growing physical violence: 'long and tedious Paper-conflicts of Declarations, Petitions, and Proclamations, . . . turn[ing] into actual and bloody Wars, and the Pens seconded by drawn swords'. The measured and leisurely paper exchanges lagged behind the political developments they were designed to control. While the Commissions of Array and Militia Ordinance by which individual noblemen and gentlemen were drafted into service might seem formally coherent, the assumption of allegiances was *ad hoc*, unpredictable, and often purely fortuitous. Hence the small sparks and fires: street skirmishes and localized struggles between individuals and groups calling themselves or being called Royalists and Parliamentarians, Cavaliers and Roundheads, without wider co-ordination or strategy.

In the process of gathering munitions prior to the raising of the militias by commission or ordinance there were two major prizes: the naval fleet and the port of Hull. The latter contained a '*Magazine of Arms of the King's for sixteen thousand Men, with Ammunition proportionable*'.[16] This meant, in contemporary terms, sufficient supply for an army.

Every year the fleet patrolled English waters twice, once in summer and once in winter. The political crisis in England and Ireland did not interrupt arrangements for the summer patrol of 1642. The Commander of the Fleet in the immediately preceding years, the Earl of Northumberland, was indisposed in 1642 and a replacement had to be chosen. As early as March, both King and Parliament proposed their choice of naval commander. Charles chose an Elizabethan veteran, Sir John Pennington, born about 1568, who had served under Sir Walter Raleigh. Pennington was to remain in nominal command of the Royalist fleet until his death in 1645. Parliament selected the Earl of Warwick, a Parliamentarian of Puritan persuasion. The King allowed the respective nominations to remain in limbo until, in June, an incident at sea brought the issue back in focus. Charles then attempted to take command of the situation by ordering Pennington to take up his commission. Clarendon recounts that 'many men wondered [the King] neglected [the matter] so long'.[17]

Pennington's attempt to take up his commission was ill-fated. Charles had failed to note the depth of the seamen's commitment to the Parliamentary cause arising from his own treatment of them. They were unpaid for long periods and punished when they rioted to obtain their entitlements. They were at times confined aboard ship, fed rotten provisions and generally abused and neglected. When in January the King had attempted to arrest the Five Members of the House of Commons, the seamen of London rallied to protect that 'great vessel, the parliament-house'. A contemporary naval pamphlet, rare at that time and known as *The Seamans Protestation*, records the unprecedented political action of the seamen 'Ebbing and Flowing to and from the Parliament House at Westminster'. On 4 July, from his Majesty's ship and Pennington's old flagship, the *James*, in the Downs, Warwick reported to the Parliamentary leader John Pym that he had gained control of the fleet, having overcome some resistance without bloodshed and notwithstanding letters from the King discharging him from command. Warwick's letter seeking Parliament's indemnity for the rebellious seamen manifests a concern for the seamen's welfare, which was a reason they had rallied behind him.[18]

The loss of the bulk of the Navy was acknowledged by Clarendon to be 'of unspeakable ill consequence to the King's affairs, and made his condition much the less considered by his allies and neighbour princes' – naval power at that time being the prime symbol of national power and sovereignty and a major source of England's influence in foreign affairs.[19] At a more practical and local level, Parliament obtained a hold over the external lines of communication for the duration of the war in England, as well as effective means to sustain its loyal outpost ports, like Hull and Plymouth, against land-based Royalist assaults.

The magazine at Hull, sufficient to supply an army, drew the parties into a contest important for both its practical and theoretical consequences. Fearing that the King would seize upon the great magazine, Parliament wanted it transported to the Tower of London, whence it could readily be dispatched to Ireland. The King returned an unusually prompt denial to this request.[20] In January, Parliament had taken the precaution of appointing one of its members, Sir John Hotham, to secure the magazine and town, instructing him not to deliver them without the King's authority as expressed by the Lords and Commons in Parliament. The Member who had been deputed to convey the order was Hotham's son, also John, who departed the chamber enthusiastically: *'Mr Speaker! fall back! fall edge! I will go down, and perform your commands'.*[21] This was the prologue to a tragic history of changed loyalties, as by January 1645 both father and son, each attempting to bargain for his life against the other, were shot by Parliament for treason.

On 23 April, Charles I arrived outside Hull with an entourage. He was rebuffed by Sir John Hotham in the first overt act of military rebellion against the King. Hotham was thereupon proclaimed a traitor. Parliament in turn declared this proclamation of treason against a servant of Parliament performing the King's commission under Parliamentary authority to be a high breach of constitutional propriety. Parliament vigorously defended its servant and its own position in the paper combat which followed, in order that 'all the World may judg where the Fault is; although we must avow, that there can be no competent Judg of this, or any the like Cause, but a Parliament'.[22]

This debate was more emphatically addressed to the nation at large than to the opposite party. It was so prolix that John Rushworth, Parliamentary Secretary and contemporary historian, relegated some of it to an appendix to his *Historical Collections*. In contrast to the formal messages and propositions between King and Parliament, these declarations and counter-declarations are heated in tone, to inflame the sympathies of their true audience. Perhaps for this reason the debate rapidly expanded beyond the specific situation at Hull to include arguments whose radical potential, as a theory of civil government, is evident. Although, in the traditional manner, much attention is given to formal precedents, arguments employing more expansive principles of constitutional behaviour assume a dominant role. The King attributes to Parliament the doctrine 'That no Precedents can be Limits to bound their Proceedings: So they may do what they please'. Parliament, rejecting what the King had allegedly laid down for principle, throws down the challenge: 'who doubts but that a Parliament may dispose of anything wherein his Majesty or any Subject hath a Right, in such a way, as that the Kingdom may not be exposed to Hazard or Danger thereby; which is our case in the disposing of the Town and Magazine of *Hull*'.[23]

The exchanges openly canvas the question of where sovereignty resides. The King complains to his readers that Parliament is acting as if 'the Sovereign Power resides in both Houses of Parliament, . . . so then we our Self must be subject to their Commands' and that the Houses intend 'to make themselves perpetual Dictators over the King and People', altering the government of church and state. The King's allegation is not unreasonable given that, on this occasion, he was replying to the Parliamentary remonstrance of 26 May concerning the business of Hull, including the following admission:

If we have made any Precedents this Parliament, we have made them for Posterity upon the same, or better grounds of Reason and Law than those were upon which our Predecessors first made any Forms: and as some Precedents ought not to be Rules for us to follow; so none can be Limits to bound our Proceedings, which may, and must vary according to the different Condition of Times.

The remonstrance also justified the publishing of Parliament's case 'for the Satisfaction of the people':

If there be no Example for it, it is because there were never any such Monsters before, that ever attempted to disaffect the People from a Parliament . . . If we have done more than ever our Ancestors have done, we have suffered more than ever they have suffered.[24]

Once they had reached this point, the exchanges became intractable. However, the practical question of Hull remained unsettled and on 11 July the King sent a message to the Houses of Parliament, together with a proclamation, concerning his advance towards Hull in order to reduce it, if it were not rendered to him. The proclamation conveyed the King's sense of profound dishonour that a town of such importance was fortified, kept and maintained against him and that the port and passage by sea was defended against him by his own ships under the command of the Earl of Warwick, who legally was discharged from his commission. On the day following the King's message, Parliament voted to raise an army 'for the safety of the King's Person, and Defence of the Parliament . . . desiring to joyn together what seemed to be at so great a distance and enmity'.[25]

Later that month Charles moved against Hull with a considerable force of horse and foot, effectively planning to besiege it. A couple of ships loyal to the King attempted to block the seaward arrival of Parliamentarian supplies. Sir Henry Slingsby recalled the King's intention 'to make some show to block up ye town of Hull, & cast up some works, burns down ye mills, guards ye river, makes cannon Burketts & Blinds'.[26] In the fighting that followed, the first blood of the Civil War was shed by a sally party commanded by the Scot, Sir John Meldrum. Charles rightly feared that Hull, unconquered, would become a military base-camp for Parliamentary incursions into the surrounding area. Once the King had departed Hull, a force from the garrison marched to the West Riding to marshal and consolidate local support.

Parliament then ordered that its own account of these events be read in all churches and chapels within England and Wales. This paralleled the King's earlier order that his Homily against Rebellion and Wilful Disobedience be read in all churches and chapels.

In this propaganda Parliament was depicted as preserving not only Hull but the whole kingdom against violence and ruin. The account claimed that, notwithstanding his solemn protestations that he did not intend to make war against Parliament, the King's action amounted to an open declaration of war. Instead of deflecting blame from the King by denouncing his 'evil counsel', this account of events portrayed Charles unequivocally as the aggressor and painted Parliament – not the King – as the victim of rebellion. This oxymoron of king rebelling against kingdom figured large in Parliamentary rhetoric and was so supported by example from his military excursion against Hull as to lose its obvious incongruity. In these circumstances, Parliament's vote to raise an army could readily be justified as a defensive measure.

Thus by July 1642 Parliament's political and constitutional disputes with Charles had shifted dramatically from their basis in the Grand Remonstrance eight months earlier. The defence of Hull by both pen and sword produced a rhetoric which in point of detail anticipated later revolutionary arguments. Parliament's claim to make its own precedents and to provide extraordinary solutions to extraordinary problems, together with the distinction it established between the person and the office of the King, foreshadows Milton's defence of regicide in *Eikonoklastes* (1649). By then Charles had been formally charged with having 'traitorously and maliciously levied war against the present Parliament and the people therein represented'. The detailed charges in the indictment, including that of high treason, were not pinpointed (as might have been expected) to August 1642 when the King set up his standard of war at Nottingham, but commenced with the incident at Beverley in Yorkshire in late June–early July 1642 when Charles beleaguered Hull.[27]

The First Civil War, 1642–6

The battle of Edgehill on 23 October 1642 was the first major battle on English soil between English armies since Bosworth in 1485. It has been described by one military historian as 'the worst fought fight in our history', reflecting military inexperience on both sides.[28] After the inconclusive battle, which neither exhausted army was anxious to renew, the Earl of Essex fell back upon Warwick, leaving open the road to London which he had hoped to block from Royalist access. The Royalists proceeded to Banbury, which they took four days later, before marching to Oxford in triumph.

The rest of this brief campaign – which lasted only during October–November 1642 – was taken up with the King's attempt to march on London, which the Parliamentary forces were determined to thwart. Within days the forward Royalist forces commanded by the King's nephew, Prince Rupert, overwhelmed Brentford, but after a stand-off encounter with the combined force of Essex's army and the London Trained Bands at Turnham Green on 13 November, the King returned to winter quarters at Oxford. Oxford was strategically close to London, loyal to the Royalist cause, and a prestigious alternative for a King dispossessed of his capital city and centre of government. It became the Royalist capital for the duration of the First Civil War. A ring of garrisons from Northamptonshire southwards to Berkshire was established to protect it and a permanent garrison was set up at Banbury, the meeting-point of the counties of Oxfordshire, Northamptonshire and

Warwickshire. Oxford remained an important strategic asset for the protection of the Royal headquarters until its fall in 1646.[29]

In contrast to the sporadic and shifting manifestation of political loyalties prior to this time, the English countryside in the winter of 1642 displayed a more settled political typography. Market towns, bridges, river crossings and the old postways and road junctions assumed strategic significance on this new-drawn political map. Towns located at or near the intersection of these political territories were among the first to be touched by the experience of war. Stratford-upon-Avon, lying between Coventry and Evesham, in a south-west axis and on a crossroad of strategic importance, was significantly affected as early as October 1642, when it quartered Essex's troops who plundered the town during their occupancy. Since the main axes of communication by and large did not change for the duration of the war, towns along those axes feature again and again as theatres of conflict. Evesham, for example, lay close to a major Parliamentary route, from Coventry to Gloucestershire, through Warwick. The Royalist route from Oxford to Worcestershire ran through Evesham. Tewkesbury, further along the south-west axis from Evesham, had changed hands six times during the year after the battle of Edgehill. The command of territory, the maintenance of its integrity and of the lines of communication as passages between loyal areas, became a prime consideration of the war efforts on both sides.

The summer of 1643 witnessed the high tide of royalist arms in the field. Although the Parliamentarians had control of the fleet and therefore of external lines of communication and supply-lines to port garrisons, and although they had the benefit of the magazine at Hull, the Royalists held territory in the northern counties of Chester, Lancashire and Yorkshire (excluding the West Riding) and areas in North Wales. Cornwall, too, was royalist. Oxford was the forward bastion, only four days' march from London. At this point, the fortunes of war might have favoured either party.

At the beginning of the campaigning season in January 1643, the Royalists had three main armies available for field operations. The Earl of Newcastle commanded a formidable army in the north and Sir Ralph Hopton led a force based in Cornwall. The King led his army in the Oxford area. The Royalist aim was to link up these three armies in an advance upon London.

The King and the Earl of Essex manoeuvred against each other in the central theatre of the Midlands, without decisive result. In the north, the Earl of Newcastle consolidated his military successes by placing garrisons in hitherto Parliamentary territory at Newark, Pontefract Castle and Tadcaster. This had the effect of opening a southwards line of communication through divided areas of Parliamentary control. Although Sir Thomas Fairfax took Leeds for Parliament in January 1643, Royalist Newark withstood Parliamentary assaults in February and May.[30] The port of Scarborough, held for Parliament by Sir Hugh Cholmley, declared for the King in March. Later in March, Fairfax was defeated at Seacroft Moor, but rallied to capture Wakefield. In June, Fairfax was defeated by Newcastle's superior army at Adwalton Moor and Fairfax's forces took refuge in Hull, whose vigilant citizens prevented the Governor from declaring for the King. Newcastle's army then besieged Hull. While Parliament retained Hull, it lost Bradford, Gainsborough, Leeds and Lincoln, and Gloucester was besieged.

In the west country, Hopton consolidated his operations in Cornwall and launched two major assaults on Devon as part of the drive east to London. Despite his failure to take Plymouth, at Stratton Down in May Hopton defeated a Parliamentary army intent upon preventing his rendezvous with Royalist forces under Prince Maurice (another of the King's nephews) in Somerset. Prince Maurice subsequently took Exeter. On 5 July, the combined forces of Hopton, Maurice and the Marquis of Hertford fought Sir William Waller's army to a standstill at the Battle of Lansdown. After Hopton was temporarily paralysed and blinded by an ammunition explosion on the day following the battle, the Royalists retreated to Devizes, seeking reinforcements from Oxford. The relief forces were quickly available and, combined with Hopton's infantry who were drawn from Devizes by the sound of battle, achieved one of the most decisive victories of the war at Roundway Down on 13 July.[31]

Waller's army was virtually destroyed at Roundway Down. The remnant of his forces retreated to the stronghold at Bristol. Lord-General Essex was unable to relieve the situation, Waller's army being 'so farre broken that no assistance at all could be given by them', particularly since Essex's own army was shrunken and debilitated by violent sickness and lack of clothing, pay and other necessities. It was considered too risky to venture 'that weake Army to the ruine of itselfe, and danger of the Kingdome; especially, since the Forces of the Associated Counties could not with safety be commanded so farre from home'. Prince Rupert's army was able subsequently to capture Bristol, 'a place of as much concernment as any in the Kingdome'.[32] By this critical stage, Parliament retained in the west only the garrisons at Lyme and Plymouth, having lost control of the counties of Devon, Dorset and Somerset.

By their run of military successes in the north and west, the King's armies had won an important strategic freedom to choose what theatre of war they would exploit in order to deliver the war-winning blow. The Earl of Newcastle seemed to be poised to invade southern England, and the Earl of Ormonde, it was believed, was ready to bring an Irish army to join the King. The King's enemies were in disarray. A party for peace emerged in the House of Lords. Thomas May records the demoralized attitudes of the King's opponents 'in this low ebbe of the Parliament'. The Royalists 'seemed to possesse an absolute Victory, and the Parliament to be in danger of being quite ruined'.[33]

The resolute defence of the city of Gloucester by Parliament's forces under Colonel Massey (who made a name for himself in the wars) during the siege from 10 August to 5 September 1643 turned the tide for Parliament. The King with his Oxford army marched on Gloucester as part of a campaign to keep open Royalist communications with South Wales. While Essex and his enfeebled army had been unable to assist Waller after the disaster at Roundway Down in July, in this later emergency the Lord-General had, by the first week of September, led a hastily assembled relief force of some 15 000 troops on an epic march to within ten miles of Gloucester. The backbone of the force was the London Trained Bands. Rather than risk encirclement, the King lifted the siege and marched away. Essex then withdrew towards London by way of Newbury. In an attempt summarily to end the war, the Royalist cavalry galloped ahead to Newbury, pre-empting Essex from entering the town and forcing him into battle on 20 September in a difficult terrain of hedges and enclosures.[34]

The first Battle of Newbury was one of the most bloody and confused battles of the war. The Royalists advanced on both flanks but were unable to dislodge the Parliamentarians from Round Hill, a prominent central feature of the battlefield, whose significance had been overlooked by the Cavaliers. The King's army withdrew to Oxford after nightfall, leaving Essex free to continue his return march to London. Gloucester and London remained safe in Parliament's hands.

One Royalist who did not share the expectation of an impending victory for the King after the events of September 1643 was the Oxford-based poet, Abraham Cowley. Sensing that the tide had turned against the Royalist cause after the first Battle of Newbury, the poet abandoned the project of an epic poem on the Civil War which he had taken up earlier in the year. As he explained in 1656, during the Cromwellian Protectorate:

I have cast away all such pieces as I wrote during the time of the late troubles, . . . as among others, *three Books of the Civil War it self*, reaching as far as the first *Battel* of *Newbury*, where the succeeding *misfortunes* of the party stopt the *work*; for it is so uncustomary, as to become almost *ridiculous*, to make *Lawrels* for the *Conquered*.

The unprinted poem was rediscovered in the twentieth century. Its archaic style does not come to terms either with the conditions of contemporary warfare or the morality of the conflict. The poet grossly denigrates the London Trained Bands whose steadiness under fire at the first Battle of Newbury saved the day for Parliament. Sneering at them and mocking their Puritan ways, the poem lacks the epic theme to sustain its grand style:

> There Stane a Col'onel and a Butcher fell;
> A mighty Man esteem'd in Israell. . . .

And

> . . . Simon Blore.
> A woemans Taylour once . . .
> Shrill was his voyce at Psalmes, as swift his Quill
> At Sermon-notes more lying than his Bill.

However, a genuine emotion informs the close of the poem, where Cowley describes an event which cast a shadow over the Cavaliers: the death of Lucius Carey, Viscount Falkland. Serving as a volunteer in Sir John Byron's brigade of horse, Falkland was shot down as he spurred through a narrow passage in the hedgerows:

> 'tis a deadly Truth! Falkland is slaine;
> His noble blood all dyes th' accursed plaine.
> Had Essex and his whole ungodly Host,
>   Had all the Puritan Name that day binne lost,
> Yet would our losse too, rightly understood,
> Cost us as much in Teares as them in Blood.[35]

Clarendon, his friend of nearly twenty years, wrote how Falkland, impatient for peace and troubled by the agony of the war, had unnecessarily courted danger in the siege of Gloucester. He observed that 'if there were no other brand upon this odious and accursed civil war than that single loss, it must be most infamous, and execrable, to all posterity'. For Clarendon, who had been a member of the charmed circle at Great Tew before the war, the death of his friend marked not only the rising toll of an accursed war but also the demise of a rich culture, destroyed in the clash of arms.[36]

Despite these premonitions of Royalist defeat, after two seasons of civil war the situation was still indecisive. Joshua Sprigge, chaplain to Fairfax, expressed his frustration that 'two Summers passed over, and we were not saved: our Victories so gallantly gotten . . . were put into a bag with holes; what we wonne one time, we lost another . . . The Game, however set up at Winter, was to be new played again the next spring.'[37] Lacking central control of strategy, both sides operated in an independent manner in different theatres of war. Each regional force had its own local interests and priorities, which created rivalries rather than co-operation between comrades-in-arms. Personal animosities between leaders exacerbated this lack of co-operation at critical stages of the campaigns. Until either party developed a centralized strategy, the pattern of the conflict resembled guerrilla warfare: the 'bag with holes' through which major victories of the field armies were dissipated. A new military approach was needed.

The supply of volunteers which filled the armies of 1642 and early 1643 had dried up, and both King and Parliament were obliged to conscript men to fight. In August 1643, Parliament ordered the impressment of more than 20 000 men from its heartland territories of London and the eastern counties. John Bunyan was one of these, being conscripted at the age of 16, and serving for two years in Parliament's army. Both sides recognized that individual counties under their control were not sufficient bases from which to finance and supply their armies, especially given the pronounced reluctance of local soldiers to march beyond their county boundaries. Late in 1643, Parliament took a crucial initiative in grouping counties strategically into two associations. The Midland Association, in one of the most contested theatres of the war, incorporated Bedfordshire, Buckinghamshire, Derbyshire, Huntingdonshire, Leicestershire, Northamptonshire, Nottinghamshire and Rutland. The Eastern Association combined Cambridgeshire, Essex, Hertfordshire, Norfolk and Suffolk into an especially effective unit, which became Cromwell's major recruiting ground for what was later to become Parliament's 'New Model Army'.

The Royalists did not have the same success in establishing and sustaining viable county associations.[38] This may have had something to do with the widely dispersed nature of Royalist territories and the depth of their regional differences, which made centralized control from Oxford more difficult. For all its prestige, Oxford lacked the settled infrastructure of government to support and implement a centralized strategy. In addition, the court culture, deeply conservative and aristocratic, was inherently reluctant to reconceptualize the pre-war *status quo*. It was the antithesis of the modern concept of a 'war machine'. Where Parliament was able to exercise increased control over its territories and command their resources, the Royalists' control over their territories loosened and they lost the resources necessary to sustain their army.

Five days after the first Battle of Newbury in September 1643, Parliament had concluded the Solemn League and Covenant with the Scots.[39] Within four months a large Scottish army had crossed the River Tweed into England to assist Parliament, dramatically altering the Royalist position in the north. With the Scottish army to the north in Northumberland and Durham, and the Parliamentarians to the south in Yorkshire, the Royalist army commanded by the Earl of Newcastle was denied its earlier freedom to choose its theatre of engagement. In April 1644, Newcastle was forced to turn back to protect the city of York from attack by Fairfax. Late in the month, York was besieged by a combined force of Scots and Parliamentarian English.

The campaigns in England in 1644 over-extended the Royalist armies as they attempted to relieve strongholds in the north and west, as well as the critical base of Oxford, threatened after the fall of Abingdon to Essex in May. As the King withdrew his forces towards Worcestershire, with Essex and Waller in pursuit, the two Parliamentary Generals quarrelled and went their separate ways. By abandoning the Parliamentary strategy of co-ordination and co-operation, they exposed their separate armies to defeat. Waller had achieved a victory for Parliament at Cheriton in March. By June he had advanced close to Banbury. On 29 June, Royalist and Parliamentarian forces, marching along opposite banks of the River Cherwell, clashed at Cropredy Bridge. It was not a decisive battle, but in its aftermath Waller's army, affected by desertion and mutiny, ceased to be an effective fighting force.[40]

In a separate campaign, Prince Rupert, acting upon unclear instructions from the King, relieved the besieged city of York. He was then forced to confront a large allied army of English and Scots in the war's largest battle, on 2 July 1644, at Marston Moor, five miles to the west of York. The outcome was a disastrous defeat for the Royalists. Newcastle's army was destroyed and the Royalist position in the north shattered as the surrender of York left only a handful of garrisons holding out for the King. Rupert and Newcastle quarrelled over the defeat and the latter took ship for exile. From this point the Royalists lacked the military resources to follow their initial strategy of a three-pronged atrack on London and seemed unable to reformulate their strategy. In this sense, the Royalists had already lost the war, although no one could have predicted as much with confidence. Cromwell, who received a superficial wound in the fight, described the victory as a great favour from the Lord to England and the Church of God: 'It had all the evidences of an absolute Victory obtained by the Lord's blessing upon the Godly Party principally'. He gave no credit to General Leslie's Scots, whose cavalry charge in fact swung the fortunes of the battle on the left flank of the allied line. The publicity given by his supporters to 'Cromwell's' victory at Marston Moor gave offence to the Scots and worsened the tensions between the allies which had emerged in previous months as a result of national and religious differences.[41]

The allied victory in the north was counterbalanced by Essex's signal defeat in the west at the end of August 1644: another case of victory dissipated by Sprigge's 'bag with holes'. Advancing westward, Essex succeeded in relieving the Parliamentary garrison of Lyme in Dorset, took Weymouth and Melcombe Regis and forced Sir Richard Grenville to abandon the siege of Plymouth. However, not content with these successes, and with an army depleted by the placement of troops at garrisons along the way, he continued rashly into Royalist Cornwall, where he found himself in difficult and hostile country. At Bodmin, he learned that the King's superior forces were within 20 miles and closing in upon him. As the Royalist grip tightened, pinching Parliament's army into a confined area, Essex's line of communication and supply could only be sustained through the port of Lostwithiel and Parliament's navy. Lostwithiel fell to the King on 21 August, trapping the main body of Essex's troops on the west bank of the Fowey river. When the earthworks defences of Castle Dore were taken on the last day of August, Essex realized that he was defeated. His cavalry, under Sir William Balfour, broke through the Royalist encirclement at night, but his infantry – some 6000 troops – surrendered and were marched off in humiliation to Portsmouth. Leaving the doughty Sir Philip Skippon to cope with the terms of capitulation, the Earl himself escaped in a fishing boat to Plymouth and safety, to face his array of critics.

This season of the breaking of armies – Waller's, Newcastle's and Essex's – was a period of bitter contention between Parliament's senior generals. Their mutual recriminations related to the overall purpose of the Civil War, as well as the conduct of particular battles. The second Battle of Newbury on 27 October 1644 brought these animosities to a head.[42] Charles I, having beaten Essex in the west, turned back to relieve his garrisons at Banbury Castle, Basing House and Donnington Castle.

Fearing that this eastward march portended another Royalist attempt on London, the widely dispersed Parliamentary armies of Essex (near Portsmouth), Manchester (at Reading) and Waller (at Shaftesbury) moved to concentrate around Basingstoke. Marching northwards to relieve Donnington Castle, the Royal army made contact with enemy forces near Newbury. The Royalists were outnumbered, but the three armies they faced were without co-ordination by a single commander. The senior generals of the Parliamentary Council of War comprised Essex, soon to retire sick to Reading, and Manchester and Waller, soon to become bitter opponents. These generals devised an elaborate and risky plan for the battle, which involved a simultaneous attack upon the front and rear of the Royalist position, from east and west. Waller, with Balfour, Cromwell and Skippon, was to march a force of 12 000 men (almost two-thirds of the combined army) over 13 miles, while Manchester with a smaller force was to hold ground at Clay Hill. Manchester was to attack at the sound of Waller's guns firing upon the village of Speen. The King, gaining intelligence of the scheme, sent Prince Maurice with his veterans of Roundway Down to defend the village.

In the event, Manchester launched his attack about an hour after Waller's assault on Speen, and was repulsed in a hard struggle. By nightfall, both sides were convinced that they had lost the day. Manchester's subsequent failure to prevent the relief of Donnington Castle, north of Speen, by a smaller Royalist force, was to be used against him by his enemies. His dilatory behaviour on the field was inspired as much by his political views as by his military capacity. As he explained to the Council of War before Donnington Castle, 'if we beat the King ninety-nine times he would be King still, and his posterity; and we subjects still. But if he beat us once, we should be hanged and our posterity undone.' As an aristocrat, belonging to one of the less radical Parliamentary factions, Manchester was not only expressing his lack of faith in a decisive victory in this protracted war, and his fear about the personal consequences, but inadvertently revealing the pre-revolutionary cast of his mind, which accepted the King's kingship even in the event of his defeat. The more radical Cromwell rejoined: 'If this be so, why did we take up arms at first?'[43]

The Committee of Both Kingdoms, which had been established by Ordinance in February 1644 after the arrival of the Scots to direct the management of the war 'for the best advantage of the three kingdoms', expressed its concern at the events at Newbury and Donnington Castle. Manchester's army critics, who included Cromwell and Waller, attacked his military record in an attempt to remove him from command of the Eastern Association army. From his seat in the Lords, Manchester vigorously counterattacked, with serious allegations against Cromwell, specifying Cromwell's open animosity against the nobility and the Scottish nation, and his favouring of radicals and Independents. The Earl claimed that Cromwell had announced that he would have in his army only men of an Independent judgement: 'that in case there should be propositions for peace or any conclusion of a peace such as might not stand with those ends that honest men should aim at, this army might prevent such a mischief'.[44]

The differences in outlook between those who, like Manchester, wished at all costs to avoid defeat, and those who, like Cromwell, desired by all means to win the war, were exacerbated by parallel differences in religious outlook. Manchester adhered to an exclusively Presbyterian church system (whereby the established Church of England would become Presbyterian), whereas Cromwell was more radical in advocating a more independent and less coercive relationship between churches, characterized by greater toleration. Loose as they were as political definitions, the labels 'Presbyterian' and 'Independent' reflected deep factions in the Parliamentary forces and mark a major change in the contemporary perception of Parliamentarian politics.

By late November 1644, the quarrels among Parliament's military leaders were recognized to be elements within a contest between peace and war factions in the Houses of Parliament. At this time, Essex planned his own attack on Cromwell. With the assistance of the Scots Commissioners, who had rallied to the peace party, and with the help of his sympathizers in the Lower House, including Bulstrode Whitelock, Essex sought to indict Cromwell as an incendiary. The Independent faction countered with the Self-Denying Ordinance, which sought to remove Members of Parliament who were from the nobility – generally, like Manchester, Presbyterian aristocrats – from holding military office. Intense political lobbying and wrangling between the factions in both Houses took place over the proposed Self-Denying Ordinance before it was passed on 3 April 1645.[45]

One of the purposes of this Ordinance, which was backed by the Commons, was to remodel Parliament's armies for a more vigorous war effort by separating military and political commands. The catch was that, because the hereditary Lords could not relinquish their place in the House, they would be obliged to relinquish their military commissions. Their Lordships took exception to the substance of the proposals as a derogation of their position and a dismissal of their contribution to the war effort. The Scots were aggrieved that they had not been consulted about the proposal. Essex relinquished his commission on the day before the Ordinance passed. Perhaps having in mind Parliament's earlier vote to live and die with him, he wryly hoped that his resignation 'may prove as good an expedient to the present distempers as some would have it believed'.[46]

The leaders of the war party in the Commons ruthlessly applied pressure on the reluctant majority of Lords to ensure the passage of the Self Denying Ordinance. One drastic move was the threat to withhold financial support from the existing armies in the field unless the Lords complied. In the interests of the Ordinance, even the negotiations for peace were jeopardized. The Commons alleged that the Ordinance was necessary to force the King to accept the impending peace treaty. This was followed by the drastic warning that the Commons were prepared to prevent the negotiations with the King at Uxbridge from proceeding at all until the armies were established on a new basis. The anomaly of the Commons insisting on military reorganization as a condition of peace cannot have been lost on the Lords. The Lords would also have been aware that the reorganized military command would have a more Independent flavour and thus, consistent with Manchester's allegations, better position Cromwell to prevent peace if the terms of that peace did not please him. Nevertheless, the threatened disruption to the peace process was a powerful inducement to the Lords, because the propositions of Uxbridge were a joint Anglo-Scots settlement embodying the agenda of the Solemn League and Covenant to which the Lords, who were predominantly Presbyterian, adhered. The Lords were caught: they were unable to proceed with a peace favourable to themselves without passing the Ordinance which threatened that peace.

Before the Ordinance was passed, the Commons proceeded with plans to create a new army financed by assessments on counties in the southeast, East Anglia and the Midlands. Sir Thomas Fairfax, a man with radical associations, was selected as Commander-in-Chief and Sir Philip Skippon was made Major-General. The position of Lieutenant-General was left vacant. Cromwell was not reappointed, but remained on active service, in spite of opposition from Essex's party in the Lords. Presumably according to a preconceived plan, several months later – on the eve of the Battle of Naseby – Cromwell was irregularly appointed by the House of Commons, without the assent of the Lords and in breach of the Self-Denying Ordinance, to the position of Lieutenant-General.

The militants also had their way over details of Fairfax's commission, against the strenuous objection of Essex and his supporters. Unlike his predecessor, the new Commander-in-Chief was not obliged by the terms of his appointment to protect the King's person. This was an ominous alteration to be understood as meaning that the Civil War for 'King and Parliament' was ending and that the New Model Army was intending to conduct a new model war. As Ian Gentles writes:

> The deletion of the clause obliging Fairfax to protect the person of the king represented the abandonment of the fiction that they were fighting the king's evil counsellors, and the first step towards the conversion of a civil war into a revolution.[47]

However portentous his new commission, Fairfax's army remained a patchwork affair. In the first place it was drawn from the shaken remnants of Parliament's three southern armies – those of Essex, Manchester and Waller. Parliament's northern forces provided few recruits. In the second place, pressed men (in the case of infantry, almost half the total number) were required to fill the proposed establishment of 12 foot regiments (14 000), 11 horse regiments (7000) and a dragoon regiment (1000). Many of the infantry were untested in war. However, the cavalry was an experienced body, which included veterans of the Eastern Association forces trained by Cromwell and a powerful siege artillery train was included.

Despite the stipulation of Parliament's Self-Denying Ordinance that soldiers take the Covenant, the oath was not imposed upon the ranks of the New Model. Nevertheless many officers submitted. Wearing red coats of good Coventry, Gloucestershire or Suffolk cloth, and grey breeches stitched from pre-shrunk fabric, and bearing different coloured regimental facings for identification, the army formed a distinctive unit easily recognized in the heat and confusion of battle. Improvised identifying tokens, like the beanstalks worn by Royalists in their hats at Naseby, were not needed. The Royalists, not sensing that the war had taken a new direction, mocked 'The New Noddle' (a dullard army) in a modish pun. The King, equally unaware, derided 'the rebels' new brutish general' and began the new year's campaign in his customary desultory manner.[48] It did not occur to them that the 'New Model' was more than a change in form: that it was a critical modernization that the Royalists did not match. Its military will was fortified by an ideology which was literally preached to the soldiers, and with regular pay and a leadership responsive to their needs, even the pressed men responded to the concept of the 'New Model' and performed accordingly.

At the resumption of war in 1645, the Royalist and Parliamentarian Councils of War were both initially indecisive. The Royalists wavered between choosing an attack on the Scots in the north, together with the relief of beleaguered Chester (as advocated by Prince Rupert and Sir Marmaduke Langdale), and an assault on the untried New Model. The compromise reached was to dispatch Lord George Goring to the western theatre – where he relished his independent command and could not be recalled to Naseby when needed – while sending Rupert north with the main army.

Having spent April organizing his army with General Skippon, Fairfax set out on 1 May still considerably short of his establishment strength. His single-minded objective to hunt down and destroy the King's army in the field was thwarted by directions from the Committee of Both Kingdoms, whose members included the discredited generals Essex and Manchester. The Committee ordered Fairfax to dispatch 2500 horse – a large part of his cavalry – to the north to reinforce the Scots army. With the remnant of his force, Fairfax was then to relieve beleaguered Taunton in the west and, following the King's departure from Oxford, to besiege the royal capital. The siege of Oxford imposed an essentially static role upon an army whose striking power lay in its cavalry. Fairfax dutifully employed the short-term siege as a useful training exercise for the New Model Army during the last days of May 1645. When the Parliamentarians took Evesham on 26 May 1645 – 'stormed and taken for want of men to defend the works' – the Royalist axis between Oxford and Banbury and Worcester and South Wales was ruptured. 'The loss of this place', wrote Clarendon, 'was an ill omen to the succeeding summer.'[49]

On 31 May, Rupert's army stormed and sacked the Parliamentarian garrison city of Leicester, after the desperate resistance of its citizens, led by Colonel Sir Robert Pye.[50] The city had been a stronghold of nonconformity, and the savagery of the attack was designed to act as a deterrent. The defaced city became a monument of the vengeance to be wreaked on rebels. The shock of Leicester prompted the Committee of Both Kingdoms to release Fairfax from the Oxford siege (5 June). The Army Council on 8 June ratified Fairfax's determination to attack the Royal army directly. At the same time, the House of Commons unilaterally agreed that Cromwell should command the Army's cavalry. The Committee of Both Kingdoms also relinquished its political control over Fairfax's movements, freeing him to follow his own strategy. By June 1645 the New Model Army was at last released for its new model war. Its objective, to destroy outright the King's capacity to wage war, marked a watershed in the First Civil War. It had serious implications for any subsequent peace settlement, because a King incapacitated for war would be a King without negotiating strength. It also had military implications, because the New Model was now a quasi-professional, quasi-revolutionary army pitted against 'unmodelled', over-stretched and dissipating Royalist forces.

On 12 June, the New Model Army came within five miles of a surprised Royal army, while the King was hunting. Two days later, Fairfax established his position at Naseby, close to the centre of England, as the Royalists approached from Market Harborough. The battle at Naseby on 14 June was the decisive battle of the war and was recognized as such by all except perhaps Charles I. It was lost for the King by Rupert's too-successful cavalry charge against Commissary General Ireton's horse on Parliament's left flank. Crashing through and continuing to Parliament's baggage-train in the rear, Rupert's Cavaliers effectively cancelled themselves from the battle.[51]

On the right flank of Parliament's position, Cromwell with nearly twice the number of horse at his disposal drove Sir Marmaduke Langdale's northern cavalry from the field after a stiff fight. Reigning in his troopers, Cromwell drove them into the unprotected left flank of Astley's outnumbered infantry, who in the centre had more than held their own at push of pike. Astley's veterans, many of them Welsh, were assaulted as well from their right by the regrouped survivors of Ireton's cavalry, followed by a charge of Okey's dragoons. The King, persuaded to retreat to a nearby hill top, watched the destruction of his infantry as they were assaulted from the front and flanks, fighting – as even their enemies acknowledged – with exemplary resolution and courage. A Royalist bluecoat regiment fought to the last man, its colours taken by Fairfax himself, who cut down the ensign. The close-up carnage must have resembled a German battlefield during the Thirty Years War.

This was the King's last battle in the field and there was no respite for him after it. He lost more than 50 colours (a real symbol of defeat), all of his artillery, much of his arms and ammunition, many of his best infantry and his baggage-carriers. Perhaps worst of all, his incriminating personal correspondence – with details of his secret dealings – was taken and soon published by his vindictive enemies to discredit him.[52] The women camp-followers found unprotected in the shambles of the Royalist army were killed outright if thought to be Irish and mutilated if thought to be harlots. The captured infantry were marched to London and paraded through the streets in a kind of Roman triumph.

The latter part of 1645 and the early part of 1646 saw a series of 'mopping-up' battles as Fairfax and the New Model took the remaining

Royalist strongholds. Royalist Bristol was taken in September 1645, a reversal of fortune described by the Secretary at War as 'the loss of all our magazines and war-like provisions, and so by consequence in very short time of South Wales, the West, and all other places in the Kingdom'. Basing and strategically placed Tiverton, town and castle, were taken in October, the former by an assault which in its brutality presaged Cromwell's Irish campaign in 1649. Dartmouth surrendered in January 1646, causing a breach in the protection hitherto afforded Exeter by the garrisons around its flanks, and the New Model soldiers endured winter cold and snow around Exeter itself. Hopton was defeated at Torrington in February 1646 and a brief campaign secured royalist Cornwall – the Prince of Wales retreating to the Scilly Isles in March. In March, Jacob Astley, intending to break through to embattled Oxford with a relief force of between two and three thousand men, was routed after a fierce engagement on the edge of Gloucestershire. The veteran Astley, who had begun his civil war at Edgehill with a memorable prayer, ended it at Stow-on-the-Wold four years later with a memorable prediction to his captors: 'You have done your work well, boys. You may go play unless you fall out among yourselves.'[53]

Quitting Oxford late in April 1646 in disguise, the King reached as far as Hillingdon near Uxbridge, before changing his mind and going north, where he reached the Scots camp at Southwell on 5 May. In June, the King ordered his remaining garrisons to surrender. His wartime capital, Oxford, was handed over to Fairfax on 24 June 1646.

Peace Negotiations, 1642–6

Throughout the years 1642–6 there were regular attempts to negotiate a peace. While some of these took place during military activity, peace negotiations naturally tended to take place at the end of each campaign season, as winter approached. The terms upon which peace was offered were often at odds with the military balance prevailing at the time. Against the tide of Royalist successes in 1643, the Parliamentarian parties presented unyielding terms to the King. Similarly, after his defeats in 1644 and 1645, Charles showed little disposition to relax his settlement demands and continued, even as a prisoner in 1646, to act as if he were able to determine essential features of his postwar dominions.

The English alliance with the Scots effectively ruled out the possibility of the King making peace separately with either of them – or with Ireland. It also charged the English peace terms with a radical ideology by defining an English settlement, especially of the Church, in Scottish terms. It imposed upon the English supporters of Parliament a specific war aim which was not what many thought they had taken up arms for.

In retrospect, the best opportunity for peace was before the Scots entered the war, when peace could have been on English terms. These terms are embodied in the propositions presented to the King in the unconcluded Treaty of Oxford in February 1643. The political solutions proposed in the Treaty hark back to the Nineteen Propositions and are concerned almost exclusively with the situation in England and Ireland. Scotland is only alluded to as one of the King's dominions threatened by the papist design to root out the Protestant religion. However, there was no pause in the fighting while these proposals were considered. According to a contemporary source, Parliament remonstrated that 'the King kept up a secret Correspondence for War', instancing the taking of Scarborough Castle and his 'bloody and barbarous' design upon Bristol. Scarborough and Bristol became icons in a war of words. Charles is recorded as complaining in reply that:

> it was a Thing as uncommon as unjust, that they should pretend; that the Treaty was to keep him under Restraint, while they were at full Liberty . . . That during the Treaty their Army committed Acts of Rebellion openly, and yet the King was in the wrong to call them Rebels. That he might be mistaken, in believing that their Soldiers had a Design upon his Life, they who had fired upon him as often as he had advanced to any Place within the Reach of their Cannon. That the Treaty could not hinder them from taking his Towns and Castles, and yet he must not recover any, nor even possess any of his Houses or Castles. That Sir *William Waller* might freely take the Towns of *Malmsbury* and *Tewkesbury*, but his Majesty must not so much as think upon *Scarborough* and *Bristol*.

Thus the peace talk became a rhetoric of escalating conflict: 'So the Treaty produced nothing but new Matter of Quarrell, both Sides were more exasperated, and the War was carried on with more Heat than ever.'[54]

Parliament's unyielding negotiating stance followed from its then current doctrines of responsible power. During the contest over Hull in

1642 it had authorized itself to reject old precedents and to construct new ones as occasion warranted. One of these new precedents was to the effect that any behaviour causing division between King and Parliament was inherently treasonable. The King was declared to be 'a person entrusted with the kingdom and discharging that trust', but his trustee-ship was to be exercised jointly with Parliament. Accordingly, he was obliged to act with and on the advice of both Houses. Insofar as the King's court advisers gave advice which differed from that of the Houses and usurped their prerogative, the advisers' behaviour was seen as traitorous and their counsel 'evil'. The Queen herself was accused of such treason after she delivered a substantial force of infantry, cavalry and artillery to the King at Edgehill.

Since a decision made without reference to Parliament was not, accord-ing to this view, a valid act of trusteeship, Parliament also found in this precedent grounds for declaring null and void whatever was sealed by the King's Great Seal. It was in this context, after the failure of the peace negotiations in 1643, that Parliament created its own Great Seal. It declared those who made use of the Royal Seal enemies of the state. Officially, Parliament continued to recognize the King's authority as trustee. But like the shots fired at His Majesty's person whenever he came within cannon range, the Parliamentary Great Seal spoke louder than words. Not only was the existence of the Seal a rival claim to supreme authority: its potent visual iconography excluded the King. The obverse bore an engraving of the House of Commons – the members sitting, and the reverse the Arms of England and Ireland. Robert Monteth claimed of the creation of the Seal:

> . . . all the People were seized with Consternation, and had Reason to believe that, at last the Divisions betwixt the King and Parliament would become irreparable, and that there would be no Hopes left of their being reconciled with one another, the Breach made in his Majesty's Authority being so great, that it portended nothing less than the Ruin of the State and the Dissolution of the Monarchy.[55]

For both parties the failure of the 1643 peace negotiations brought to light a revolutionary subtext.

When, in February 1644, after the entry of the Scots, Parliament estab-lished the Committee of Both Kingdoms to direct the management of the war, the Ordinance forbade the Committee to negotiate for peace or arrange any cessation of arms without the express direction of both

Houses of Parliament. However, the second Committee which was appointed three months later was empowered to negotiate peace directly under delegation from Parliament. Since the Scottish interests on the Committee were powerful and well organized, the effect of this delegation was to entrench the Scottish agenda in the peace process. The propositions presented to the King at Oxford in November 1644, and discussed at Uxbridge (the so-called Treaty of Uxbridge) in late January and February 1645, incorporated the English and Scottish agendas into a document almost twice as long as its predecessor, the Treaty of Oxford. One significant addition was the reformation of religion on the Scottish model: both kingdoms were mutually obliged 'to endeavour the utmost conformity and uniformity in matters of religion'. The King was to take the Covenant, as were all the subjects of the three kingdoms. The Book of Common Prayer was to be replaced by a Directory of Worship rushed through the Westminster Assembly of Divines. A second measure was the naming of war criminals from amongst Charles's supporters in the British Isles. More than one hundred named persons 'shall expect no pardon' – a direct assault not only on the King's supporters, but on his prerogative of mercy. The King's nephews, Princes Rupert and Maurice, were included, along with William Laud, Archbishop of Canterbury, Edward Lord Littleton (who had dispatched the Great Seal to the King at Oxford), General Ralph Hopton and Edward Hyde (later the Earl of Clarendon).[56] On 10 January 1645, in the interval between the November propositions and the Treaty of Uxbridge, Archbishop Laud was ignominiously removed from imprisonment in the Tower and publicly executed for treason on Tower Hill. This was in defiance of the King's pardon given under the Great Seal after Laud's conviction by Parliament in 1642 and symbolically encapsulated Parliament's rejection of the authority of that Seal.

On 21 January 1645, the King sent from Oxford six propositions of his own for discussion at Uxbridge, the last of which called for a cessation of arms so that the Treaty would not be disrupted by allegations of a 'secret correspondence of war', as at the Treaty of Oxford. In contrast to Parliament's hectoring and prolix assertions, the King's propositions were open-ended and succinct: deliberately forcing the contrast upon their audience. The first three demanded the restoration to the King of his Navy, towns and lands, the recognition and return of his full legal rights and powers, and the disclaimer and discharge of all convictions and other outcomes achieved through the improper exercise of power by Parliament or its committees. However, in propositions four and five the King left the key questions of church reform and the punishment of the alleged criminals open to later resolution and the devising of 'appropriate laws'. Notably, also, he refrained from any reference to the execution of Laud, notwithstanding the nearness of that event in time and its extreme pertinence. The seemingly ameliorative tone of propositions four and five was tactically astute: defusing the attack, accepting Parliamentary terminology while effectively parrying its application, and deferring the formulation of active remedy.[57]

January 1645 had been a particularly busy time. Despite the inclement season and sporadic attempts at a ceasefire, military activity continued with unusual intensity. Parliament was engaged in the exercise of making its military machine more effective with the creation of the New Model Army. Parliament was also occupied with the question of church reform, adopting a Presbyterian model as satisfying the Word of God. The House of Commons dispatched its completed version of a Directory of Public Worship to the Lords for consideration. The arrangements for a peace treaty were debated in the midst of all this other business.

Uxbridge, midway between the rival camps of Oxford and Westminster, was selected on the recommendation of the Committee of Both Kingdoms. The Commissioners met on 29 January 1645 in rigidly controlled conditions: Parliament's retinue on the north side of the town and the Royalists on the south side, 'and no inter-mixture of the one party of their attendants with the other'. Twenty days were all that were allowed for the discussion of the three heads of the agenda: religion, militia and Ireland. The recollections of Bulstrode Whitelock and Edward Hyde, Uxbridge Commissioners respectively for Parliament and the King, reveal the straitened and pressured circumstances in which the peace teams debated, struggled to reach agreement and keep their principals informed, and raced against the clock. In the event, little progress was made during the 20 working days, except some hint of royal concessions over the militia. The negotiations got bogged down in debate over definitions: what was meant by 'presbyterial government', or 'provincial or synodical assemblies', or by the 'bounds of parishes'? Since the spokesmen for episcopacy and the spokesmen for presbytery each claimed divine sanction for their churches, the conference made little progress when it turned to the details of church reform. An attempt was even made to resolve the difficulties by conducting the ecclesiastical debate in syllogisms! When Hyde and Whitelock locked horns in legal argument over the militia question, the Commissioners put aside the debate and attempted, without success, to settle details. The Royal Commissioners' request for more time was dismissed peremptorily by Parliament on the grounds that the King's party had not granted any of Parliament's propositions. As Whitelock recorded, 'most sober men lamented the sudden breach of the treaty'.[58]

After the routing of the King's forces at Naseby in June 1645, and the succession of Royalist losses in the winter of 1645–6, the King was effectively on the run. In March 1646, after Lord Astley's defeat, Charles wrote from Oxford to a confidante of his intention to make for London, 'being not without hope that I shall be able so to draw either the Presbyterians or Independents to side with me, for extirpating the one or the other, that I shall be really King again'.[59] This wildly optimistic hope turned out to have some foundation, as the events of 1648 were to show. What is even more extraordinary is the equality of the King's expectation of a potential alliance with each faction. Nothing could indicate more dramatically the shift in the locus of conflict and debate from King and Parliament and their rival Seals to the rival ideologies of Parliamentarian factions on the subject of church reform. What is also clear is that the conflict was perceived as so intense that the King, who had then been at war with them for four years, could envisage either party embracing such an enemy to secure a pragmatic victory.

Whatever caused Charles to abandon this strategy and surrender to the Scots, he was effectively a prisoner when Parliament delivered its peace terms to him at Newcastle in July 1646. He found these Newcastle Propositions particularly galling. His first reply early the following month concluded that the Propositions:

> do import so great alterations in government both in the Church and kingdom, as it is very difficult to return a particular and positive answer, before a full debate, . . . and that His Majesty (upon a full view of the whole propositions) may know what is left, as well as what is taken away and changed.

Since the Commissioners could neither give him reasons for the demands they conveyed, nor hearken to his own wishes, the King sought to come to London for a direct and personal conference with the Houses of Parliament upon the questions raised. This request implicitly recognized that the problem, as at Uxbridge, was the Commissioners' inability to negotiate in the true sense, tied as they were to the inflexible dictates of a remote Parliament. Consistent with its steely determination to have peace upon its own terms, Parliament refused the request. Parliament was also unwilling to expose London to the spectacle of a supplicant King, with the political risks that that might entail.

The Newcastle Propositions embraced two separate settlements: one for England and Ireland, and one for Scotland. The three matters forming the heads of the Uxbridge agenda – religion, militia and Ireland – were to be determined at the discretion of each regional parliament: by the Scottish Parliament for Scotland, and by the English Parliament for England and Ireland. Formally the King's assent was no longer required for the enactment of laws, although his assent to the Propositions was sought to give the semblance of constitutional propriety. Accordingly, the King was required to agree in advance to such articles of settlement as the Parliaments at their discretion might enact. A lengthy part of the Propositions was devoted to naming and condemning Royalists in all three kingdoms and to ensuring that anyone who had deserted Parliament would be excluded from office or state employment. The King had to acknowledge that Scotland and England had taken up arms in their just and lawful defence, and to accept the imputation that the guilty parties were to be found among his supporters. Turning the screw, Parliament demanded that the estates of Lord Littleton and William Laud be forfeited to pay public debts and damages.

Not surprisingly, the King saw these terms as 'destructive to his just regal power, if he should give a full consent to these propositions as they now stand'. He responded to the stalemate caused by the refusal of his request to negotiate in person with the Houses by reiterating that request in a second reply to the Propositions in December 1646.[60]

The Newcastle Propositions embodied an essentially Presbyterian platform, entrenching the Solemn League and Covenant, which had been the price of Scotland's entry into the war. For the Scots, they were not just peace terms, but the legitimation of the war: the realization of a scriptural ideal which had dictated how the war itself was perceived. The Scots held them up as the only legitimate programme accepted by both kingdoms waging war as morally required by the Covenant, and the only terms upon which the war could be legitimately concluded. However, this high status was to be challenged during the interregnum of 1647, when the captive King was courted by powerful interests with alternative settlement proposals.

Ireland

From the beginning of the Irish rebellion late in 1641, Parliament was determined to settle the Irish question on its own terms, without reference to the King. The King's initial offer to take personal command of the situation was swept aside. In April 1642, after the King had conceded the conduct of the Irish war to Parliament, he complained that he had not 'intended to exclude ourself, or not to be concerned in your counsels'. That exclusion, as previously noted, is encapsulated in the iconography of Parliament's Great Seal, which excluded the King but bore the arms not only of England but of Ireland. Making the most of the opportunity of intervention in Ireland, Parliament mounted a profound assault on Irish culture. It resolved to exclude from pardon anyone supporting the Irish rebels, and raised loans in England to finance intervention in Ireland, on the security of Irish land to be confiscated. The aim, as confirmed by the Solemn League and Covenant of 1643, was to extirpate popery and prelacy 'that the Lord may be one, and His name one in the three kingdoms'. Since what was under attack included policies encouraged by the King in seeking Irish support and popish institutions with which the King was a suspected sympathizer, the King was of necessity excluded.

The threat of just such a puritanical crusade had prompted many of the Irish to rise anew against English rule. The Covenant confirmed their worst fears about their faith and their future. On the other hand, the King's position was deeply ambiguous and his ability to intervene uncertain. He was slow to condemn the rebels and his later public statements were reticent on the Irish question, perhaps because negotiations were taking place in secret. Ireland was, after all, a potential – and to some extent actual – provider of Royalist troops. As late as 1647, in his negotiations for peace with Parliament, Charles undertook with respect to Ireland only to give 'satisfaction therein' once other matters were settled. Yet to the extent that he offered to give Parliament 'satisfaction', he was prepared ultimately to consider treasonable the challenge to English sovereignty mounted partly in his name.

A year after the first Irish rising and the day after the battle of Edgehill, the Irish rebels formed an assembly to take charge of the rebellion.[61] The General Assembly of the Confederated Catholics met at Kilkenny in October 1642. Its seal emblazoned the motto, *Irishmen unanimous for God, the King, and the Country (Pro Deo, rege et patria, Hiberni unanimes)*. An order to raise an army in Leinster was one of the first acts made under this Great Seal. Resolving that the Roman Catholic Church was to regain its rights and by defining its enemy as the 'puritanical party', the Assembly sharpened the religious focus of the nationalist rebellion. For example, it considered – but for the time being left open – the question of whether

Irish protestants would be allowed religious liberty in a reformed Ireland. The Assembly acted as an independent government, minting its own currency and establishing printing presses. It issued letters of marque, licensing its armed vessels to attack enemy shipping. Generals were appointed to command the Confederate forces in Connaught, Leinster, Munster and Ulster: the very provinces that Parliament in England planned to settle with Protestant plantations when the rebellion was suppressed, the Act for this purpose having received the King's assent.

In addition, the Confederate government published its cause overseas, sending agents and ambassadors to Rome, Louis XIV of France, the Emperor Ferdinand III and other principalities and notables. Agents were also sent to Charles I to explain the Irish 'holy war' and at the same time to profess their allegiance to the Crown of England. Before adjourning in January 1643, the Assembly published a declaration of independence under the English Crown, declaring that during the troubles no temporal government should be exercised in Ireland without the authority of the Confederation. The Kilkenny Assembly presented a rival parliament to the Dublin Parliament controlled by English interests, which described the members of the Assembly as rebels. It was a parliament of the Irish people, with representatives of all the areas not controlled by the enemy and deferentially calling itself an Assembly only because it was not summoned by the King's Writs.

Fortified by a papal blessing and with a papal nuncio at hand to sustain their resolve, the Irish leaders pressed for genuine religious and legislative independence from England, while (for some of them) retaining a connection with the Crown. The national statehood that the confederated Irish struggled for in these circumstances bore a distinct likeness to that sought by the covenanted Scots; both sharing an ideal of political and religious self-determination within the British Isles, while retaining links with the Stuart Crown. While it was a model acceptable to Parliament when applied to the Scots, which would later become enshrined in the Solemn League and Covenant, applied to the papist Irish it was anathema. For the King's part, having gone to war with the puritan Scots to deny them a separate assembly, he was hardly in a position to concur openly with a separate assembly for the Irish. He was, however, far more dilatory in condemning the Irish Catholics as traitors than he had been the Protestant Scots.

Although publicly condemning the Irish rebellion, Charles issued confidential instructions to his main lieutenant, James Butler, twelfth Earl of Ormonde and a leading member of the Protestant ascendancy, and other

Commissioners to negotiate with the Confederate authorities. His offer to treat with the Catholic leaders recognized – and even went so far as to legitimize – the Assembly as a *de facto* government of one of his dominions. Ormonde was authorized to negotiate, with the utmost secrecy, a cessation of arms for one year between the King and the Irish rebels. After much wrangling, the treaty was signed in September 1643, shortly before the House of Commons took the Solemn League and Covenant. The cessation was subsequently renewed in the interests of both parties until the end of January 1645. The King's correspondence with Ormonde in January 1645 reveals his deep concern that resolution of the Irish problem would be a stumbling block in the Uxbridge negotiations. He explained that 'one of the first and chiefest articles they [the Parliament] will insist on, will be to continue the Irish war; which is a point not popular with me to break on'.[62]

For the King to accept the Uxbridge Propositions would have been to undermine his secret Irish diplomacy. The Propositions required him, in the first place, to accept all treaties made between the Parliaments of England and Scotland and, in the second place, to accept any Act of Parliament voiding the cessation of arms in Ireland and any other non-parliamentary treaties with the rebels there. If he agreed, the King would have to relinquish his continuing hope of an Irish contribution to his war with Parliament. Charles urged Ormonde to make peace with the Irish, or at least secure an extension of the ceasefire, in the hope of releasing his own and Irish troops for use in other theatres of war.

Ormonde, however, had singularly little to bargain with on the prime grievances of the Irish in arms. The King had confessed that his cause in England would be ruined if he agreed to abrogate the Irish penal statutes: Poyning's law of 1494, for example, which stipulated that Acts passed by an Irish Parliament were validated only when confirmed by an English Parliament; or the even older (1353, 1365 and 1393) statutes of Praemunire directed with severe penalties against appeals to Roman jurisdiction in certain ecclesiastical causes. Furthermore, the King would not on principle give unqualified assent to the return of plantation lands to the dispossessed Irish. As a matter of royal policy he was committed to retaining control over Irish land, politics and religion.

Charles reassured Ormonde that his main purpose in seeking peace with the Confederated Catholics was to ensure the Protestant interest in Ireland. However, at the same time and unknown to Ormonde, he granted to the Catholic Edward Somerset, Earl of Glamorgan, extraordinary powers to negotiate with the Irish and engaged secretly to ratify Glamorgan's dealings.

The disastrous outcome at Naseby in June 1645 intensified the King's importunities to Ormonde. If the Earl could dispatch Irish forces within two months, Charles was confident that 'my last loss would be soon forgotten', and that he could restore his affairs before winter. In July he advised Ormonde that 'if my expectation of relief out of Ireland be not in some good measure and speedily answered, I am likely to be reduced to great extremities'. At whatever hazard to Ireland, Ormonde was absolutely commanded to bring to the King all the forces he could draw together. The King had plans also to join forces with Montrose in Scotland. After Montrose and the Royalist cause in Scotland had been defeated at Philiphaugh in September 1645, Ireland seemed the King's last resource to continue the armed struggle. From Oxford in December 1645 he informed Ormonde that an Irish peace, concluded without a guarantee of considerable assistance from Ireland (he required 6000 well-armed troops before April 1646) would be 'fruitless, depriving me of the most principal means of persuading the English rebels to return to their wits'.[63] In March 1646, Ormonde concluded a peace treaty with the Irish, one of the terms of which was that the Confederates would dispatch 10 000 Irish troops to England for the Royal service. However, in the circumstances of the Confederacy's own war with Parliamentarian forces, this promise was unreal and unkept. The treaty itself was not proclaimed in Dublin until 30 July 1646, by which time the King was a prisoner of the Scots and Oxford had been surrendered. There was no Irish solution to the King's British problem.

Breaking the Seal

When Oxford was delivered to Fairfax on 24 June 1646, the civilized articles for the surrender allowed the garrison the honours of war. The defeated Royalist forces were permitted to march out of the city with flying colours, trumpets sounding, drums beating and bearing arms, with lighted matches and with bullets in their mouths. It was a dignified exit from the capital, but the articles included a clause (number four) of greater political significance than these pleasing military courtesies. The Great Seal and other seals of the royal government were to be locked up in a chest and left in the public library. One of the Commissioners of the Army then collected and presented the captured seals to the Parliament, which ordered that these symbols of Royal authority be broken. In August, after the King had expressed his difficulties with the Newcastle

Propositions, the Royal Seals brought from Oxford were broken into pieces by a smith in the presence of both Houses of Parliament. This public spectacle was an iconoclastic action charged with revolutionary significance. The Parliamentarian Bulstrode Whitelock, who in 1642 feared that more than a civil war was in prospect, reported this extraordinary scene without comment. But the incident, wrote the Royalist James Heath, 'made too deep an impression to be so easily obliterated'.[64]

2

INTERREGNUM, 1646–7

The word 'interregnum', which denotes the time during which a state has no normal ruler, is commonly applied to the period in English history between 1649 and 1660. It is also an apt description of the period between the First and Second Civil Wars in all three kingdoms of the British Isles. King Charles, having lost control of Ireland and having been defeated in England and Scotland, became a prisoner first of the Scots and then of the English and was reduced to soliciting each of his captors to restore his authority on the best terms available.

In Ireland, the bitter war between the Confederates and Parliament had continued unabated, with notable victories by Confederate troops – such as the rout of General Monroe's Anglo-Scots army at Benburgh near the Blackwater early in June 1646[1] – causing the Protestant interest to lose ground. Facing the prospect of a Protestant defeat, Ormonde in February 1647 entered a new round of negotiations, this time with Parliament, to secure the Protestant ascendancy by yielding Dublin (the Irish seat of Crown authority) to Commissioners appointed by Parliament. At this same time, the Scots, having failed to persuade the captive King to accept their conditions for his restoration, yielded him into Parliamentary custody at Holmby (Holdenby) House in Northamptonshire, not far from Naseby, and marched back over the Tweed to Scotland.[2]

Dublin was unconditionally given over in June 1647, and shortly thereafter Ormonde departed Ireland. The effect was to abdicate the Royal authority in Ireland in favour of Parliament and thus to institutionalize Parliamentary power in Ireland. With the Royal authority in abeyance, the Royalist cause in Ireland became subordinated to the prime struggle between Catholic and Puritan.

Although the King was to remain in custody for the rest of his life, he exerted a profound influence upon his captors' plans for postwar England, an influence deriving from the fact that at that stage neither the English nor the Scots could envisage postwar society excluding the King. Accordingly, the various factions among the Scots and within the Parliamentarian ranks sought compacts with the King which would embody their different and competing convictions concerning the postwar terms of settlement. The King's own person figured in these factional conflicts when radicals from the New Model Army kidnapped him in June 1647 from his Parliamentarian custodians. As the *Eikon Basilike* later observed, this incident '[told] the world, that a KING cannot be so low, but He is considerable; adding weight to that Party where He appeares'.[3]

There was, however, a critical difference between the King's perception of the meaning of the Civil War and that of the various Parliamentarian parties. It is clear from Charles's behaviour in the negotiations that he did not see the voluntary surrender of his person as essentially compromising his prewar status. In his own view he had not forfeited the trust he held for his people and retained all the credentials of a king. In a real sense, he sought to set the war aside: to dismiss his defeat and to resume peace on the basis of the Constitution as it appeared in August 1641, after the initial reform measures of the Parliament were completed. This was the spirit of his counter-proposals to the terms put to him both at Uxbridge in 1645 and later at Newcastle. His adversaries, however, had conducted the war on the basis that they had become trustees of the public good in place of a king seduced by evil counsel into separation from his people. In winning the war, the Parliamentarians saw Parliament's assumption of such responsibilities as providentially certified. From the Parliamentarian side, any settlement therefore would require the defeated royalists to acknowledge explicitly the moral judgement delivered through history by the hand of God.

This acknowledgement was specifically sought as part of the Newcastle Propositions and was, of course, the very thing that the King could not concede: his guilt. To concede that would be to concede the legitimacy of the Puritan charge that he had compromised, if not completely forfeited, his God-given status as royal trustee. It would make his kingship – if not the institution of kingship at large – assailable as never before.

The Newcastle Propositions adopted the premise that decisions taken under the Royal Seal after 20 May 1642 – being the date when both Houses of Parliament declared that the King 'seduced by evil counsel intended to raise war against the Parliament' – were invalid, not only because Parliament's assent to the affixing of the Seal was not obtained, but on moral grounds, in that after that date the King was acting wrongfully to the detriment of his subjects.

This moral dimension differentiates the Newcastle Propositions from the Uxbridge Propositions. With the judgement of history apparent in the defeat of the King, the peace terms were not primarily directed to practical power-sharing from the midst of conflict, but in effect arraigned the King and invited him to submit to judgement. By submitting to judgement, the King would notionally accept limitations on his power, which were justified as preventing him from again succumbing to that seduction. In acknowledging his guilt, he was required to accept the propriety of his being returned to kingship on probation.

It was after Charles withheld his assent to the Newcastle Propositions that the symbol of his authority, the Great Seal, was literally broken in pieces, and the silver fragments ordered to be delivered to the Speakers of both Houses.[4] This gave stark notice of an interregnum: the King was not only imprisoned but deprived of the prime instrument by which his power was validated and his authority conveyed. Except in the West Country, where they were still in abeyance, the assizes which had been abandoned between 1643 and 1645 were resumed on the orders of Parliament: a symptom of prewar order returning, but under new governance. The King acknowledged his subordinate position by seeking permission to 'come to London, or any of his houses thereabouts, upon the public faith and security of his two Houses of Parliament and the Scots Commissioners, that he shall be there with honour, freedom and safety'.

In seeking a postwar accommodation of his royal presence, Charles relied naively upon the 'candour of his intentions', which he believed would be recognized by those who were 'good Christians and subjects'. To that audience of faithful subjects in whom belief in divine kingship still survived, he offered 'his personal presence' as a talisman whereby he would 'raise a mutual confidence between him and his people'.

In making this offer, the King was attempting to invoke the magic of his kingship, as if the world of postwar England were no different from the theatrical world of the prewar courtly masques, where Strife, Dissimulation and Envy disappeared at the wave of a royal hand. Just as after Naseby, when he predicted against incontrovertible evidence that the tide would turn in his favour, Charles was confident not only that God would make his efforts prosper, but 'it will be the readiest means by which the kingdoms may again become a comfort to their friends, and a terror to their enemies'. He did not entertain the prospect of a society of which he was no longer the protagonist. In his mind, the readiest means to unity lay in his restoration.

By taking no real account of the issues raised by the war, and especially by his defeat, Charles failed in his appeal to those of his subjects whose experience and thinking had been transformed by the years of Civil War.

As noted, Charles's probity and good faith had been casualties of the propaganda war. Parliament's publication of his correspondence captured at Naseby had delivered a mortal stroke to his image as a trustworthy King, by revealing his secret dealings with the Irish, his private opinions and judgements denigrating his supporters and the directness and nakedness of his plans to play his adversaries against one another to further his own ends. The *Eikon Basilike* acknowledged this propaganda *coup*, reflecting upon the calculated damage to the royal reputation by the malice of his enemies:

> The taking away of my Credit is but a necessary preparation to the taking away of my Life, and my Kingdoms. . . . I must seem neither fit to Live, nor worthy to Reign.[5]

Despite his continual protestations, a King seen to have shed the blood of his subjects and to whom God had denied victory could not easily appeal to his record as ruler to substantiate his Royal integrity.

The *Eikon Basilike* devotes an entire chapter to the peace process, in which the King accuses his enemies of 'setting Peace at, as high a rate, as the worst effects of Warre'.[6] This is a fascinating complaint, given that the 'worst effects of Warre' had been manifested in the King's defeat, so that to the victors peace at any lesser rate was virtually unthinkable. Yet it is clear that the King expected a settlement far more favourable than the military outcome would support, and that, for its part, Parliament compromised its military victory by negotiation, simply because it could not at that stage imagine an England without a King, whatever role the King might play. Parliament therefore accorded the King a negotiating power which his military position did not warrant. Mistaking this as a reflection of the intactness of his prewar kingship, the King was outraged by Parliament's demand for dishonourable concessions, asking for what he felt, in reason, he must deny.

This discrepancy in expectations pinpoints the King's and Parliament's differing conceptions of the meaning of the war. For the King it was a contest. There was a victor and a vanquished, but the battle for power had a political, not moral dimension. It was a forceful effort to make 'the English rebels . . . return to their wits': the means to decide a question, not the mould which shaped the answer. For Parliament, the price of peace was directly related to the cost of the war. Since Parliamentarians conceived that cost not only in the number of lives lost, but as the King's betrayal of his office and his trust, the fact of the war and God's certification of the outcome made it impossible to restore the King's kingship unconditionally – especially when the King refused to recognize the breach that had occurred. This moral dimension also meant that Parliamentarians viewed the vanquished not as persons who had played by the rules and lost honourably, but as accomplices in the crimes perpetrated by the King against his kingdom, and therefore to be proscribed and prosecuted. Hence the open-ended list of war criminals against whom Parliament reserved the right to proceed, which formed one of the stumbling-blocks of the Newcastle peace proposals. As the Parliamentarians would have it, the King's prerogative of Mercy must yield to the divinely sanctioned justice of Parliament.

Nine months of protracted and dilatory negotiations took place between Charles's first answer to the Newcastle Propositions in August 1646 and his third answer in May 1647. In his third reply he was beginning to make concessions in religious matters and regarding the militia. He declared his readiness to accept the Presbyterian Government of the Church of England for three years (presumably on a trial basis), together with the Assembly of Divines at Westminster and the Directory of Worship as proposed by Parliament. He would settle for Parliamentary control of the militia on sea and land for ten years, rather than 20 as required by the Propositions. As for Ireland, 'other things being agreed, His Majesty will give satisfaction therein', whatever that might have meant.[7]

However, just after the King began to make these concessions, Parliament's monopoly of the peace-making was challenged by alternative proposals made in August 1647 by the New Model Army. These proposals were the culmination of several months of tension between the Army and Parliament, as the victorious and under-occupied (but not demobilized) Army found its own voice in the political debate. Religious differences lay at the basis of this developing conflict between Parliament and the Army, although political factors also played a part and the escalation of the conflict was directly attributable to Parliament's inept handling of the soldiers' professional grievances.

While Parliament was dominated by Presbyterians, the Army was dominated by religious Independents. After Naseby in June and the storm of Bristol in September 1645, Cromwell coupled his notice of victory to Parliament with a plea for religious toleration. As a symptom of the widening difference between Parliament and the Army, reflecting the divergence of opinion between Presbyterian and Independents, these pleas were omitted from the official Parliamentary newsletters. The New Model Army became a nursery of nonconformity, giving sectaries a voice by permitting officers and ordinary soldiers to preach without official licence. Cromwell later reflected that religion, although 'not the thing at first contested for . . . at last . . . proved that which was most dear to us'.[8] The religion he sought to preserve was the broad church formed around the conscience of the individual believer, which generations of Puritan writers had invoked in opposition to the ecclesiastical rules and ceremonies imposed by episcopal authority. It was a short and logical step for adherents of this tradition to assert the primacy of conscience over *all* external authority in matters of religion, including the Presbyterian authority which Parliament aimed to impose.

On 21 March 1647, General Fairfax and more than 40 officers met at Saffron Walden church to receive a deputation dispatched by the Presbyterian-led Parliament to enlist volunteers for service in Ireland. The officers agreed to induce their men to enlist, but none of them would personally volunteer until they had obtained satisfactory answers on four matters. These were: which regiments were to remain in commission in England; who was to lead the Parliamentary forces in Ireland; what assurances could be given for the subsistence and payment of troops once in Ireland; and, finally, what satisfaction would be given concerning the outstanding arrears of pay for their Civil War service – then 43 weeks for horse and dragoons and 18 for foot-soldiers – and indemnity for acts committed during that service. A meeting of officers on the following day, which included General Ireton, confirmed this resolution and took the further step of agreeing to present a petition on these matters to Parliament as a whole. Learning of the petition, the Parliamentary Commissioners took offence and appealed to General Fairfax, disputing the soldiers' right to question Parliament's orders. Fairfax denied knowledge of the petition and undertook to ensure that it contained no matter that would give Parliament offence. Within 12 hours 29 officers had abandoned their demand for answers and agreed to volunteer for service in Ireland in a spirit of professed confidence in Parliament's response on the matters raised.

The rank and file, who had more at stake in the four demands than their superiors, reacted to this recantation by circulating a petition of their own. They also drew up *An Apology of the Soldiers to all their Commission Officers*, urging the officers to 'go along with us in this business, or at the least to let us quietly alone in this our design, we desiring no more than what is just and right, according to all their declarations and protestations to the whole world'. However, the officers intervened to have the language of the petition modified and to encourage the soldiers to direct it to Fairfax rather than Parliament in a bid to confine the political damage, keep the terms of the dialogue with Parliament within the control of the Army command,[9] and perhaps to defend all parties from allegations of insubordination to Parliament's orders, in that a petition addressed to the Commander was an internal matter and its authors could be disciplined militarily rather than prosecuted as treasonable.

Upon hearing of it, Parliament ordered Fairfax to suppress the petition, declaring that persons proceeding with the petition would be regarded as enemies of the state. Although the Lords voted to summon Fairfax to account for what was occurring, the Commons ordered that the officers concerned in the petition be sent up to the Bar of the House for examination. That Fairfax succeeded in suppressing the petition testifies as much to the political heat it generated and perhaps to behind-the-scenes officer involvement, as to Fairfax's personal standing in being able to persuade his troops.[10]

Fairfax's reply to the Speaker's letter conveying these orders referred to his soldiers'

> very deep sense of their unhappiness in being misunderstood in their very clear intentions, which were no other than by way of petition to represent unto me those inconveniences which would necessarily befall most of the army after disbanding; desiring that as much as I should judge fit and seasonable might be submissively made known to the house of commons

and reassured the Commons of the Army's 'constant perseverance in [its] accustomed obedience unto all your commands'. As ordered, Fairfax dispatched five senior officers to give it '(as far as they are acquainted therewith) a full and candid account of the whole proceedings in this petition'.[11] When interviewed by the Commons, these officers denied involvement in any petition or that there were 'menacing or threatening words used' and were eventually given leave to return to their regiments, charged with 'care for the suppressing [of the petition], or any other of the like Nature for the future'.[12]

Meanwhile, the rank and file began to formalize their representation, to ensure their voice was heard and to give it strength, consistency and scope outside the narrow ambit of complaints about pay arrears and indemnities. In April they took the highly unusual step of electing regimental representatives (known as Agitators) who would place before the officers the soldiers' 'rights and desires', extending to issues such as the political terms of the postwar settlement.[13]

The *Apology of the Soldiers to their Officers*, printed on 3 May 1647 as an addition to the similarly named *Apology* of 28 April 1647, reflects the more militant tone of relations between the rank and file and their officers, the widened political agenda and corrosive animosity towards the Parliament. It speaks of the end of 'all tyrannies and oppressions', so that 'the meanest subject should fully enjoy his right, liberty and properties, in all things; which the Parliament have made known to all the world' and for which the war, in the authors' view, was fought.

> But instead of it, to the great grief and saddening of our hearts, we see that oppression is as great as ever, if not greater, yea, and that upon the cordial friends to the Parliament and us . . . the best and most candid intentions and actions of theirs and ours, grossly and foully mis-construed, even to such a height as deserving no less than to be declared as troublers of, and enemies to, the state and kingdom.

It complained that

> . . . many of our fellow soldiers that have been disbanded have been so rigorously dealt withal as imprisoned, indicted, and hanged, for things done in . . . necessity of the Parliament's service

and asked

> Was there ever such things done by a Parliament . . . ? . . . Is it not better to die like men than to be enslaved and hanged like dogs? Which must and will be yours and our portion if not now looked into, even before our disbanding.[14]

The common thread in the soldiers' religious and political complaints was their new-found equation of freedom and selfhood. Edmund Ludlow observed that about this time the men in the ranks rejected the term 'common souldiers', for that of 'private souldiers'. In their regimental grievances presented to the Army Generals at Saffron Walden on 13–14 May 1647, they placed themselves in the category of 'freemen of England . . . deprived of their liberties and freedom': regarding themselves not as 'subjects' or 'soldiers', defined by their duties, but as citizens entitled to – and currently deprived of – their rights. They also expressed resentment that the Presbyterian-dominated Parliament 'denied the liberty which Christ hath purchased for us . . . to enforce us to a human conformity never enjoined by Christ' and expressed the fear that 'the consciences of men shall be pressed beyond the light they have received from the rule of the Word'.[15] These concepts expressed the developing coalition of radical interests, as the religious radicals in the Army took up the language of social and political radicals like the Levellers – the 'first democratic political movement in modern history'[16] – and the political pamphleteers began to support the Army and circulate its grievances. They also mark the extent to which the radical faction within the Army diverged from the alleged joint war aims of the English Parliamentarians and the Scots as enshrined in the Covenant.

By mid-May 1647 there was, therefore, escalating tension between the increasingly radical rank and file and their commanders, most of whom still wished to reach an accommodation with the King. Exhortation to the commanders could quickly become threatening:

> Therefore, brave Commanders, the Lord put a spirit of courage into your hearts, that you may stand fast in your integrity that you have manifested to us your soldiers; and we do declare to you that if any of you shall not, he shall be marked with a brand of infamy forever as a traitor to his country and an enemy to this Army.[17]

It was in this context that the Agitator Cornet George Joyce and his troopers, possibly acting in collusion with radical officers, sought in June 1647 to increase the bargaining power of the radical faction by seizing the King from Parliamentary custody.[18]

The task of preserving Army unity and co-ordinating policy in these extraordinary circumstances fell to General Fairfax as commanding officer. However, the intellectual formulation of the Army position fell to General Ireton, who, as a superior officer and orthodox Congregationalist, had an important stake both in consolidating Army morale to maximize pressure on the Presbyterian camp and in maintaining discipline, soothing grievances and seeking to lower the political temperature among his subordinates to keep open the option of accommodating a restored King. Ireton was almost certainly responsible for the *Solemn Engagement of the Army*, which was accepted at general rendezvous on 5 June 1647 and its companion piece, issued on 14 June, 1647, *A Declaration, or Representation from Sir Thomas Fairfax and the Army under his Command*, which together set forth the terms upon which the Army would disband or accept service in Ireland and the principles to be applied in any peace settlement. By accepting the Agitators as part of the General Council which the *Solemn Engagement* established, but balancing them with commissioned officers, these manifestos both entrenched and diluted Army radicalism. Most significantly, they immeasurably strengthened the Army's position by unifying it under one policy.

On the religious question, the *Solemn Engagement* offered reassurance that the Army was not captive to particular persons or interests and did not seek to establish Independency in place of Presbyterianism. The Army's aim was to preserve 'common and equal right, freedom and safety'. But its stance towards Parliament was starkly insubordinate in refusing to disband until its grievances were addressed. The *Declaration* similarly upheld the Army's right, if necessary, to resist Parliament's orders – on the remarkable and now famous basis that 'we were not a mere mercenary army . . . but called forth and conjured by the several declarations of Parliament to the defence of our own and the people's just rights and liberties'. Moreover, the *Declaration* demanded the reform of Parliament which, under Leveller influence, the Army radicals had come to regard as arbitrary and corrupt. The reform of Parliament became an integral part of the Army's proposed peace settlement and plan for postwar England. Further, the *Declaration* proposed, as a matter of political priority, that only after the people's rights and liberties had been settled and established should the rights of the King and his posterity be considered.[19]

Thus, by mid-1647 the peace settlement was clouded by the prospect of a renewed Civil War on ideological lines between, on the one hand, the Presbyterians of the Long Parliament and those in the City of London and in Scotland and, on the other, the New Model Army and its supporters. Parliament and the City colluded in a plan to purge the Trained Bands – a force of some 18 000 men who were under their direct control – of Independents and to create their own 'New Model' to oppose the New Model Army militarily. The Northern Army, which was kept at two-thirds the strength of the New Model Army, was led by General Poyntz, who was associated with the Presbyterian interest.[20] The English Presbyterians were also in the process of securing military support from Scotland. A 'New Model' Scots army created from the force which had left England in February 1647 under the command of General Leslie (a doctrinaire Presbyterian) was preparing for deployment in England if necessary.

But differences between the Army leadership and the lower ranks re-emerged at a meeting of the Army at Reading on 16 July 1647: the so-called Reading Debates. There was division on a number of questions.

The radicals wanted a military push – a demonstration of raw military power – in the form of a march on London to overawe the Parliament, support the minority in Parliament who were the Army's political allies (whom they called 'the honest party in the House') and impeach their prominent Presbyterian opponents. This purge of the Parliament was to be accompanied by an assumption of control of the London militia, then mobilizing in the Presbyterian cause under the direction of a predominantly Presbyterian Parliament. The officers, especially Cromwell, wanted to avoid such drastic action against Parliament and to continue negotiating with the King, despite opposition from the Agitators to any continued negotiation. To further their more conservative objectives, the Army Generals proposed new terms for peace drawn up by General Ireton, to be forwarded to the King as an act of Army diplomacy, sidestepping Parliament. These were called *The Heads of the Proposals* and were presented to the General Council on 17 July 1647 – their hasty introduction possibly a reaction to the contrary arguments of the Agitators on the previous day and the need to circumvent their impatience for direct action.

The *Proposals* were shown to the King and his advisers informally on about 23 July, and were formally presented to him by an Army deputation on 28 July. This deputation, which included General Ireton, spent three hours negotiating with the King. However, when the King ill-advisedly pronounced 'You cannot do without me. You will fall to ruin if I do not sustain you',[21] Colonel Rainborowe left the meeting in protest and reported back to the Army the ill-treatment with which, in his view, its deputation had met.

The King was buoyed by hopes of armed support from Scotland after his recent correspondence with the Scots, and of support within London. In July 1647, a crowd of Londoners signed a *Solemn Engagement of the City [of London]*, engaging to restore King and Covenant but using the King as a tool to achieve a settlement on different terms from the wishes of the Army as expressed in *its Solemn Engagement*. This intensification of military and political pressure towards a Presbyterian settlement is sometimes styled 'the Presbyterian counter-revolution'. In reaction to this pressure, the two Speakers, eight Peers and 57 Members of Parliament of Independent persuasion quitted the Parliament by 30 July and took refuge with the Army, thus polarizing the warring camps and providing a rationale for Army intervention in Parliament, as previously advocated by the Agitators. The General Council of the Army adopted *The Heads of the Proposals* on 1 August, which were printed the following day as a public statement of the Army's programme. The Army marched on London and occupied Westminster briefly from 6 August 1647. The Independent Members of Parliament were reinstated during this invasion and the Presbyterian Parliamentarians subjected to intimidation.

These developments provided the King with welcome bargaining opportunities. During August and September 1647 the King's view that he was indispensable to the settlement of peace seemed to be justified.[22] Presbyterian Parliamentarians and Army generals alike vied for his attention, courting the Royal approval for their competing proposals. Consulting with the King as much as a Member of Parliament as in his capacity of general officer, Cromwell (together with Ireton) profoundly offended army and civilian radicals and gravely damaged his reputation amongst them. Hugh Peters, a fiery Army chaplain, described them as 'too great courtiers'.

On 7 September 1647, Parliament sent revised Newcastle Propositions to the King in response to the King's third answer to the Propositions and requested an answer within six days. The King's prompt reply to these little-changed Propositions was to express a preference for the Army's *Heads of Proposals* as a more suitable foundation for a lasting peace; a decision which angered the Presbyterian Members of Parliament. He described the latest Parliamentary propositions as 'in many respects more disagreeable to the present condition of affairs than when they were formerly presented to him, as being destructive to the main principal interests of the army, and of all those whose affections concur with them'.[23] In this the King was being tactical. With the New Model Army at odds with Parliament, he was able to regain a voice in the peace process. By preferring the Army proposals, he could also escape Parliament's insistence that the Covenant be imposed on all three kingdoms and could seek a settlement with Scotland on terms more acceptable to him.

At Putney on 16 September the Council of the Army resolved to ask Parliament to draw up bills securing the subjects' liberties and the privileges of Parliament, and settling the militia, with the understanding that after these bills obtained the Royal assent subsequent bills would secure the King's rights. The decision to proceed in this way caused a row in the Council. A minority led by Rainborowe strongly opposed Cromwell, on the basis that further negotiations with the King were useless. During the dispute, a heated Rainborowe told Cromwell that 'one of them must not live'.[24]

The Independent party in Parliament also fractured around this issue. After both Houses of Parliament sitting on 21 September recognized that the King's reply amounted to a rejection of the Newcastle Propositions, Henry Martin, who with Rainborowe led the new republican group of

Independents, proposed that no further addresses should be made to the King. The King was described as 'the Achan in Israel' (1 Chronicles 2:7): in other words, a cursed disturber of God's chosen people. Cromwell, Ireton and others of the old Independent leadership opposed Martin's motion, Cromwell collecting the 'no' votes, which were 84 to 34. As late as 22 September, Cromwell and Ireton were reported as opposing moves in the House of Commons to break off negotiations with the King. It was in this context that *The Heads of the Proposals* was republished by the Army leaders on 24 September as an appeal to public opinion.

The Heads of the Proposals was primarily concerned with settling the peace in England and Ireland. Scotland was mentioned only briefly, with generalized reference to the need to keep the peace between Scotland and England. Dealing with the issues of the militia, Ireland and the Church – the three issues left unresolved since Uxbridge – the *Proposals* gave Parliament control of the militia for ten years, left the prosecution of the war in Ireland to Parliament, and repudiated the Presbyterian claim to monopolize the Church settlement.

The Thirteenth Clause of *The Heads of the Proposals* stipulated that no one was to be required to take the Covenant, and that no penalties were to be imposed for refusing it. The reason offered was to prevent individuals being 'restrained to take it against their judgments or consciences'. This publicly laid the axe to the root of the Covenant justification of the Civil War, shattered the idea of a joint settlement and raised the question, retrospectively, of whether there had ever truly been a joint war.[25]

By proposing to take away the traditional coercive powers of the bishops and ecclesiastical officers, *The Heads of the Proposals* also effectively envisaged the separation of church and state. The Eleventh Clause proposed the repeal of all laws enabling civil magistrates to impose civil penalties for breaches of ecclesiastical law. The Twelfth Clause prevented Parliament from enjoining the use of the Book of Common Prayer and provided that no penalties were to be imposed for absences from church services (although anti-papist legislation was to remain in force, to prevent papists 'from disturbing the State').

The civilian Leveller, John Wildman, later attributed the King's receptiveness to *The Heads of the Proposals* to the fact that he had previewed and modified them. He denied that they were in reality *Army* proposals, since he 'scarce believe[d] they passed a General Council before they were published'. According to Wildman, the modifications included according the King a full veto over legislation (where the draft proposals gave effect to legislation passed by two consecutive parliaments, notwith-

standing the King's refusal of consent); halving the period for which
enemies of Parliament were to be excluded from office and allowing the
Council of State to appoint such persons to positions of trust within the
exclusion period; allowing the office and functions of the bishops to continue, with only their civil jurisdiction abolished (whereas it was the desire
of the Agitators to eradicate the bishops entirely); and giving the Lords
– 'the very offspring of the King's corrupt will' – power over the militia
'co-ordinate and co-equal to the Representative of all the nation, the
Commons in Parliament' and a 'judicial power in exposition and application of law . . . so that any sentence of the Commons, representing all
England, may be contradicted by five or six Lords, by virtue of the King's
patent'. These, Wildman claimed, were wounds received from 'pretended
friends' – the Army Generals – for the sake of the King, whom he termed
'the capital enemy'.[26]

The political opposition within the rank and file to *The Heads of the
Proposals* was expressed in the election of new and yet more radical
Agitators from five elite regiments – including Cromwell's and Ireton's
own – raising the question of how effective a control of their regiments
the Generals had by this time. The new Agitators – whom Rushworth
terms the 'dissenting Agitators of the Army of the Five Regiments' – were
strongly influenced by the views of Lieutenant-Colonel John Lilburne,
whom Wildman accused Cromwell of allowing to languish in prison at
the will of the Lords in Parliament. The new Agitators met regularly in
London with the civilian Levellers. They regarded *The Heads of the
Proposals* as promoting the King's interests before the Army's and as a
denial of rights that the people 'have purchased by blood', which the
restoration of the King would deny. This case is made out in *The Case
of the Army Truly Stated* dated 15 October 1647 by John Wildman, which
evidences the 'ideological bridge' between the Army radicals and the
Leveller movement.[27] The proposals contained in the document were
separately issued, in abbreviated form, as *Propositions from the Agitators of
Five Regiments,* dated 18 October 1647.

Essentially, the *Case* calls upon the Army not to resile from its *Solemn
Engagement* of 5 June 1647 or disband 'before satisfaction or security is
given to the whole Army in relation to themselves or other the freeborn
people, either in respect to their grievances or desires'. It complains that
the train of artillery is to be disbanded before satisfaction has been given:

> And when the strength or sinews of the Army be broken, what effec-
> tual good can be secured for themselves or the people in case of oppo-
> sition? . . .

The whole intent of the Engagement, and the equitable sense of it, hath been perverted openly by affirming, and by sinister means making seeming determinations in the Council, that the Army was not to insist upon, or demand any security for, any of their own or other the freeborn people's freedoms and rights . . .

It also cites alleged breaches of the undertakings in the *Declaration* of 14 June, and 'many discouragements of the Agitators of the regiments in consulting about the most effectual means for procuring the speedy redress of the people's grievances'. It notes, in particular, that

. . . in the Declaration of June 14 . . . it was desired that the rights and liberties of the people might be secured before the King's business should be considered. But now the grievances of the people are propounded to be considered after the restoring him to the regal power . . .

and that

[the] engagement for purging the House from those delinquents, whose interest engages them to be designing mischief against the people and Army, is declined and broken, to the black reproach and foulest infamy of the Army.

Later it speaks of the 'poor nation and oppressed people' expressing their miseries 'in petitions, first to the King, then to the Parliament and then to the Army; yet they have all been like broken reeds, even the Army itself, upon whom they leaned, have pierced their hands'.[28]

It is clear from this that the Army was no longer speaking with one voice, but had become a battleground of opposing convictions and proposals. Not only the unity of the Army, but its control was at issue, as the dissenting Agitators vied with the Generals. An army victorious in war was beginning to defeat itself in peace. The image of 'pierced hands' could not be lost upon an audience accustomed to interpret its political life through biblical metaphor. The Army, in the eyes of its rank and file, was crucifying its own.

The emphasis in the radical manifestos upon the soldiers' desires as well as their grievances reflects the dissenting Agitators' wider agenda of public justice through political reform: an agenda earlier proclaimed in their *Advertisements for managing the counsels of the Army* of 4 May 1647. After reciting the usual litany of grievances concerning Parliament's failure to grant indemnities and provide security for arrears, *The Case of the Army Truly Stated* turns quickly to 'the rights and freedoms of ourselves and the people, that we declared we would insist upon': these being, a finite date for the dissolution of the present Parliament; the reform of Parliament; and relief from 'public burdens or oppressions by arbitrary committees, injustice in the law, tithes, monopolies and restraint of free trade, burdensome oaths, inequality of assessments, excise (and otherwise)'. Among the proposals it put forward was one for fixed parliamentary terms and regular elections, with a franchise extending to all freeborn males over 21 years of age except those who had disqualified themselves 'by delinquency' – that is, notoriety in the Royalist cause.

In the three-cornered contest between King, Parliament and the Army, the Army during August and September 1647 enjoyed the greatest practical power. It had the King in its custody, and had asserted its power over Parliament by occupying Westminster. The King had expressed a preference for its terms of settlement over those of Parliament, turning the tide against the Covenant settlement. But this power was dependent on Army unity. Without a unified voice and a capacity for united action, the Army's 'strength and sinews' would be broken and its power lost. The Agitators and Generals could not but be aware of this, as the fragile unity affirmed in the *Solemn Engagement* and the *Declaration* broke apart into renewed accusations of betrayal and the radical faction increased numerically, with a further eight regiments electing radical Agitators.

Fairfax's mistrust of the dissenting Agitators is encapsulated in his letter of 7 October 1647 to the Parliament, where he writes of 'the great Advantages some that study Anarchy and Distractions, take upon [the needs of the soldiers], to make their Impressions upon this Army'.[29] The letter from the Agitators of the Five Regiments, which accompanied *The Case of the Army Truly Stated*, included the startling statement that the soldiery would not obey orders from either their Commander-in-Chief or the Parliament to disband or keep silent, because neither source could 'discharge us of our Duties to God or to our own Natures'.[30]

The General Council of the Army planned to discuss further negotiations with the King at its meeting on 14 October 1647, following the King's indication of his preference for the Army's proposals over those of Parliament. However, the arrival in London on 11 October of two new Scottish Commissioners raised the spectre of a Scottish invasion on the King's behalf. Concern on this head displaced any consideration of further negotiations with the King.

At its following meeting on 21 October, and three days after Fairfax had received the document, the General Council considered *The Case of the Army Truly Stated.* Its first reaction was to punish the junior officers believed to have promoted the work; but after debate – in which Ireton may be presumed to have played a significant part – it was agreed to appoint a committee of senior officers and soldier and officer Agitators, to consider the case, take action in relation to such matters as the arrears of pay, and defend the Army against the aspersions cast upon it. It was, however, agreed to purge from the Army, as suspected infiltrators and subversives, all cavalry troops recruited during and after the Army's march on London on 6 August.

This committee of officers and Agitators met at Ireton's quarters immediately after the General Council and, on hearing that a meeting of dissenting Agitators was also taking place, advised them in writing of what had occurred at the General Council and invited them to meet with the committee 'to go on in a way that might tend to unity'. The Agitators effectively declined the invitation, on the basis that their demands were clear and simply required the Council's concurrence. Little might therefore be gained from dialogue. However, they were, in Ireton's words, subsequently 'induced to descend a little from the height' and agreed to appear, together with some of their civilian supporters, before the next meeting of the General Council on 28 October 1647, to debate the matters in question.[31] It is clear from the manifestos produced to coincide with the first day of what became known as the 'Putney Debates' that this occasion was viewed with high seriousness, at least in radical quarters, and temporarily eclipsed the Army's dialogue with the King and Parliament.

The Army had been headquartered at Putney since August, when the King was removed to Hampton Court. Located on the Thames halfway between Hampton Court and Westminster, Putney effectively symbolized the Army's ideological distance from both King and Parliament. For several days between 28 October and 1 November 1647, Putney Church echoed with radical sentiments unheard of five years earlier, and which possess a haunting eloquence that resonates across the interval between that time and this.

3

THE ARMY IN DEBATE

Only days after *The Case of the Army Truly Stated* was published, Cromwell spoke for three hours in the House of Commons in his capacity as a Member of Parliament. He denied that either he or his senior officers had any part in the manifesto, explicitly disavowed it and dissociated himself and the Army leadership from the soldiers' arguments. In Army terms it was a very divisive speech and since Parliament at that time leaked copiously, news of it soon circulated.

When the General Council of the Army met at Putney on 28 October 1647 with Agitators and civilian Levellers in its midst, there was a preliminary skirmish between the parties on this issue. The opening address by Edward Sexby, a trooper from Fairfax's regiment and one of the leading dissenting Agitators, was directed particularly to Cromwell and Ireton. He informed them:

> Your credits and reputation have been much blasted, upon these two considerations. . . . for seeking to settle this kingdom in such a way wherein we thought to have satisfied all men, and we have dissatisfied them – I mean in relation to the King. The other is in reference to a Parliamentary authority, which most here would lose their lives for . . .[1]

Cromwell took up the point, claiming not to know why he and Ireton had been singled out 'except you think we have done somewhat, or acted somewhat, different from the sense and resolution of the General Council'. In defending himself, Cromwell distinguished between representations he had made behalf of the Army and those made 'in another

64

capacity as a member of the House'. His support for further negotiations with the King was of the second kind and, he added, 'what I delivered as my own sense I am not ashamed of'. Colonel Rainborowe interposed that nevertheless 'it *was* urged in the House that it was the sense of the Army that it should be so'; whereupon Ireton, seeking to deflect the issue, 'desire[d] not to speak of these things', yet ventured to say that if he *had* indicated the Army's support for a further approach to the King – which he had not – it would have reflected 'what I thought. And if I thought otherwise of the Army . . . I protest I should have been ashamed of the Army and detested it.'[2]

The apparently conciliatory clearing of the air was therefore replete with tensions and challenges. Two letters from the Agents of the Five Regiments had appeared on the eve of the debates. The first, *A Letter from the Agents to the Whole Soldiery*, exhorted the rank and file not to be persuaded that it was 'irregular and disorderly' to argue with their officers, but to remember 'that if you had not joined together at first, and chose your Agents to act for you when your officers thought it not safe for them to appear, you had been now in no capacity to plead for your own or the people's freedom'. The letter foreshadowed that 'some will be muttering that we have designed to divide the Army, or the soldiers from the officers'; but reminded the soldiers that the Agitators' demands were merely for performance of those things in which the Army had previously 'joined unanimously', concluding rhetorically 'And is this to divide?'[3] A second letter, from the noted Independent preacher John Saltmarsh to the Council of War, invited the officers to '[l]ook over your first Engagements, and compare them with your proceedings, that you may see what you have done, what you must do'.[4]

Further pressure was exerted on the officers by the advent of the *First Agreement of the People*. Also produced on the eve of the Debates, this agreement listed the regiments that subscribed to *The Case of the Army Truly Stated*: all the elite cavalry regiments and a significant number of foot regiments. It made apparent both the numerical strength of the radical element and their military muscle. With such numbers of soldiers, including elite horse regiments, in dispute with their nominal commanders in the Army and their nominal political leadership in Parliament, the situation was clearly threatening.

Historians differ in the significance they ascribe to the Putney Debates.[5] In part this reflects the absence or inaccessibility of any record of the debates when histories of the Civil War were first written. A shorthand record was taken by the Secretary to the General Council, William Clarke, and a fair copy later made – although precisely when is unclear.[6]

After Clarke's death the fair copy was donated to Worcester College, Oxford, along with other papers, where it languished until brought to light by C. H. Firth at the end of the nineteenth century. John Rushworth does not appear to have had access to the record for his *Historical Collections* covering the years 1645–8 (although there may have been other reasons for the omission, since *The Case of the Army Truly Stated* does not appear in his collection either). He records the events taking place at Putney in summary as 'understandings' of things taking place at a remove from his own location at Westminster, and which – for reasons that are political as well as geographical – he chooses not to elaborate. For the 28 October he notes that '[t]he dissenting Agitators of the Army of the Five Regiments put forth some further Papers this Day' and then reproduces the brief Answer of the Five Agitators to allegations that they are fostering division in the ranks. For the 29 October, he reports that the General Council 'sate very close from Morning until Night' and that in addition to consideration of papers from the Agitators of the Five Regiments

> . . . some other things fell in . . . which occasioned a very high Debate, but the Particulars are not thought fit to be mentioned until the further Sense of the General Council be known concerning the same.[7]

Rushworth's reticence in recording the matters in dispute (like the caution of the newspapers in reporting the proceedings) may certainly have contributed to the scant regard paid to the Debates in subsequent histories and the obscurity in which the fair copy transcript was permitted to remain. Nothing is made of them in Henry Cary's *Memorials of the Great Civil War in England from 1646 to 1652* published in 1842 or in Thomas Carlyle's 1845 compilation of Cromwell's letters and speeches. Firth himself appears not to have appreciated the full value of his discovery, which was made when he was editing the Clarke papers for the Camden Society, which published the first text of the Debates in 1891. S. R. Gardiner, however, acclaimed the newly published Clarke papers as 'bring[ing] us, as we have never been brought before, into the very heart of [the New Model Army] . . . and enabl[ing] us to trace the movements of political thought which afterwards developed themselves in the constitutional experiments of the Commonwealth'. Gardiner devoted some 16 pages to the debates. A. S. P. Woodhouse, similarly, wrote in his Introduction:

> The Debates have a special value, even beyond the pamphlet literature of the day, in giving us a spontaneous and unconscious revelation of

the Puritan mind as it wrestles with its problems, practical and theoretic, in an effort not merely to justify a policy and batter down opposition, but to arrive at truth and agreement.[8]

To this writer the Debates provide not only a vivid glimpse into the radical mentality of the English Civil War and Revolution, but represent a critical moment in English political history. The participants are people on the threshold of power after a bloody war, determined to secure the vision of a future England for which they fought. Their moral intensity is grounded in the 'sacrifice in blood' by which their victory was purchased and their cause sanctified. They believe they owe a duty to providence which has brought them so far, a belief that gives their political convictions the quality of 'conscience'. They are in awe at the magnitude of the divine plan. As Sexby says: 'We have been by Providence put upon strange things, such as the ancientest here doth scarce remember.'[9] But their common journey has produced differing visions and incompatible ends: one vehemently republican; the other seeking a reformed constitutional monarchy.

At 48, Cromwell was one of the oldest present. Ireton was 36; and the radical Leveller John Wildman was 24. With 'theirs and the people's freedoms' at stake, the radicals had no scope for astute compromise or adroit manoeuvre. The Army leadership was more politically shrewd and equally tenacious, mistrustful of the universalism and secularism of the Leveller proposals. Cromwell's radical religious Independency would later assert itself in a foreshadowed 'reign of grace' by the godly minority that providence selected, placing him in irreconcilable opposition to Leveller democracy. But at this stage Cromwell and Ireton were seeking a settlement that involved the King. If all had gone as the leadership planned, Ireton might have been Secretary of State in a restored and purified monarchy. The dialectical interplay between these two Army factions, with differing philosophical bases, reflecting back on the reasons for which they fought the war and postulating rival futures for England, reveals the truly extraordinary nature, scale and controversy of the issues raised by the defeat of the King. It also emphasizes the unprecedented position in which the victors found themselves, as men still young but hardened by war and grappling with their own power, suddenly faced with the task of defining and bringing into being a true model of godly statehood.

The Debates commence with a tone of polite containment, with both parties seeking to dampen the dispute and reach a resolution. Sexby desired his leaders to 'consider those things that shall be offered to

[them]; and if [they] saw anything of reason, [to] . . . join with us, that the kingdom may be eased and our fellow soldiers may be quieted in spirit'. He was sure that it was not only the officers' proper business but 'in all [their] hearts' to satisfy the soldiers' needs and demands. But there is little reason in his uncompromising formulation of those demands. In the midst of the opening formalities his position is stark:

> The cause of our misery [is] upon two things. We sought to satisfy all men, and it was well; but in going [about] to do it we have dissatisfied all men. We have laboured to please a king, and I think, except we go about to cut all our throats, we shall not please him; and we have gone to support an house, which will prove rotten studs – I mean the Parliament, which consists of a company of rotten members.[10]

Cromwell, as a more artful politician, delays his reply, making an indirect rejoinder in the course of his self-defence against the charge of misrepresenting the Army's position in Parliament. He rehearses the immediate past history leading up to the General Council, then tactfully and tactically moves that the invitees be heard. Ireton adopts a similar approach, commencing with self-defence and ending with a motion admitting the visitors. But Ireton's position is conveyed almost as immediately, and certainly as directly, as Sexby's:

> . . . yet I shall declare it again that I do not seek, or would not seek, nor will join with them that do seek, the destruction either of Parliament or King. Neither will I consent with those, or concur with them, who will not attempt all the ways that are possible to preserve both, and to make good use, and the best use that can be, of both for the kingdom. And I did not hear anything from that gentleman (Mr Sexby) that could induce or incline me to [abandon] that resolution.[11]

Thus the battle-lines and the stand-off are apparent in the opening minutes.

Having reduced their case to a set of principles in *An Agreement of the People*, the radicals were keen that that document set the framework for the debate. Robert Everard, the Agent for Cromwell's Regiment, exhorted the Council to 'fall directly upon the matter presented to [it]' and lay aside 'all carping of words', that the Army might 'go on together'. His short statement, before the *Agreement* was read out, seeks to pre-empt the debate by defining its starting-point and dictating its terms:

According to my expectations and your engagements, you are resolved every one to purchase our inheritances which have been lost, and free this nation from the tyranny that lies upon us. I question not but that it is all your desires. And for that purpose we desire you to do nothing but what we present to your consideration.[12]

Cromwell's reaction is to note that '[t]hese things that you have now offered . . . are new to us: . . . this is the first time we have had a view of them'. He also comments on the magnitude of the proposals, which contain

. . . very great alterations of the very government of the kingdom, alterations from that government that it hath been under, I believe I may almost say, since it was a nation . . . And what the consequences of such an alteration as this would be, if there were nothing else to be considered, wise men and godly men ought to consider. I say, *if* there were nothing else . . . It is not enough to propose things that are good in the end, but suppose this model were an excellent model, and fit for England and the kingdom to receive, it is our duty as Christians and men to consider consequences and consider the way.[13]

Cromwell's 'something else' requiring consideration is what he sees as the work at hand: the task of unifying the Army by considering that which 'tends to the uniting of us' (rather than to disputation, as in the case of the *Agreement*) and of determining 'what obligations lie upon us, and how far we are engaged . . . and how far we are free'.[14]

This immediately sparks a debate that is both procedural and philosophical. Procedurally, each party is anxious to command the terms of the debate and to defer consideration of the other's propositions until after critical groundwork has been set. Wildman summarizes the position as follows:

I conceive the chief weight of your Honour's speech lay in this, that you were first to consider what obligations lay upon you, and how far you were engaged, before you could consider what was just in this paper now propounded . . . To that I must only offer this . . . the first thing is to consider the honesty of what is offered . . . By the consideration of the justice of what is offered, [it] shall appear whether [those obligations] were just or no.[15]

Later in the Debate, he is even more forthright:

> And whereas it is desired that engagements may be considered, I shall
> desire only that the justice of the thing that is proposed may be con-
> sidered . . . Whether the thing be just or the people's due? And then
> there can be no engagement to bind from it.[16]

The parties differ in what they perceive as fundamental. To the radicals it is preservation of 'the people's rights', and any engagement dero-
gating from those rights and therefore destructive of the kingdom,
should, as a matter of conscience, be breached. To the leadership – for
whom Ireton is the key spokesman – the honouring of laws and covenants
is the cornerstone of social order. To feel free to break an engagement
without considering amends is, Ireton says, 'a principle that will take away
all commonwealth[s], and will take away the fruit of this [very] engagement if it were entered into'.[17]

Underlying the very abstract and prolix debate on the force of prior
engagements and the circumstances in which they may or should be
breached is the radicals' concern that these engagements may involve a
secret compact with the King and the leadership's desire to deflect debate
from the radical platform contained in the *Agreement* to an accommodation with King and Parliament based on the Army's past propositions.
Rainborowe astutely notes the obstacles the leadership is putting in the
way of a debate on the merits of the radicals' proposals:

> It hath been said, that if a man be engaged he must perform his
> engagements. I am wholly confident that every honest man is bound
> in duty to God and his conscience, let him be engaged in what he will,
> to decline it when [he sees it to be evil] . . . There are two [further]
> objections are made against it.
>
> The one is *division*. Truly I think we are utterly undone if we divide,
> but I hope that honest things have carried us on thus long, and will
> keep us together, and I hope that we will not divide. Another thing is
> *difficulties*. Oh, unhappy men are we that ever began this war! If ever
> we [had] looked upon difficulties, I do not know that ever we should
> have looked an enemy in the face. Truly, I think the Parliament were
> very indiscreet to contest with the King if they did not consider first
> that they should go through difficulties . . .[18]

Rainborowe's unmistakable irony culminates in an image which clev-
erly reverses, but reverberates with, the Parliament's failure to pay its

Army: 'For I think it is a poor service to God and the kingdom, to take their pay and to decline the work'. He goes on to claim that

> ... there have been many scufflings between the honest men of England and those that have tyrannized over them; and if it be [true what I have] read, there is none of those just and equitable laws that the people of England are born to, but are entrenchment[s on the once enjoyed privileges of their rulers] altogether. But [even] if they were those which the people have always been under, if the people find that they are [not] suitable to freemen as they are, I know no reason [that] should deter me ... from endeavouring by all means to gain anything that might be of more advantage to them than the government under which they live.[19]

In fact, as Maximilian Petty (one of the two civilian Levellers present) later conceded, there was 'somewhat' in the *Agreement* 'against the King, the power of the King, and somewhat against the power of the Lords'. The 'principles of common freedome' adopted by the *Agreement* from *The Case of the Army Truly Stated* included the proposition that:

> all power is originally and essentially in the whole body of the people of this nation ... and ... the supreme power of the people's representers, or Commons assembled in Parliament [ought forthwith be declared].[20]

The intention to exclude the monarchy is made quite plain some sentences later:

> This power of Commons in Parliament is the thing against which the King hath contended, and the people have defended with their lives, and therefore ought now be demanded as the price of their blood.[21]

As the radicals see it, these are rights *defended* with the people's lives, which the people are now in a moral position to *demand*. Any settlement is to reflect the cost of the war – the 'price of their blood' – not simply the fact of the King's defeat.

Cromwell responds to Rainborowe's speech with an assurance that his objections of difficulty and danger '[and] of the consequences' are not 'forged to deter from consideration of the business' but are 'things fitting consideration'. He is clearly not convinced that the radicals speak for the general populace when they claim to speak for 'the people'. He concedes that '[p]erhaps we are upon engagements that we cannot with honesty break', but claims that he is 'as free from engagements to the King as any man in all the world': the Army's engagements are to the kingdom and the Parliament. Because 'the kingdom is in the danger it is in', he proposes that a committee be formed out of the General Council to consider the prior engagements, and another to engage in 'liberal and free debate' with the Agents, followed by a short day for the General Council. Rather than 'have this kingdom break in pieces', he offers to withdraw from the Army and lay down his commission, leaving the way open for the radicals. But he is also buying delay.[22]

The differences and mutual suspicion are such that even a proposal to convene a prayer-meeting to seek divine assistance meets with dissension, both as to the place of worship and whether opportunity would be taken to alter the soldiers' minds. Cromwell comments 'it seems as much to us in this as anything, we are not all of a mind', and again expresses the hope that 'whilst we are going one way, and you another, we be not both destroyed'. The debate that was to have been deferred breaks out anew between Wildman and Ireton, with Wildman objecting to the proposition that the Army may be engaged to submit to laws Parliament has made unjustly, which

> is contrary to what the Army first declared: that they stood upon such principles of right and freedom, and the Laws of Nature and Nations, whereby men were to preserve themselves though the persons to whom authority belonged should fail in it . . .[23]

Wildman then 'speak[s] plainly' of his fears that 'two or three days may lose the kingdom':

> . . . there may be an agreement between the King [and the Parliament] by propositions, with a power to hinder the making of any laws that are good, and the tendering of any good [laws]. And therefore because none of the people's grievances are redressed, they do apprehend that thus a few days may be the loss of the kingdom.[24]

Hence his concern to have the principles in the *Agreement* endorsed, 'to secure the rights of the people in their Parliaments' in accordance with the Army's declaration of 14 June. In this context, 'the kingdom' that the radicals see as being lost is not only the land and power won militarily, but their utopian concept of a just state that is almost within physical reach but is threatened from every direction: by King, Parliament, and the Army itself.

The rights of which Wildman speaks are akin to those inalienable rights that were later enshrined in the American constitution. They are informed by concepts of natural justice and equality and were fuelled by the predicament of soldiers who had served providence and 'preserved the kingdom', but who lacked property and were therefore without the franchise. Ireton, on the other hand, sees 'the great fountain of justice' as having its source in covenants and contracts between man and man, and in the civil law which intervenes against 'that [right] which another man may claim by the Law of Nature, of taking my goods':

> And therefore when I hear men speak of laying aside all engagements to [consider only] that wild or vast notion of what in every man's conception is just or unjust, I am afraid and do tremble at the boundless and endless consequences of it.[25]

Ireton's and Wildman's exchanges express the timeless conflict between radical free thought based on general concepts of natural justice and the structured conservatism of the lawyer's and law-maker's conception of social and political change.

Ireton's adherence to the civil constitution, albeit with some modifications, is strongly apparent during the second day of the Debates when the tactic of consulting prior engagements exhausts itself and attention turns to the principles in the *Agreement*. Article One was a proposition Ireton claimed not to understand. The text clearly implied universal (male) franchise:

> That the People of England, being at this day very unequally distributed by Counties, Cities & Burroughs, for the election of their Deputies in Parliament, ought to be more indifferently proportioned, according to the number of the Inhabitants, the circumstances whereof, for number, place and manner, are to be set down before the end of this present Parliament.[26]

Ireton wanted to know what was meant by 'more indifferently proportioned': whether the meaning was 'that every man that is an inhabitant is to be equally considered, and to have an equal voice in the election of those representers' (in which case he had an objection); or whether 'it be only that those people who by the civil constitution of this kingdom' were previously the electors, who were meant. Rainborowe summed up what was meant in the remarkable words:

> I think that the poorest he that is in England hath a life to live as the greatest he; and therefore truly, sir, I think it's clear, that every man that is to live under a government ought first by his own consent to put himself under that government.[27]

Ireton, somewhat incredulous, responds that 'if you make this the rule I think you must fly for refuge to an absolute natural right, and you must deny all civil right'[28] – unable as he is to detach the notion of the franchise from property rights and the continuation of property under the civil law.

It is clear from this part of the Debates that the radicals and the leadership have a fundamentally different understanding of certain key concepts, among which are 'birthright', 'constitution' and 'representative'. Behind these differences are their varying understandings of why they fought the war. Ireton's view is that 'no person hath a right [to participate in government by electing representatives] that hath not a permanent fixed interest in this kingdom':

> . . . those that choose the representers for the making of laws by which this state and kingdom are to be governed, are the persons who, taken together, do comprehend the local interest of this kingdom: that is, the persons in whom all land lies, and those in corporations in whom all trading lies.[29]

Property and the property basis of the franchise are a 'fundamental part of the civil constitution' which if taken away will lead to general anarchy or – only marginally better – the domination of policy by disinterested foreigners. As Ireton later says, 'All the main thing that I speak for, is because I would have an eye to property',[30] the great mainstay of common law rights. As to 'birthright',

> Men may justly have by birthright, by their very being born in England, that we should not seclude them out of England, that we should not refuse to give them air and place and ground, and the freedom of the highways and other things, to live amongst us.[31]

But that is all. Put somewhat negatively, his 'birthright' amounts to the right to starve unmolested on a public highway. What the soldiers fought for was, in his view, to prevent 'one man's will [being] a law': that they should have the benefit of the representative of those that had the interest of the kingdom, though that representative was not of their choosing:

> Here was a right that induced men to fight, and those men that had this interest, though this not be the uttermost interest that other men have, yet they had *some* interest.[32]

In other words, a Parliament of others' making was still a benefit to them, as compared with an autocratic King.

The constitutional dispute between Ireton and the Agitators turned upon different perceptions of English history, and in particular the Norman Conquest, which had become increasingly a focus of debate from Elizabeth's reign onwards. Foreign conquest posed problems in defining the nature of post-conquest feudal law and the property rights flowing from it. In the early part of the century this debate was specialized and legalistic: the province of antiquarians, historians and lawyers. But by the 1640s it had gained a place in populist rhetoric and became a vital tool in questioning and subverting the prevailing order. The radicals saw the Conquest as a total usurpation of ancient English liberties by foreign warlords. Cowling adopted this view in asserting that 'Since the Conquest the greatest part of the kingdom was in vassalage'. Charles I and his Lords were the legatees of 'William the Bastard' and his men, and their power was a continuation of the 'Norman Yoke'. Victory over King and Lords in the Civil War was therefore hailed as the occasion for redeeming these lost liberties and rewriting the record to reflect that Conquest from the vantage-point of the conquered. Thus Wildman says:

> Our case is to be considered thus, that we have been under slavery. That's acknowledged by all. Our very laws were made by our conquerors . . . We are now engaged for our freedom. That's the end of Parliaments: not to constitute what is already [established, but to act] according to the just rules of government. Every person in England hath as clear a right to elect his representative as the greatest person in England. I conceive that's the undeniable maxim of government: that all government is in the free consent of the people.[33]

Ireton, trained in law, rejected 'talk of laws by ancient constitution' when there was no evidence of their content, and talk 'of usurpation', when there was no evidence – other than indirect evidence in the form of the words of the King's oath – that formerly laws were made without the

King's consent.[34] The Norman Conquest was legitimized politically and legally through a mediaeval statute which limited 'legal memory', thereby limiting the making of legal claims and the legality of any 'record' including land title to the period after 3 September 1139 when Richard I acceded to the throne. Ireton's definition of the seventeenth-century civil constitution depends on this legal fiction. It enables him to claim that it is 'original and fundamental, and beyond [it] I am sure no memory of record goes'.[35] The constitution before the Conquest is 'beyond memory' and therefore has no legitimacy either as a precedent or record.

The radicals' knowledge of pre-Conquest England is obviously scant. Ireton remarks pointedly to Cowling, 'If subjection to a King be a tyranny, [we had a King before the Norman Conquest]'.[36] But pre-Conquest England had by this time assumed a quasi-mythic status in folklore as an indigenous and egalitarian society, based on a pre-feudal system of independent freehold estates and decentralized administration, where each man enjoyed a 'birthright' of liberty, independence and self-respect. It was common for radical pamphleteers to speak of the need to 'recover' that birthright. Sexby's account of why the radicals fought the war is consistent with this:

> We have engaged in this kingdom and ventured our lives and it was all for this: to recover our birthrights and privileges as Englishmen.[37]

The contemporary manifestation of the Norman yoke, in Rainborowe's eyes, was the subjection of the people to laws in which they had no voice at all.[38] Universal male suffrage was proposed 'for the preservation of all the [native] freeborn men', to '[make] good unto them', for – as a second Rainborowe (Major William) put it – 'the chief end of this government is to preserve persons as well as estates, and if any law shall take hold of my person it is more dear than my estate'.[39] Moreover, Rainborowe reasoned, if the foundation of all law lies in the people – a proposition with which no one present disagreed – then the people at large must consent to the authority of the law-makers and the law-makers must be representative. But perhaps the most compelling argument of all was the 'miserable distressed condition' in which, Rainborowe alleged, many a soldier 'whose zeal and affection to God and this kingdom hath carried him forth in this cause' would be placed on finding himself without an estate after years in the Army and therefore without an interest in the future of the kingdom or a voice in elections. Indeed, Rainborowe makes several pleas to Ireton on this basis.

Ireton's intransigence on this point draws complaint from the radicals. As Sexby says, in a haunting reversal of the Army's claim in its *Declaration of 14 June 1647* to be more than a mercenary army:

> There are many thousands of us soldiers that have ventured our lives; we have had little propriety in the kingdom as to our estates, yet we have had a birthright. But it seems now, except a man hath a fixed estate in this kingdom, he hath no right in this kingdom. I wonder we were so much deceived. If we had not a right to the kingdom, we were mere mercenary soldiers.[40]

Rainborowe likewise asks 'what the soldier hath fought for all this while?':

> He hath fought to enslave himself, to give power to men of riches, men of estates, to make him a perpetual slave . . . When these gentlemen fall out among themselves they shall press the poor scrubs to come and kill [one another for] them.[41]

Sexby's bitter reflection that if Ireton's views had been advertised earlier 'you would have [had] fewer under your command to have commanded'[42] feels entirely justified when Ireton later argues – with extraordinary insensitivity, and apparently unconscious of the situational irony – that to give a voice in elections to any man without property in the kingdom is to 'put it into the hands . . . [not] of men desirous to preserve their liberty, [but of men] who will give it away'.[43]

To the radicals, Ireton appears to enjoy an advantage by supporting the *status quo*. By having to persuade him they expose themselves to the charge of being wilful and divisive: of not subjugating their wishes to God's will, as manifested in the consensus at which open hearts and minds might arrive, were it not for the radicals' strong convictions. Rainborowe comments of himself and Ireton:

> There is a great deal of difference between us two. If a man hath all he desire, [he may wish to sit still]; but [if] I think I have nothing at all of what I fought for, I do not think the argument holds that I must desist as well as he.[44]

Yet for all the appearance that Ireton is in the position of power, the army command is constantly on the back foot – due, in large part, to the *Agreement* and its authors' firm instructions to the Agents that they were 'obliged absolutely to procure for [the people]' the things it contained. The radicals succeed in having the debate on their own terms and are tantalizingly close to having their proposals accepted. But Ireton doggedly stands his ground, to the mounting frustration not only of the radicals but of others who wish the matter resolved and are impatient of Ireton's determination to take issue at every turn. It is in this context that the debate towards the end of the second day becomes acrimonious, with Robert Everard, an Agent of Cromwell's Regiment, alleging that 'there are meetings daily and contrivances against us' by those he calls 'our adversaries'[45] and Ireton exploding in denunciation of the authors of *The Case of the Army Truly Stated* who have 'gone [about] to divide the Army':

> I say plainly, the way [they have taken] hath been the way of disunion and division, and [the dissolution] of that order and government by which we shall be enabled to act at all.[46]

Order and government, he says, are 'as essential to an army as life is to a man – which if it be taken away I think that such a company are no more an army than a rotten carcass is a man'.[47] One of the Agitators is quick with the obvious rejoinder:

> It was the dissatisfactions that were in the Army which provoked, which occasioned, those meetings, which you suppose tends so much to dividing; and the reason[s] of such dissatisfactions are because those whom they had to trust to act for them were not true to them.[48]

Ireton's means of dealing with this impasse is to suggest that there is little substantive difference between *The Heads of the Proposals* and the *Agreement*: continuing his previously expressed view that the divisions in the Army centre less on issues than personalities: 'whether such [men] or such shall have the managing of the business'.[49] But he stumbles immediately into the question which triggers the remainder of that day's debate: whether (as proposed in the *Agreement*) the Commons should be enabled to make laws without the consent of the King or Lords; or whether the consent of the King should be restored (as proposed in *The Heads of the Proposals*).

This issue immediately raises again the question of prior engagements and the future role of the King, and further polarizes the parties. Ireton's view is that till we can acquit ourselves justly from any engagement, old or new, that we stand in, to preserve the person of the King, the persons of the Lords, and their rights, so far as they are consistent with the common right [and the safety of the kingdom] – till *that* be done, I think there is reason [that] that exception [in their favour] should continue . . .[50]

Maximilian Petty immediately puts the Leveller counter-view:

Whereas you seem to make the King and Lords so light a thing as that it may be without prejudice [to keep them, though] to the destruction of the kingdom to throw them out; for my part I cannot but think that both the power of King and Lords was ever a branch of tyranny. And if ever a people shall free themselves from tyranny, certainly it is after seven years' war and fighting for their liberty. For my part [I think that] if the constitution of this kingdom shall be established as formerly, it might rivet tyranny into this kingdom more strongly than before.[51]

Wildman follows with an analysis of how the 'foundation of slavery' is 'riveted more strongly than before' through *The Heads of the Proposals*, citing the following as cause for 'future quarrels':

- militia instated in the King and Lords, not the Commons;
- the King to have control of the militia before any redress of the people's grievances;
- the King to have a 'negative voice' (i.e. power of veto) over the laws passed by Parliament;
- the King's consent sought to an Act of Indemnity protecting the soldiers from the consequences of things done during the war.

The solution in his view was an Agreement of the People limiting the power of Parliament 'so [the people] might be destroyed neither by the King's prerogative nor Parliament's privileges [including those of the Lords]', and releasing it to perform its proper task of redressing the people's grievances.

Ireton in turn denies that these are the effects of *The Heads of the Proposals*. They do not give the King a 'negative voice':

we do but take the King as a man with whom we have been at a difference; . . . We do not demand that he shall have no negative, but we do not say that he shall have any.[52]

To the allegation that the King's rights are addressed before the grievances of the people, he replies that 'things that are essential to peace'
are put before the King's rights, but

> There were many other grievances and particular matters [of] which
> we did not think [it] so necessary that they should precede the settling
> of a peace, [the lack of] which is the greatest grievance of the kingdom.
> Our way was to take away that [first] . . . What we thought in our con-
> sciences to be essential to the peace of the kingdom we did put pre-
> ceding to the consideration of the King's personal right; and the
> concurrence of [the King to] those is a condition without which we
> cannot have any right at all, and without [which] there can be no
> peace.[53]

As to the indemnity, while it was desired to obtain the Royal consent to
the proposed Act of Indemnity, 'we should account the authority of the
Parliament valid without it'.[54] But it is Wildman who has the last word of
the day, commenting:

> whereas you say it is a scandal for [us to assert that you would have]
> the King to come in with his personal rights [before the grievances of
> the people are redressed, it is said in the *Proposals*] that, the King con-
> senting to those things, the King [is] to be restored to all his personal
> rights. There's his restoration. Not a bare consideration what his rights
> are before the people's grievances [are considered], but a restoration
> to his personal rights . . .[55]

The third day of the Debates – and the final one of which we have a
complete record – commences with various speakers communicating
their experiences arising from prayers overnight, for what they may indicate of the divine will. Cromwell uses the opportunity to take stock. While
he concedes that there may have been some 'pleasing' of the King, his
future kingship would be upon new terms: 'for I think [it hath been made
clear] that the King is king by contract'.[56] This sober formulation, and
the contrasting echo of the 'divine right', convey with a sudden shock the
philosophical distance that even the Army conservatives have travelled.
Having dealt with the King, he turns to Parliament, with a suggestion that
the Army has need of the Parliament and should conform to it:

> Either they are a Parliament or no Parliament. If they be no Parliament
> they are nothing, and we are nothing likewise. If they be a Parliament,

we are [not to proceed without them in our plan of settlement, but]
to offer it to them.[57]

Cromwell would like to see a 'visible presence' of the people to satisfy his
conscience of their wishes and affections, 'for in the government of
nations that which is to be looked after is the affections of the people'.
The present electorates were 'very unequal' and care must be taken to
secure proper representation. If a more representative and perpetual
Parliament could be secured through a compact between the present
Parliament and the King 'there is much may be said for the[ir] doing of
it'.[58] As for the condition of the Army, he had

> been informed by some of the King's party, that if they give us rope
> enough we will hang ourselves. . . . And therefore I shall move [that]
> what we shall centre upon [must be the rules of war and our author-
> ity from the Parliament. We must not let go of that] if it have but the
> face of authority. [We are like a drowning man]: if it be but an hare
> swimming over the Thames, he will take hold of it rather than let it
> go.[59]

Sexby's response to this attempt to foster acceptance of King and
Parliament is to merge his Leveller convictions with the radical logic
of religious Independency and discredit the King through biblical
metaphor:

> We find in the word of God, 'I would heal Babylon, but she would not
> be healed.' I think that we have gone about to heal Babylon when she
> would not. We have gone about to wash a blackamoor, to wash him
> white, which he will not. We are going about to set up that power which
> God will destroy.[60]

This is an important moment in the Debates. It is the first identification of the King not merely with tyranny – which pertains to his office –
but with irredeemable sin, which pertains to him personally. It conflates
the Leveller desire to escape tyranny with the Independents' need to see
the state purged of its sinful past. It also demonstrates the potent and
fearsome Puritan habit of reacting to the world through biblical arche-
types, which carries a conviction that otherwise confusing and ambiguous reality has been reduced to its metaphysical essence. It is the process
by which Charles swiftly becomes 'the man of blood' who must be purged
by execution. Being named in this way is like being emblazoned with a

symbol which suppresses all contrary signals and presents itself as the true reality. In this instance Cromwell tries to detach the label before the damage is done but not before, in his intensely Puritan way, he contemplates the issues of conscience that would arise if the identification were correct:

> The gentleman applied [the text] to us, as that we had been men that would have healed Babylon, and God would not have had her healed. Truly, though that be not the intent of that scripture, yet I think it is true that whosoever would have gone about to heal Babylon when God hath determined [to destroy her], he doth fight against God, because God will not have her healed. And yet certainly in general to desire an healing, it is not evil . . .[61]

He wrestles openly with the vexed issue of how they are to judge whether the words of those present are 'of God or no', when 'it doth not carry its evidence with it, of the power of God to convince us clearly'. In such a case, he thinks, 'our best way is to judge the conformity or disformity of [it with] the law written within us, which is the law of the Spirit of God, the mind of God, the mind of Christ'.[62] This task of judging 'the God without' by reference to 'the God within', in what is already a conscience debate, is highly onerous, if not paradoxical. But Cromwell is right in thinking 'it hath pleased God to lead me to a true and clear stating [of] our agreement and our difference', which he puts as follows:

> The end is to deliver this nation from oppression and slavery, to accomplish that work that God hath carried us on in, to establish our hopes of an end of justice and righteousness in it. We agree thus far. Further too: that we all apprehend danger from the person of the King and from the Lords – I think we may go thus far farther. . . . If it were free before us whether we should set up one or [the] other, I do to my best observation find an unanimity amongst us all, that we would set up neither. Thus far I find us to be agreed; and thus far as we are agreed, I think it is of God. But there are circumstances in which we differ as in relation to this . . . So that part of the difference that seems to be amongst us is whether there can be a preservation [of them with safety to the kingdom].[63]

But the radicals clearly mistrust his carefully crafted consensus and his cajoling towards reconciliation. Captain George Bishop roughly disrupts it by describing the Debates as 'distracted' and laying the blame for that

in 'a compliance to preserve that man of blood, and those principles of
tyranny, which God from heaven by his many successes [given] hath mani-
festly declared against, and which, I am confident, may [yet] be our
destruction [if they be preserved]'.[64]

Wildman follows through by proclaiming:

> Whatever another man hath received from the Spirit, that man cannot
> demonstrate [it] to me but by some other way than merely relating to
> me that which he conceives to be the mind of God[65]

and noting that discerning the will of God in civil matters has its particular difficulties, 'for we cannot find anything in the word of God [of]
what is fit to be done in civil matters'. But reverting to the Babylonian
reference, he finds it 'very questionable whether there be a way left for
mercy upon that person that we now insist upon'. The warrant for the
King's execution already exists in his mind:

> [I would know] whether it is demonstrable by reason or justice, [that
> it is right] to punish with death those that according to his command
> do make war, or those that do but hold compliance with them, and
> then [to say] that there is a way left for mercy for him who was the
> great actor of this, and who was the great contriver of all?[66]

The fragile near-consensus has fractured into open debate between those
who would preserve the King and his office and those who would see
both perish.

This sparks a series of altercations between Ireton and Wildman as the
heat is turned up. Ireton is determined to correct the record, that the
subject of the debate is not 'punishment', but whether the King and
Lords can with safety be given an interest in the public affairs of the
kingdom.[67] Wildman distinguishes between the Lords and the King, 'for
. . . none have any exception against the persons of the Lords'. As to the
King, the point is silently maintained. Wildman's argument is then that
the proposed settlement will accord the King and Lords more power than
they enjoyed before. Ireton insists that the issue is whether 'that interest
that they have in this (if they have any), whether it should be now positively insisted upon to be clearly taken away',[68] an argument harking back
to the issue of 'prior engagements'. He also maintains the curiously
double-sided position that although the Royal assent would be required
to complete the legislative process, and although the King would be
bound by oath to give his assent to Parliament's laws, the Commons 'are,

in point of safety, a law without him'. The *Proposals*, he says, are framed on that basis.

The record contains no further speech from Cromwell. The closing stages of the third day's debate are occupied with proposals coming from the Committee that had been appointed to review the previous declarations of the Army and their consistency with the present and future security of the kingdom. These appear to have embodied much of the radical platform. The present Parliament was to end on the following 1 September. Election of members to the Commons were to be 'according to some rule of equality of proportion, so as to render the House of Commons, as near as may be, an equal Representative of the whole body of the people that are to elect'.[69] The qualifications of those to constitute the electorate were to be determined by the Commons in the present Parliament 'so as to give as much enlargement to common freedom as may be' and so as to include all those who had 'served the Parliament in the late war for the liberties of the kingdom' and were in service before 14 June 1645 or have otherwise voluntarily assisted the Parliament: such service to be certified by the Commons for that purpose. (Conversely, those deprived of their freedoms for their 'delinquency in the late war or otherwise', were not to have any voice in the election or be capable of being elected.) No Lords made since 21 May 1642, or at any time in the future, were to be capable to sit or vote in Parliament without the consent of both Houses. The Commons were to legislate 'as to the whole interest, of all the Commons of England' and to have the 'conclusive exposition and declaration of law', and the power of final judgement without further appeal. No law could be repealed or new law made to bind the Commons of England without the particular concurrence and consent of the House of Commons. Ministers of State (including the King) were to be accountable to the power and judgement of the House of Commons 'for any maladministration of [their] place to the hurt or damage of the commonwealth'; and no person adjudged by the Parliament could receive a pardon, or have his sentence or fine remitted by the King without the advice or consent of Parliament.

But there were major exceptions to what the radicals had sought. The King and Lords were to be accommodated within the legislative system; the Lords were to be exempted from the operation of laws to which they had not consented; elections to the Commons were to be triennial; and a property qualification of £20 per annum was proposed for members of the House of Commons. Rainborowe, predictably, took exception to the property qualification, and Wildman to the interest accorded the King and Lords, which he alleged to be 'surer than before'.[70] To Ireton's reassurance that the powers of the King and Lords were a 'shadow' that could do no more than keep their own persons and property free from the Commons, Wildman replied that, 'Whether it be a shadow or no', it was of substance that no law would be made but by address to the King. This, he said, 'will be very shameful in future chronicles, that after so much blood there should be no better an issue for the Commons'.[71] For his own part, he would 'venture myself and [my] share in the common bottom'.[72]

The record of the Debates ends at this point, with a motion of adjournment. While it is profoundly unsatisfying that it ends before the adoption of the 2 November 1647 resolutions, and that the final words of the manuscript should be so comparatively inconclusive, it is nevertheless appropriate that that vigorously unpretentious image of the 'common bottom' should constitute the last word. For Wildman's words are effectively the epitaph of the Leveller cause, which reached its zenith at Putney but was soon to be suppressed, its language and images disappearing into the underground stream of alternative history flowing from pre-Conquest England into which the later European and American revolutions, and nineteenth-century working-class history in Britain, would tap.

According to John Rushworth, at the meeting on 2 November, it was agreed that a number of points should be conveyed to Parliament in a Declaration. It appears that a further long debate took place on the scope of the electorate, after which it was resolved '*That all soldiers and others, if they be not servants or beggars, ought to have voices in electing those which shall represent them in Parliament, although they have not forty shillings per annum in freehold land*'.[73] The Agitators claim in their letter to their regiments that 'there were but three voices against this your native freedom'.[74] The other matters were referred to a committee and were to be finally approved on 5 November. On 4 November, the General Council considered the treaty with the King and formulated measures for coping with Army arrears. On 5 November, Rainborowe persuaded the General Council, under protest from Ireton who left the meeting, to write to Parliament making it clear that the Army was not urging a further approach to the King. Given that the Council had considered terms for a treaty the previous day, and that Cromwell was now absent at the House of Commons, it seems likely that Rainborowe's action was in response to a perceived threat that Cromwell might represent to the House (as it was alleged that he had done previously) that the Army would support such an approach.

The radicals then sought an open debate on the issue 'Whether it were safe either for the Army or people to suffer any power to be given to the

King?'[75] The debate was set for the following Monday (8th November),
with Cromwell and Ireton pledging to take part:

> but when they met they wholly refused, and instead of that, spake very
> reproachfully of us and our actings, and declaimed against that which
> was passed, the Council before, concerning the voices of those in elec-
> tions which have not forty shillings a year freehold; and against the
> letter sent by the Council to the Parliament. . . . The next day they still
> waived and refused the free debate of the aforesaid question, and dis-
> solved the Council for above a fortnight, and for a time resolved that
> they would only prepare some fair propositions to the Army about
> arrears and pay.[76]

The decision to disperse the officers and Agitators to their several commands and regiments and dissolve the Council was taken with the express
intention of 'quieting' the soldiers 'forasmuch as many distempers are
reported to be in the several regiments, whereby much dissatisfaction is
given both to the Parliament and the kingdom through some misrepre-
sentations'.[77] Before it dissolved, the General Council on 9 November
declared:

> If any by that letter bearing date 5th November do make any construc-
> tion as if we intended that we were against the Parliament's sending
> propositions to the King . . . it was no part of our intentions in the said
> letter, but that the same is utterly a mistake of our intention and
> meaning therein, our intentions being only to assert the freedom of
> Parliament.[78]

It is difficult to avoid the conclusion that Cromwell and Ireton were
determined to thwart the outcome of the debates, which was at least to
a degree unexpected. Ian Gentles[79] expresses surprise that Cromwell's
motion to send the officers and Agitators back to their quarters was able
to gain support. He speculates that the threat of mounting disunity and
the increasingly ugly attacks on the King may have influenced the vote,
along with the prestige of Fairfax, who probably lent Cromwell support,
and the promise of a general rendezvous to follow in the near future.
The action Fairfax was taking with respect to pay and arrears may also
have had its impact. Concern that the soldiers might be placated by the
meeting of these limited demands and thereby abandon the larger platform underlies the Agitators' exhortation to the soldiers in their letter to
the regiments of 11 November to remember that they 'have been fed with

paper too long'. The same letter urges them not to disperse 'till our Arrears be actually secured, and the foundations of our freedom, peace and security in the Agreement established':

> We know some fair overtures will be made to you about pay, arrears, seeming freedom and security; but we hope, as you formerly rejected such overtures from the Parliament, knowing that without a settlement of freedom no constant pay or arrears will be provided – so now we are confident you will not be deceived. . . . that we may all agree together in fulfilling our Declarations and Engagements to the people.[80]

If the soldiers became satisfied, the cause of the Agitators and of their allies the civilian Levellers would be lost.

Ironically, just as the Army was being 'quieted', the King took flight from Hampton Court, apparently in fear of his life. While there were mounting rumours of plans to assassinate the King, the trigger for his departure may have been a letter from Cromwell to the King's keeper, expressing fear 'of some intended attempt on his Majesty's person . . . a most horrid act'.[81] Cromwell's intention may well have been to ingratiate the Army leadership with the King as his would-be defenders, and more importantly to put pressure on the King for a speedy settlement on Army terms. If so, his tactic backfired when the King fled to Carisbrooke Castle on the Isle of Wight (where he arrived on 14 November), and positioned himself either to flee to Europe or to resume negotiations with the Scots. The opportunity represented by the King's preference for the Army terms over those of Parliament was lost.

In London, meanwhile, Leveller sympathy was on the increase, especially after the Commons refused Fairfax's request for church lands as security for the Army arrears. There was an attempt to mobilize the craft guilds to attend the Army rendezvous at Ware in Hertfordshire, which was to be the first of three separate meetings planned in place of the general rendezvous sought by the Agitators. By having nominated regiments to meet at three separate times and places, and excluding several of the more radical regiments (Harrison's, Lilburne's, Ingoldsby's, Scrope's and Twisleton's), the leadership minimized the opportunity for an Army-wide demonstration of support for the *Agreement* and, more importantly, the opportunity for general mutiny. Mutiny was certainly in the air. Robert Lilburne's regiment, which Fairfax had ordered to Newcastle, ceased their northward march at the behest of their Agents, engaged in a skirmish with other troops sent to enforce Fairfax's orders, and proceeded instead to Ware under the direction of their only remaining officer (and suspected ringleader), Captain-Lieutenant William Bray. Harrison's regiment, likewise, appeared at Ware uninvited and without its officers, which was an incipiently mutinous act.

The gathering at Ware on 15 November was a military occasion with modern political overtones.[82] Before the formalities commenced, speeches were delivered in support of the *Agreement*, signatures to a petition were collected, and the petition was delivered to Fairfax by a delegation headed by Rainborowe, who had no authority to be present. Others whose attendance was irregular, including agents from Skippon's and Waller's uninvited regiments and three London agents, were either escorted from the scene or arrested. In a dramatic and threatening show of support for the *Agreement*, Harrison's uninvited regiment appeared without their officers and with copies of the document pinned to their hats, bearing the slogan 'England's Freedoms, Soldiers' Rights'. Had their arrival coincided with that of Lilburne's regiment, a mutiny may have taken fire. As it was, Harrison's regiment found little support for insurrection among the seven assembled regiments and were quickly subordinated to Fairfax's commands. When Lilburne's regiment arrived well into the afternoon, also with papers in their hats, there was sporadic violence as they refused at first to be brought to discipline, but there was no insurrection for them to join and they too were brought to account. Bray was arrested and a number of ringleaders were summarily court-martialled and condemned to death. One poor scapegoat – Richard Arnold, who was chosen by lot – was summarily executed and the rest pardoned. But it was enough to ensure that the second and third rendezvous – at Ruislip Heath near Watford, and Kingston, Surrey – were without incident, notwithstanding the attendance at Kingston of Ireton's and Whalley's regiments, which were known to have radical sympathies.

Without exception, the regiments that attended the rendezvous subscribed to the Remonstrance which had been drawn up, at Fairfax's behest, by a committee of 18 appointed by the General Council on 8 November. The committee included only two Agitators and two radical officers. In addition to proposing constant pay, security for arrears and improved indemnity, it proposed 'for the kingdom':

- a time limit for the present parliament;
- future parliaments to meet and dissolve at prearranged times and sit for fixed periods; and
- provision also for the freedom and equality of elections.

This modest agenda was the 'fruit' of the debate at Putney.

When the civilian Levellers turned from their defeat at Ware to petition the House of Commons to debate the *Agreement* and investigate the Army court martials, the House resolved to imprison their leaders. Cromwell contributed to the debate, denouncing the Levellers' 'drive at a levelling and parity' and outlining the history of the view he now held that they must be suppressed.

Over the next two months the Army leadership made a concerted effort to have the issues of the soldiers' pay and arrears addressed in the Commons. Fortunately for the leadership, the obvious solution to the state's mounting indebtedness to the Army was to reduce Army numbers drastically, which provided the opportunity to purge the Army politically even as its ordinary grievances were being addressed. There was some internal reconciliation by which officers who made apology were reinstated (among them Rainborowe) and prayer meetings were held with the aim of unifying the troops. None of the sentences arising from mutinous behaviour at Ware were carried out, except that which was performed on the day, and those charged were sent back to their regiments. But the greatest aid to political unity in the Army was the 50 per cent reduction in its numbers in January–February 1648, which was implemented so as to remove first those regiments which had not partaken of the reconciliation; then the provincial troops not connected to the New Model Army; and finally, parts of the New Model regiments chosen selectively so as to eliminate radical elements. Gentles notes that Harrison's regiment suffered the most severe cuts, and was reduced by half.[83]

4

THE SECOND CIVIL WAR

The day after the fateful rendezvous at Ware, which curtailed Army opposition to the reinstatement of the King, Charles I (now at Carisbrooke) sent new proposals to Parliament which sought to modify *The Heads of the Proposals*. His first object was to maintain episcopacy, but he would allow the Presbyterian system of government adopted in the English Church to remain for three years, pending a detailed settlement between himself and Parliament. That agreement would preserve 'full liberty to all those who shall differ upon conscientious grounds from that settlement', excepting papists, atheists and blasphemers. As a mark of his good faith, he offered to relinquish to Parliament his rights over the militia and his power to appoint officers of state and Privy Councillors during his lifetime, on the understanding that those powers would return to the Crown after his reign. He was willing to do 'any thing that can be done without the violation of his conscience and honour' to meet the Army arrears, and would undertake to pay £400000 in arrears within 18 months, if the Parliament would remit him monies received from the sequestration of Royalist estates. Any insufficiency he would meet by sale of the Crown forests (church lands, however, were sacrosanct, and he would not permit them to be alienated). There would be an Act of Oblivion extending to all subjects and a statute nullifying all Oaths, Declarations and Proclamations made against Parliament or its sympathizers. He would give unspecified 'satisfaction' in relation to Ireland and

> although His Majesty cannot consent in honour and justice to avoid [i.e. annul] all his own grants and acts passed under his Great Seal

since 22nd May 1642, or to the confirming of all the grants and acts passed under that made by the two Houses, yet His Majesty is confident that upon perusal of particulars, he shall give full satisfaction to his two Houses to what may be reasonably desired in that particular.[1]

These things were offered in earnest of his intentions 'to give full security and satisfaction to all interests' and were to be accommodated along with other 'just and reasonable demands' in a personal treaty which His Majesty would enter if permitted to come to London 'in honour, freedom and safety'. Once the treaty was in place, the Army proposals concerning the succession of Parliaments and Parliamentary elections would be considered. The King would also 'very readily apply himself to give all reasonable satisfaction' concerning the kingdom of Scotland 'when the desires of the two Houses of Parliament on their behalf, or of the Commissioners of that kingdom, or both joined together, shall be made known'.[2] In all, while there were one or two undertakings of substance, it was a very loose and inconclusive set of proposals, with much scope for subsequent reservations based on the King's conscience and what he considered 'just and reasonable'.

The House of Lords received the document on 17 November 1647, but did not deal with it until 25 November. On that day it was resolved to appoint a Committee to select key propositions from Parliament's earlier proposals to the King, which would be presented again to him, as a test of his integrity on those issues, it being felt that the present offer left too much unspecified. The Lords were unwilling to have the King come to London before detailed understandings were in place, because of the risk that Royalist demonstrations would occur and tip the balance in his favour. Royalist and Presbyterian sentiment was still strong in the capital.

On 14 December, Parliament passed Four Bills to be sent to the King for his assent, and approved more than 20 accompanying propositions derived from the Newcastle Propositions. Once he assented to the Bills, Parliamentary Commissioners would attend the King at the Isle of Wight to negotiate a treaty based on the propositions. The Four Bills concerned control of the militia (which was to be vested in Parliament for 20 years); the revocation of oaths, declarations and other proceedings against Parliament and its supporters; the nullifying of honours and titles conferred after 20 May 1642 when the Great Seal was removed from Parliament; and, finally, the right of Parliament, at its discretion, to adjourn lawfully to any other place within England (thereby enabling it to remove from London if the political atmosphere there presented difficulty). By formulating legislation on these matters, Parliament left no detail to chance, and put the King on his mettle by requesting that he give his royal assent to the Bills 'by [his] Letters Patent under the Great Seal of England, and signed by [his] hand, and declared and notified to the Lords and Commons assembled together in the House of Peers, according to the law declared in that behalf'.[3] It was indicated pointedly that any other form of assent – that is, assent lacking the force of law – would '[stand] not with the safety and security of the kingdom and Parliament'.[4]

The propositions repeated a great deal of the substance of the Newcastle Propositions and flatly rejected the King's proposal to restore episcopacy and maintain church lands. The Third Newcastle Proposition – that an Act of Parliament be passed 'for the utter abolishing and taking away of all Archbishops, Bishops &c.' – became article nine of the new propositions. Articles ten and eleven obliged the King to confirm or pass statutes appropriating church lands for the use of the Commonwealth and article eight provided for them to be used to secure and pay Army arrears. Articles fourteen and fifteen required the King to consent to Acts establishing and entrenching Presbyterian Church government through- out England and Ireland and empowered the Parliament to appoint Irish and Scottish Commissioners and to discipline Jesuits and papists. The substance of these articles was derived from the Newcastle Propositions, but was now extended to Ireland. The cessation of the war in Ireland, as negotiated by the King, was to be declared void (article four, reproduc- ing the seventeenth Newcastle Proposition); and the King was to declare his approbation of the making of treaties 'between England and Scotland &c.' (article seven).

Otherwise, the propositions sought to secure the position of Parliament by ensuring that the King would consent to Acts for the raising of monies (article two), curtailing the King's own sources of revenue (article six) and obtaining recognition of the Parliamentary Great Seal. Article one reproduced the nineteenth Newcastle Proposition by which it was to be declared and enacted that instruments sealed by the Parliamentary Great Seal were as effective as any instrument to which any previous Great Seal had been affixed; that the Parliamentary Great Seal was to continue in use as the Great Seal of England; and that any instru- ment sealed by the King's Great Seal after 22 May 1642 was void and of no effect. Articles three, five, twelve and thirteen dealt with war-related matters including indemnities for the Parliamentarian soldiers, restora- tion of pensions or offices withdrawn from those who sympathized with Parliament, the identification of delinquents and of the value of their estates, and agreement that certain named persons and their estates be proceeded against 'as both Houses of Parliament shall think fit' and that the King be incapable of pardoning them.

The King was provided with the Four Bills and accompanying propositions and given four days in which to answer. In fact, he did not answer until 28 December, at which time he provided Parliament with a refusal in writing.[5] Explaining that he was unable to pass the Bills, he referred to the difficulty 'of complying with all engaged interests in these great distempers', claiming that the Scottish Commissioners had objected to the Four Bills and that on those grounds alone he would not pass them. Furthermore, since he was unable to give his assent in person in the House of Lords and lacked a Great Seal ('unless his two Houses intend that His Majesty shall allow of a Great Seal made without his authority', i.e. he is refusing to sanction the use of the Parliamentary Great Seal) he could not pass the Bills in either of the 'ancient and known ways'. These procedural problems aside, the Bills as they were composed represented 'the divesting himself of all sovereignty' and conferred 'an arbitrary and unlimited power in the two Houses for ever, to raise and levy forces for land and sea service'. They also threatened 'the liberty and prosperity of the subject, and His Majesty's trust in protecting them'. Finally, reiterating his belief that a personal treaty was the best means to a well-founded peace, he advised that he was 'very much at ease within himself, for having fulfilled the offices both of a Christian and of a King' and was therefore content to wait upon the pleasure of Almighty God to influence the 'hearts of his two houses to consider their King'.

But before writing these pious and complacent words he had made other arrangements with the Scots. In December, when the Four Bills were before him, he was negotiating in secret with the Scottish Commissioners and signed an Engagement with them on 26 December, two days before his letter of reply to Parliament. (Enclosed in lead, the signed document was buried in a garden at Carisbrooke Castle, until arrangements could be made for its safe removal from England.) By this Engagement the Scots promised the King military assistance if necessary to recover his Royal authority in England in exchange for the King's promise that, when restored to power, he would confirm the Presbyterian government of the English Church for a period of three years, pending final settlement of ecclesiastical matters. The Covenant was to be affirmed by an Act of Parliament in both kingdoms, fostering the alliance between the English and Scottish churches, but no individual was to be compelled to take it. Although the King had espoused toleration in his letter of 16 November to the English Parliament (no doubt with an eye to appeasing the Army), he now engaged to suppress the opinions and practices of sectaries, Arminians, separatists and even Independents – the latter a significant inclusion, given the strength of Independency within the Army.

In fact, the Engagement manifests a strong animus against the Army as the King's real adversary (rather than the Parliament). It notes that the Army refused to disband as Parliament had ordered; that it carried away and detained the King against his will; that it violently forced Members of Parliament away from the Houses; and it 'possessed [itself] of the City of London and all the strengths and garrisons of the kingdom'. The Engagement alleges that through its power and influence Propositions and Bills have been sent to the King without the agreement of the Scots 'which are destructive to religion, His Majesty's just rights, the privileges of Parliament, and liberty of the subject, from which Propositions and Bills the said Scots Commissioners have dissented in the name of the kingdom of Scotland'.[6]

The Scots engaged themselves to address this situation 'first in a peaceable way', by facilitating Charles's safe passage to London to make a personal treaty with the Houses of Parliament and the Commissioners of Scotland, upon propositions to be mutually agreed by His Majesty and the two kingdoms. The Engagement refers to James I's vision of 'a complete union of the kingdoms, so they may be one under His Majesty and his posterity'.[7] The Scots were committed ideologically to a Presbyterian Church settlement uniting the three kingdoms and in need economically of the benefits of a 'common market' with England. This was their opportunity not only to promote a 'united kingdom', but to ensure that such a union would take maximum account of Scottish interests and be in part on Scottish terms.

If the restoration of the King could not be achieved on peaceful terms, the Scottish Parliament would denounce the 'unjust proceedings of the two Houses of Parliament towards His Majesty and the kingdom of Scotland' and would declare the powers of the King in 'the militia, the Great Seal, bestowing of honours and offices of trust, choice of Privy Councillors, [and] the right of the King's negative voice in Parliament'. Such a declaration was obviously intended to take effect extra-territorially in England and would be an intensely provocative infringement of the powers of the English Parliament. The Scottish Army would then invade England

for preservation and establishment of religion, for defence of His Majesty's person and authority, and restoring him to his government, to the just rights of the Crown and his full revenues, for defence of the privileges of Parliament and liberties of the subject, for making a firm union between the kingdoms, under His Majesty and his posterity, and settling a lasting peace.[8]

Indeed, the invading army was to be on the march from Scotland even before the peaceful overtures were made, in anticipation that military intervention would be required. Under the terms of the Engagement the King authorized it in advance to possess Berwick, Carlisle, Newcastle upon Tyne, Tynemouth, and Hartlepool as 'places of retreat and magazine'. The Engagement also provided for payment to be made by the King to the kingdom of Scotland 'for the charge and expense of their army in this future war'[9] and to compensate losses it might sustain. The Scottish Army in Ireland was also to be granted 'due satisfaction . . . out of the land of that kingdom or otherwise'. The King's financial obligations under the Engagement were such that the Scottish Army was effectively a mercenary army replacing the defeated Royalist force. Finally, the Engagement incited sympathizers in England and Ireland to join the insurgency on the promise that the King would protect their persons and estates.

By signing this document the King implicitly declared a second civil war. The Scottish Commissioners, on their return to London and before departing on 24 January 1648, made secret arrangements for insurrections in England to coincide with the Scottish invasion. Parties within the Eastern Association counties – formerly a Parliamentarian stronghold – and in Kent, for example, were organized to take up arms on a pre-arranged signal.

Meanwhile, Parliament was reacting to the King's refusal of the Four Bills. On 3 January there was a debate on a motion from the aptly named Sir Thomas Wroth that the King be impeached and the kingdom settled without him. Both Cromwell and Ireton appear to have supported the motion.[10] According to Clarendon, Cromwell explained his loss of confidence in the King as arising from the fact that he had pretended to deal with Parliament while making 'secret treaties with the Scots' commissioners how he might embroil the nation in a new war and destroy the Parliament',[11] suggesting that the Engagement with Scotland had quickly become known. Rather than voting to impeach Charles (which the Presbyterian Members would not have accepted), Parliament resolved upon a vote of no addresses. Parliament would make no further addresses to the King; anyone making such addresses without Parliament's leave would be guilty of high treason; and no more messages were to be received from the King. Rainborowe, who had tried from Putney to achieve this outcome, must have felt vindicated. The motion was passed by 141 to 91 votes in a full House, which meant that even the Presbyterians in Parliament were angered by Charles's pact with the Scots. The vote of no addresses was carried in the Lords on 15 January and thus became a resolution of both Houses. It was reaffirmed in the Commons on 11 February 1648, passing by 80 votes to 50. The occasion of its reaffirmation is not clear, but it may have been the receipt of the report of the Committee appointed to devise a defence of the vote of no addresses.

Without a dissenting voice, the House of Commons also acted to dissolve the Committee of Both Kingdoms which had co-ordinated the Parliamentarian war effort in the three kingdoms during the First Civil War. This meant that the Scottish Commissioners were dispatched from England. The Committee which replaced it, which was first called the Committee of Safety and subsequently became known from its place of meeting as the 'Derby House Committee', consisted of the English members of the former committee, with the addition of three Independents. This Committee became the permanent executive with the task of responding to the developing emergency.

The emergency created by Charles's agreement with the Scots was fuelled by a more general sense of civic unrest, commencing with the Kentish Christmas riots of December 1647. These were sparked by Puritan orders suppressing Christmas revels and requiring businesses to operate on Christmas Day, Christmas being regarded as a popish festival marked by undisciplined and licentious conduct. In the polarized political environment, it was natural for displeasure with Puritan restraints to manifest itself in Royalist slogans. In Canterbury, rioters condemned Parliament and its taxes and shouted support for the King. When a further disturbance occurred within a matter of days, 3000 of the Trained Bands were brought in to quell the rioting.

This was the very period during which the New Model Army was undergoing the purge which drastically reduced its numbers. Officially, it was no longer the 'New Model Army', but a standing army incorporating regiments from outside the New Model, some of them from the Northern Association. It consisted of 14 regiments of horse, 17 of infantry, and 30 unattached companies,[12] the total establishment being about 24 000 men.[13]

The flashpoint in this very delicate exercise of reshaping the Army was Wales where regiments which had been associated with the Presbyterian counter-revolution were in the process of being purged. Fairfax's orders were greeted by a threat of general mutiny in Wales, but all but Major-General Roland Laugharne's regiment succumbed to Fairfax's subsequent orders threatening arrest for refusal to disband. Laugharne petitioned Parliament to pay his men's arrears before they were disbanded. One of his colonels – John Poyer, the Governor of Pembroke Castle – dissented more vigorously by refusing to disband his troops before they were paid and seeking support from the Royalists.

This was symptomatic of the realignments taking place at this critical juncture. Cromwell was involved in negotiations with the Prince of Wales (Charles's first son, later to become Charles II), hoping to bypass the recalcitrant Charles I and restore the monarchy through his more pliant son. This plan came to grief when the Prince was implicated in a plot for the escape of the Duke of York (Charles's second son, later James II), but was revived in February, again without success, by Independents who would rather 'trust [the monarchy] than the rigid Presbyterian yoke that will prove to our party a most antichristian bondage'.[14] An intercepted letter to the King from his agent at The Hague suggests that Royalists looked to Prince William II of Orange and also to the Irish Army for support, but the extraordinary state of political uncertainty is epitomized by the agent begging the King to remain constant to his own cause.[15] The Earl of Ormonde, who was then in France, having strategically yielded the Irish war against the Catholic Confederacy to his Puritan opponents, dispatched Colonel Barry to promote co-operation between Irish Royalists and sympathizers among the Irish Confederate troops. The Confederates were split between the papal faction, which looked to Catholic government of Ireland, and the landowning faction, dependent on the Crown for its titles and therefore more open to approach from the King.

The Scottish Commissioners, who had served the Parliamentary cause since the Solemn League and Covenant in 1643, on returning to Scotland did all they could to rally support for the King. In a speech delivered on 15 February, Commissioner Lauderdale claimed the four things that English Parliamentarians could not endure were the Covenant, Presbytery, monarchical government and the Scots.[16] These four things define the new political fault-line between English and Scottish interests: the English Parliamentarians being now linked to Independency, toleration, 'English' birthright and republicanism, while the Scottish Parliament declared for the King, the Covenant (designed to unite the three kingdoms under a common Presbyterian discipline) and Scottish national interests. Charles had by this time recovered the support of the Scottish nobility which he and Archbishop Laud had forfeited in 1637 with their attempt to impose English episcopacy on the Scottish Church. Yet the nobility was divided from the clergy, who had reservations about supporting a King who had personally refused the Covenant and would not commit to the long-term future of Presbyterianism. The 'war' party within the Scottish Parliament (broadly speaking, the nobility) urged the King to modify his stance on religious matters to answer the concerns of the clergy, who did not support the proposed invasion. The nobility were, however, the majority party in the Parliament and preparations for war continued.

As the realignments materialized, hostilities intensified. In mid-March 1648, Fairfax reluctantly determined to deal with Poyer's defiant occupation of Pembroke Castle and ordered Laugharne and other officers to take action. Instead of acting in accordance with Fairfax's orders, Laugharne and his troops joined Poyer in driving Fairfax's men from the city and declared for the King, supporting his demand for a personal treaty. Poyer and Laugharne then mustered support throughout the county, which was of such a magnitude that further troops would have to be dispatched before the rebellion could be put down.

On 3 April, Lord Inchiquin, who had led Parliamentarian forces in Ireland in several notable victories (and atrocities, as at the Rock of Cashel in 1647), responded to Colonel Barry's advances by announcing his support for the King and for an alliance between the Irish Confederates and the Scots.

On 11 April the Scottish Parliament passed resolutions declaring that the English Parliament had breached the 1643 Covenant Treaty with Scotland, demanding the establishment of Presbyterianism in England and the suppression of heresy and the Book of Common Prayer, asking the English Parliament to reverse its policy of no addresses and enter further negotiations with the King, urging it to disband its 'Army of *Sectaries*'.[17] Anticipating the refusal of these demands, a week later it named the colonels of the future regiments of the invasion force. News of these appointments reached Westminster on 25 April, where the House of Commons resolved immediately to strengthen the defences at Newcastle, where two Parliamentary regiments were still garrisoned.

On 28 April, Sir Marmaduke Langdale, who had commanded the left-wing of the Royalist cavalry against Cromwell at Naseby, took control of Berwick. The next day the English Royalists also seized Carlisle, thereby gaining control of both cities on the English side of the Scottish border and securing access to England for the invasion force.

On 1 May, the Parliamentary Army held a general rendezvous at Windsor, apparently less in response to the imminent military crisis than to the crisis in Army morale: that 'low weak, divided, perplexed condition' to which it was reduced by loss of the people's affections, such that some 'judg[ed] it a duty to lay down [their] arms' or to imitate Christ and seal their active testimony through suffering, while others thought the only path to extrication lay in 'search[ing] out our iniquities, and humbl[ing] our souls before the Lord'.[18] As at Putney, but in a humbler and more introspective spirit, the Army debated over several days in accordance with an agreed procedure, described in the testimony of William Allen:

> To look back and consider what time it was when with joint satisfaction we could last say to the best of our judgments, The presence of the Lord *was* amongst us, and rebukes and judgments were not as then upon us . . . and having done so, to proceed, as we then judged it our duty, to search into all our public actions as an Army, afterwards. Duly weighing (as the Lord helped us) each of them, with their grounds, rules and ends, as near we could.
>
> By which means we were . . . led to find out the very steps . . . by which we had departed from the Lord . . . Which we found to be those cursed carnal Conferences our own conceited wisdom, our fears, and want of faith had prompted us, the year before, to entertain with the King and his Party.[19]

On the third day, the prayer-meeting unanimously reached two momentous decisions:

> That it was the duty of our day, with the forces we had, to go out and fight against those potent enemies, which that year in all places appeared against us . . . [and] That it was our duty, if ever the Lord brought us back again to peace, to call Charles Stuart, that man of blood, to an account for that blood he had shed, and mischief he had done to his utmost, against the Lord's Cause and People in these poor Nations.[20]

Thus both the resumption of fighting and the decision to put Charles on trial were the outcome of Army self-scrutiny and prayer conducted in a spirit of solemnity both befitting the occasion and strangely at odds with the immediacy of the military threat.

At the conclusion of the meeting Cromwell was dispatched to Wales to put down Poyer's rebellion, one of Fairfax's loyal officers (Adjutant-General Fleming) having been killed by the insurgents. Cromwell reached Gloucester on 8 May, with about 6500 troops. Hoping to deal with Colonel Thomas Horton's regiment before Cromwell's reinforcements arrived, a force of 7000 Welsh Royalists led by Laugharne attacked Horton's much smaller New Model force of about 2500 at St Fagans,[21] near Cardiff on 8 May, but the Royalists were driven back, with many killed and about 3000 taken prisoner. Laugharne himself was wounded and fled.[22] This was a significant blow to the Royalist party, and caused public opinion to shift back in the direction of Parliament and the Army, to whom God again appeared to have given the victory, despite the Royalists being vastly in the majority. Horton and Cromwell then linked forces and proceeded over the next two months successfully to lay siege to Welsh Royalist strongholds.

On 3 May 1648, the Scottish Parliament had forwarded a letter to the English Parliament relaying its resolutions of 11 April with a deadline for response of no more than 15 days. It demanded that arrangements be made for the King to come to London for further negotiations and that the excluded Members of Parliament be readmitted to the House for that purpose. Notwithstanding this, on 4 May the Scottish Parliament resolved that the Scottish Army should number 30 000, with the Duke of Hamilton (leader of the nobility faction) as its Commander-in-Chief. Significantly, the Commander of Cavalry desired by the Scottish Parliament – David Leslie, who had distinguished himself at Marston Moor – would not serve a cause which did not have the blessing of the Scottish clergy. The discontent of the clergy impacted generally on the supply of men and money, so that the invasion occurred later than intended. As Gardiner notes, the English Royalists holding Berwick and Carlisle were left without Scottish support for some time.[23]

This lack of co-ordination was characteristic of the Royalist campaign and can at least in part be explained by the circumstance of Charles's imprisonment, leaving the Royalists without a co-ordinated command. There were marches upon Parliament bearing petitions in support of the King, which added to the atmosphere of crisis and growing Royalist support outside Wales. One of the largest of these, on 4 May, was the Essex petition involving 2000 men (and claiming to represent 30 000 inhabitants), emanating from the former stronghold of the Eastern Association. On 16 May, petitioners from Surrey marched on Westminster. Eight or ten were killed and about one hundred wounded in the scuffle that ensued. However, with Wales being brought under control, there was little chance of a successful English rebellion without Scottish and Irish assistance. The difficulty was to prevent the spontaneous and premature occurrence of Royalist rebellions, before the awaited Scottish support was available.

This Royalist fear materialized in the Kentish rising of 21 May, following an attempt by the unpopular County Committee (appointed by Parliament) to suppress a popular petition similar to the Essex and Surrey petitions. This followed the dismissal by a local jury of charges brought against those who had been involved in the Christmas riots. The Derby House Committee supported the County Committee in its attempt to suppress the petition, advising it to 'do what in you lyeth for the preserving the peace of that county'.[24] The County Committee is alleged to have planned to 'hang two in every Parish that were promoters of [the petition], and sequester the rest'.[25] The Derby House Committee also empowered the County Committee to summon further military aid, at its discretion.[26] Rumours that military reinforcements had been sent for fuelled the insurrection. On 22 May, a number of local gentry placed themselves at the head of the movement and the county magazine at Canterbury was seized. On 23 May, leaders of the petitioners at Canterbury issued a Declaration and granted commissions for the raising of troops. They also ordered a general rendezvous to take place the following day.

The wide powers given to the County Committee by the Derby House Committee reflected the strategic importance of Kent. Like Essex and Surrey, it was alarmingly close to London; but even more importantly it was where the naval fleet was stationed (at the Downs) and naval stores and munitions, capable of supplying an insurgent force, were heavily concentrated along the Thames estuary. Just as before the First Civil War, the fleet was a prized asset, the capture of which could turn the tide of political and military fortune. If anything, its significance was enhanced because of the King's location on the Isle of Wight, and the need to prevent his escape abroad, from whence he might muster additional support and work more mischief.

Until 1647 the Navy bore few of the signs of the political change that had transformed the Army. Although the King's inattention to the needs of his seamen before the First Civil War had caused the Navy to defect to Parliament, it continued to maintain the fiction that it was fighting for both King and Parliament. The exigencies of war, and the departure of gentlemen commanders in favour of the King, had swept away the convention that high command must devolve upon gentlemen and many of the commanders were men of humble origin, but the Navy had no agitators or affiliations with radical civilian factions to split its ranks. In a letter of 18 June 1647, addressed to the Masters of Trinity House, Army Agitators explained 'the work that we are about' and sought their 'concurrent assistance', hoping that 'false suggestions' would not divide those who had defended freedom and justice 'you by sea and we by land, for these five years last past'.[27] The fact of the explanation, and the apparent lack of response, suggests the remoteness of the Navy from the Army agitations.

The appointment of William Batten as Vice-Admiral in 1645, following the Earl of Warwick's resignation as Lord High Admiral, had been a compromise measure until differences between the two Houses of Parliament as to the future command structure could be worked out. Batten, who was 'notoriously friendly to the Presbyterians',[28] served until September 1647 when an Independent-dominated Parliament pressured him into resigning and appointed Thomas Rainborowe in his place. Rainborowe's remarks at Putney suggest that he was not pleased to be transferred from the Army and that the appointment may have received support from those wishing to remove him from influence as much as from those wishing to magnify it. Although startling, the transfer was not entirely improbable. Rainborowe's father William had been a naval commander and Rainborowe himself had served in the Navy before joining the Army. It was also a far from smooth transition. In November, the House of Commons resolved to question Rainborowe following a report from Fairfax on his behaviour at Putney and Ware, and in December 1647 it resolved to delay his appointment to go to sea. However, his path and that of the Parliament and the Navy were converging. Once the King entered his Agreement with the Scots the obstacles to Rainborowe assuming his commission disappeared. A small Royalist demonstration at the Isle of Wight on 1 January 1648 provided the pretext for the Commons to order him to sea without the approval of the House of Lords. This foreshadowed the unilateral governance by the House of Commons which followed the vote of no addresses carried within the next few days.

The political symbolism of Rainborowe's appointment was not lost on his contemporaries, one of whom commented 'the Bell-weather of the *Republicans*, is set over the fleet'.[29] A Royalist newspaper referred to Batten having been 'cast over-board by a Committee of land-pirates':[30] a reference to the Committee for the Admiralty, to which the Commons had recently appointed five new members and the Lords four, which meant that the Committee which forced Batten's resignation had a majority of new members.

A further resolution of the House of Commons on 8 February 1648 that the ships henceforth be called 'the Parliament's ships', omitting the King's name and title, continued the new-modelling of the Navy, and reflected the general hardening of Parliamentary attitudes towards the

King. An anonymous pamphlet drew attention to this as further evidence of a systematic conspiracy, incorporating Rainborowe's appointment, to surround the King with a retinue so disloyal that every one of them 'in probabilitie would not scruple to bee his assassinate, so it might be done in private'.[31] This fear that a navy of Independents might assassinate the King was the Royalist counterpart of the radicals' fear that a navy of Royalists might help him escape.

Rainborowe's appointment was confirmed in April, amid the atmosphere of crisis generated by the Welsh insurrection and Inchiquin's defection. A major naval effort was required in the Irish Sea. But Rainborowe had difficulty mobilizing his fleet and sought Parliament's support in calling the commanders to their ships: an early sign of Royalist sympathies or general conservatism among the naval officers making them reluctant to serve a cause unambiguously hostile to the King. On 4 May, Henry Oxinden wrote to his wife that 'the sea men begin to be mutinous against Rainborowe who came to the houses to acquaint them therewith'.[32]

It is therefore not remarkable that the Kentish rising caught up the mutinous seamen, gave point and force to their discontent, and led at the end of May to a revolt of a portion of the Fleet in the Downs. Although the Derby House Committee issued instructions for the secret removal of ships and the protection of munitions and stores, the petitioners plundered the stores and seized several vessels. Peter Pett, who was in charge of the Chatham yard, reported 'haveing no power to resist them, being forsaken almost by the whole Navy'.[33] By the third week of May, a newsletter reported that the petitioners were 'universally in arms' and had 'seized on all Magazines as well those of the Navy as others'.[34] A letter from Rochester dated 21 May stated that the petitioners were joined by officers and others of vessels in the river there.[35] A pamphlet dated 24 May reported that 'there are in Rochester, and the parts hereabouts ... at the least a thousand that are risen, besides their interest in some Seamen'.[36] The support of the seamen in the fleet gave the movement national importance. The author of a newsletter recognized the moment as potentially critical: 'if one thing be true, that the Navy is revolted and Rainsborow set ashore, then I conceive all is at an end'.[37]

Rainborowe had indeed been 'set ashore' on 25 May when the crew of his ship, the *Swallow*, mutinied while he was ashore securing the castles in the Downs and debarred his return to the ship. His was one of several vessels that declared for the King. On 28 May, the mutinous captains signed articles of association with the Kentish gentlemen. A group of seamen, including the officers of the *Swallow* and the *Constant*

Reformation, also produced a document entitled *The Declaration of the Navie* explaining their mutinous action. This declaration – which can be seen as the conservative counterpart of *The Case of the Army Truly Stated* – demanded a personal treaty for the King, the disbanding of Fairfax's Army and payment of its arrears, the establishment of the known laws, and the preservation of the liberties of the subject and the privileges of Parliament. The seamen also demanded Batten or Warwick to command them in place of Rainborowe. On 29 May, Parliament sought to placate them by meeting this last demand and sending Warwick (who had been Lord Admiral before the Self-Denying Ordinance, and was now hurriedly appointed Lord High Admiral) to them. However, the mutineers made their acceptance of Warwick conditional upon his agreeing to engage in support of the petitioners, which demand he rejected.

Within a short time the petitioners had control of most of the principal places of east Kent, including Dover, where the castle alone (garrisoned by two companies sent to the county after the Christmas riots) held out for Parliament. Other groups had raised substantial forces in central and west Kent and had all but gained control of Chatham dock. Sir Richard Hardres, summoning Dover castle on 26 May, declared that 'all the County is ours, onely this castle, and one castle in the Downes, and this Evening all the Ships in the Downes have declared for us'.[38]

But like other episodes in this period of Royalist uprising, the insurrection in Kent was fragmentary and ill-timed. When the petitioners began to raise troops, the Earl of Thanet – one of their leaders, who had been among the first to rise – took fear and made full discovery of the matter to the Derby House Committee. On the same day (24 May) a cessation was signed between representatives of the petitioners and some members of the Committee of Kent with a moratorium on further recruiting. Following the Earl's disclosures and other reports from the region, Parliament dispatched troops to the area on 25 May, with orders to suppress the rioters. Some of the petitioners, who had marched as close to the City as Greenwich and Deptford in an armed demonstration, approached Parliament seeking an indemnity, which was granted on condition that they lay down their arms. A brief lull ensued, as many of the petitioners returned home. But others determined to proceed with the march, with the support of their leadership.

At this point Parliament determined to give 'this Business of the reducing of *Kent*' to Fairfax. A post from the House of Commons was sent to the gentlemen in command of the rising directing them to treat with Fairfax and the Derby House Committee. The prospect of facing the full might of the Army 'quite turned the Ballance',[39] making the petitioners amenable to negotiate with Fairfax as invited. But Fairfax would have none of it, 'answering, that he knew no authority they had to appoint commissioners for such a purpose'[40] and refusing to negotiate while the petitioners remained in arms. He led his 4000 troops to rendezvous on Blackheath on 30 May, in a preliminary show of force which caused a general retreat among the petitioners, who were also fragmenting into factions. Driving deeper into Kent and causing the petitioners to retreat, he eased the threatening prospect that the City of London would answer the call to arms in Kent.

A critical battle took place at Maidstone on 1 June between some 2000 Kentish troops and an Army force almost double that size. The fighting was intense, with pitched battles from street to street once Fairfax's troops had penetrated the town. The resistance was much stronger than Fairfax expected. Gentles suggests that '[o]ne reason why the defenders of Maidstone fought so grimly may be that most of them were not coun-trymen but "seamen, apprentices and . . . commanders in the king's army"'.[41] In a sense, it was a battle between army and navy. Notwithstanding this, Maidstone's defenders were subdued after several hours.

Royalist strategists had hoped for a demonstration in Kent after the Army had marched north against the Scots. The rapid growth of the Kentish movement caught them unprepared. Perceiving its significance, Fairfax postponed his movement north to meet the Scots and was able to use the Army to subdue the rebellion in Kent and intimidate the City of London from joining in (except for those apprentices who ventured to Kent for the fray). By rising too early the insurgents in Kent precluded their Scots allies from coming to their aid. Moreover, while the insurgents in Kent numbered about 11 000, they were dispersed between several towns and were thus more readily outnumbered, as at Maidstone. After Maidstone took its toll in casualties and desertions, their total number was reduced to about 3000.[42]

With the threat of general risings in Essex and Surrey, which could trigger a rising in London, Parliament ordered the fortification of London Bridge and the termination of ferry services across the Thames. With their route to London blocked, the insurgents under the leadership of the Earl of Norwich made their way secretly by boat across the Thames into Essex, heading for Chelmsford and Colchester. The Essex Royalists responded by seizing the members of the County Committee and pledg-ing themselves to the preservation and defence of those principles espoused in the Kentish petition and *The Declaration of the Navie*. While a small Parliamentarian force led by Colonel Whalley followed Norwich into Essex, Fairfax undertook the 'mopping up' in Kent. After Dover

Castle was relieved on 5 June, the remaining insurgent troops in Kent converged on Canterbury, where they were again defeated. With this, Kent was effectively subdued.

Yet the situation at large was far from under control. The rising in Essex was gaining in support, the situation in London was precarious, Poyer was holding Cromwell at bay in Wales, the mutinous seamen still held a number of ships which were subsequently placed at the disposition of the Prince of Wales, the Scottish invasion was imminent and petitions were emanating from several counties. The Royalists were mustering support in Surrey and were concentrated at Kingston in the expectation that the Prince of Wales would sail up the Thames to join them and that London would then rise. From mid-July until 3 September the Prince's fleet was in fact hovering about the east coast, threatening to relieve Royalist hotspots or inspire further insurrection, but the Prince had no land force or resources to sustain an insurrection and his presence proved ineffectual. Parliamentarian troops dispatched to Kingston met and defeated the Royalists there before their plan materialized. The day before his departure back to Holland in September, the Prince was persuaded, on threat of mutiny, to sail up the Thames estuary to engage Warwick, but a storm arose which made attack impossible. This was the closest he came to striking a blow in the Royalist cause.

Strategically, Whalley's presence in Essex was important in keeping Norwich away from London; but militarily he played a waiting game until Fairfax had finished in Kent. This allowed the Parliamentarian forces to consolidate before taking any real action in Essex. Fairfax crossed into Essex on 11 June, met up with Whalley and Sir Thomas Honywood's Essex brigade and proceeded to Colchester, where a bitter siege ensued, lasting 11 weeks and causing terrible suffering on both sides. Gentles notes that Fairfax could not risk storming the town, because the strength of the Royalists meant that the outcome must be uncertain. A Parliamentarian defeat at Colchester might be the small trigger needed to spark revolution in London.[43] So the soldiers on both sides and the tragically trapped civilians were set to experience 'perhaps the bitterest episode of either civil war'.[44]

In co-ordinating the disposition of troops to these many flashpoints, the Derby House Committtee had a most unenviable task. It had to pressure Cromwell to release troops for the defence of the north when he had need of them in Wales. At the beginning of June, Sir Marmaduke Langdale, in a daring ploy, had seized the fortress at Pontefract. With Scarborough also declaring for the King, there were now two secured routes for Scottish penetration into England and the situation in the north was obviously unstable. But events or providence favoured the Parliamentarians. The long delay before the Scottish invasion force entered England on 8 July – caused by wrangling among Scottish factions – allowed them basically to deal with Wales and the south-east (with the exception of Colchester) before containment in the north became critical. When Tenby fell to the Parliamentarians on 31 May, troops were released to assist Cromwell at Pembroke, the last bastion of the Welsh rebellion. Poyer surrendered Pembroke to Cromwell on 11 July, just three days after the Scottish invasion. This timing was critical in permitting Cromwell to proceed north with a further 4200 men to help redress the gross imbalance in the numbers of Royalist and Parliamentarian troops there.

The Parliamentarian forces in the north consisted of John Lambert's northern army of about 3000 troops, which engaged Langdale defensively while awaiting reinforcements from the south that would enable a more vigorous offensive; Hesilrige's small force which had been sent north with the object of defending Newcastle; and locally raised troops, the largest contingent of which (about 1500) came from Lancashire, the least Royalist of the northern counties. This force was facing an invading army of 9000 to 10 000 men, whose ranks could be expected to swell as they moved south. Within days of the invasion Lambert's forces were increased by 1000 troops whom Cromwell had sent north while the siege of Pembroke was still in progress, and a reinforcement of horse from Yorkshire. But the critical element in evening up the numbers was an advance party of 30 troops of horse (about 2400 men) whom Cromwell was able to send to Lambert because the engagement in Wales had ended.

An extraordinarily wet summer hindered troop movements and dampened powder and match. Gentles sums up the situation facing the Scots very colourfully:

> Torrential rains made the summer of 1648 the wettest in living memory. Rivers and streams that were easy to ford in normal years were turned into raging floods; roads became quagmires; match and powder were soaked; and life for the rank and file, shivering in their sodden clothes, was hellish. The English suffered from the weather too, but they at least were fighting on home ground.[45]

Heavy rain had prevented the general rendezvous of Royalists in Kent on 24 May. Unusual conditions and inclement weather were also to play a part at the battle at Preston in Lancashire where the defeat of the Scottish force took place.

The Scottish force was led by the Duke of Hamilton. This choice itself reflected divisions among the Scots. Leaders more able than Hamilton refused to head an invasion to support a King who did not support the Covenant. For the same reason the invading force was not well provisioned from Scotland and soon alienated the local English by plundering supplies from the countryside through which it passed. Hamilton had chosen imprudently to march south through Lancashire: the least friendly to the Royalist cause of the two gateways south and the least geographically hospitable for cavalry. It had been pointed out to him at his Council of War, when the competing routes were debated, that 'Lancashire was a close country, full of ditches and hedges; which was a great advantage the English would have over our raw and undisciplined musketeers . . . while, on the other hand, Yorkshire was a more open country and full of heaths, where we might both make better use of our horse and come sooner to push of pike'.[46] Hamilton apparently misjudged the extent of Royalist support in Lancashire and the political complexion of Manchester, which led him to choose as he did. In the event, the unhelpful terrain in Lancashire was decisive against the Royalists, making it necessary for the cavalry to proceed ahead to places where the horses could forage and thus causing the army to be strung out over many miles, making it vulnerable to splinter by lateral attack. This is precisely what occurred at Preston. The terrain, the weather and the shortage of food also impacted on the morale of the Scottish troops and contributed to their dispersal.

Cromwell had been advancing steadily north, gathering men and provisions along the way. He met up with Lambert on 13 August at Ripon. Sir Marmaduke Langdale, meanwhile, marshalled his troops in Yorkshire and directed them towards Preston, to link up with the main Scottish force. He was advised on 13 August that Cromwell was nearby, but apparently discounted the advice as rumour and failed to warn his Scottish allies. On 16 August he was only six miles east of the main force when a surprise encounter between Royalist and Parliamentarian troops made him aware that Cromwell, who had resolved with Lambert to mount a combined offensive on the Scottish force at Preston and cut off its line of retreat to Scotland, was within three miles of his troops, further to the east. The following morning he withdrew towards Preston and positioned his troops for battle, so as to block the road to the town, and went to forewarn the Scottish commanders. The Scottish force, however, was not ready to assist him. Its cavalry were quartered 16 miles further south at Wigan, and Hamilton decided that the lateral attack was only a probe by Cromwell's forces, which Langdale could deal with. The Scottish foot-soldiers crossed the Ribble at Preston Bridge to continue their march south while the attack on Langdale's troops proceeded.

Langdale's and Cromwell's troops engaged in heavy fighting in a sunken lane, with thickly hedged enclosures and muddy ditches, thrusting horse against musketeers and pikemen, with little room for manoeuvre. But as Langdale's troops were driven gradually to more open ground, Cromwell's superior cavalry came into their own and Langdale's force was decimated. From his position on Preston Moor, Hamilton sent fresh troops and ammunition and resolved to give battle to what he now perceived was Cromwell's main force. But he was persuaded from this course of action by the argument that the Moor would maximize Cromwell's opportunity to use cavalry against Scottish foot-soldiers unsupported by their own cavalry. He therefore resolved to allow the southward passage of foot-soldiers to proceed, to put the Ribble between the two armies and to regroup the Scottish infantry and cavalry before committing them to a major battle. Hamilton remained on the Moor with a rear-guard and some of his life guards, and two brigades were posted to hold Preston Bridge.

Predictably, Cromwell soon entered Preston, cutting Hamilton off from Preston Bridge and from the greater part of his army. Hamilton sent some of his horse north to General Monroe (at Kirkby Lonsdale), whence the remnant of Langdale's horse were fleeing. After Cromwell's men had captured Preston Bridge, he and others of his horse eventually swam the Ribble to rejoin the Scottish force. By nightfall about 4000 of Hamilton's troops had been captured and about 1000 killed. Hamilton then resolved to make a night withdrawal of his troops to join up with Middleton's cavalry from Wigan. This was done so precipitately that wagons of ammunition were left for Cromwell to find. In a further example of mismanagement which sums up the Scottish misadventure, Hamilton's troops took a different road to Wigan from the one up which Middleton was proceeding to meet them. Middleton thus found himself facing Cromwell instead of Hamilton and further losses ensued.

With Cromwell in pursuit, Middleton retreated to Wigan Moor where Hamilton's infantry had by then gathered, its ranks thinned by desertions during the night march. Hamilton's fatigued and dispirited troops were in no position to make a stand against Cromwell. They set off through Wigan for Warrington, leaving Middleton's horse to engage Cromwell just north of the town. The next day, Scottish foot-soldiers engaged Cromwell at Winwick, three miles from Warrington. Cromwell claimed that 1000 Scots were killed and 2000 taken prisoner. At this point Hamilton determined to cut his losses by abandoning his foot-soldiers at

Warrington (who swelled the ranks of Cromwell's prisoners by between 2500 and 4000) and proceeded with his cavalry towards Cheshire, where the Royalist rising upon which he was depending had in fact already failed. Lambert was sent to pursue Hamilton and local commanders were instructed to hunt down all remnants of the defeated force. Cromwell himself went north to deal with Monroe and those who had escaped to join him. Nearly all of the Scottish commanders were captured or surrendered by the end of August, but Monroe escaped back to Scotland, where the Scottish defeat in England provoked a short-lived civil war. Cromwell crossed the border, lending the Duke of Argyle military assistance in exchange for Berwick and Carlisle. His brief campaign against pro-Royalist forces in Scotland was such that Argyle's authority in Edinburgh and England's security in the north were at least temporarily assured. Pontefract, however, remained in Royalist hands and took further time to subdue.

After the defeat of the Scots invaders there was no course open to the defenders of Colchester but to surrender. They were already on the brink of surrender from famine and other deprivations (including denial of water) to which Fairfax had brutally subjected both its Royalist defenders and civilian inhabitants. But the news of the defeat at Preston was decisive. The surrender took place on 27 August 1648 and effectively marked the end of the Second Civil War. But the nature of that end symbolized the more brutal injustice the Army would now dispense in anger at the renewed warfare. All surrendering soldiers and officers below the rank of captain were assured of their lives. But Fairfax declared of the remainder that 'justice must be done on such exemplary offenders who have embroiled the kingdom in a second bloody war'.[47] They were men of blood to whom small mercy should be shown, particularly if they had borne arms against those who had been their captors and released them after the First Civil War. Two of the leaders who were not peers were summarily shot by firing squad. The peers, in deference to their privileges, were turned over to Parliament. The King, whom the Army officers regarded as the author of these secondary crimes, was not yet called to account. But the fate suffered by the officers at Colchester presaged the treatment that Charles himself would later receive.

This 'savage spirit of exasperation'[48] was not reserved merely for the Royalists, but extended to the perceived hesitancy and gullibility of the Parliament. On 14 August, a number of the excluded Presbyterian members of Parliament resumed their seats and on 24 August, in the wake of the Parliamentarian victories in the north, the vote of no addresses was repealed to make way for a treaty with the King. On 29

August, Parliament passed a comprehensive Ordinance establishing a Presbyterian system in England without the toleration looked for by the Independents. This was clearly done in the hope that a treaty embodying these terms for a religious settlement could be entered before the Army could turn from military to political matters and perhaps intervene to prevent the treaty.

The Independents in Parliament first approached the Army to intervene to prevent the negotiations at about the time of the surrender of Colchester on 27 August, well before negotiations commenced on 18 September. Fairfax gave no undertakings, but Ireton conceded that military intervention would probably be necessary. However, he thought intervention should be delayed until the King again displayed bad faith during negotiations, when both he and those who tried to treat with him would again lose popularity. The London Levellers petitioned the House unsuccessfully to refrain from negotiations and implement a platform derived from the *Agreement of the People*, abolishing the powers of the King and the Lords. But the Parliament, dominated by the Presbyterians, pushed the negotiations forward, granting the King parole to travel to Newport for the purpose.

From Newport the King played for time while the Queen tried to arrange a foreign military intervention and, failing that, to obtain from the Irish an agreement to invade in the following year, which would necessitate the King's escape until the time was ripe. One week into the negotiations the King indicated that he would consider nothing to which he agreed binding upon him until a whole agreement was finalized. This left him free to pretend to negotiate in detail: as the Independents claimed, it had 'a mere dilatory object'.[49] He replied to Parliament's proposals with counter-proposals that provided no direct answer and depended on the security of his word. As Parliament pointed out in rejecting his counter-proposals on 2 October, in the circumstances his 'bare word'[50] was not enough.

The Army too was becoming restive. Regiments from Newcastle and Berwick petitioned Fairfax to support the Leveller petition and purge the Parliament. By now Ireton was positive in his support for a purge and wrote a long letter to that effect to Fairfax on 27 September. Petitions from Oxford and Leicestershire were tabled in the House on 30 September. A document titled *The Declaration of the Army* was tabled on 3 October, and in mid-October Ireton's regiment petitioned Fairfax to resist those who had voted to repeal the vote of no addresses and see that justice was 'done on all criminal Persons' and that they received the same punishment 'in the Person of King or Lord, as the poorest commoner'.[51]

Still the negotiations went on, with the King rejecting a proposition excepting a large number of his supporters from pardon, and Parliament on 27 October rejecting the King's counter-proposal on episcopacy. On that day it became known that Ormonde had again landed in Ireland and was brokering agreements with Inchiquin and the Confederates with a view to the King's relief. The King wrote to Ormonde telling him not to be 'startled at my great concessions concerning Ireland, for that they will come to nothing'.[52] He referred expressly throughout October to his plans to escape rather than be bound by the impending personal treaty. Gardiner quotes someone present at Newport as summarizing the situation astutely:

> It is the opinion of wise men that if the King be resolved not to agree with Parliament he will escape hence to the Prince's fleet, leaving the Parliament and the army to their divisions, and to the discontents and hatred of the distracted people; his Majesty hoping by the next spring to have as fair a game to play over again as he had this summer.[53]

In November the Army debated a manifesto penned by Ireton known as *The Remonstrance of the Army*. This document is discussed in some detail in the next chapter. Its two themes were the danger of continuing to treat with the King and the need to bring him to trial. When Fairfax would not rule out an accommodation with His Majesty a compromise was reached by which it was agreed that the Army would put certain propositions directly to the King which, if accepted, should then be forwarded to Parliament. In the meantime, Cromwell and Ireton fostered an alliance with the Levellers and held several conferences with them where the *Remonstrance* was discussed and amended. They obviously assumed — and with good reason — that the Army propositions to the King would be rejected, and that the Army would then vote to proceed with the *Remonstrance*. At the first of the conferences with the Levellers the attitude of the soldiers was blunt: the King's head should be cut off and the Parliament purged or dissolved. Lilburne countered with a separation of powers argument, that it was necessary to 'keep up one tyrant to balance another' and that some other source of power was needed than the 'wills and swords' of the Army.[54]

In the short term, however, those wills and swords prevailed. The Army propositions were put to the King on 16 November and were rejected the following day. They included a demand for a permanent constitutional settlement rather than interim arrangements which left the King free to do whatever he pleased on recovering his power. The present Parliament was to cease on a date fixed under statute and to be replaced by biennial parliaments with a revised distribution of seats (but no liberalization of the electorate). A Council of State would control the militia, and the important officers of the Crown would be selected by Parliament for the first ten years and thereafter by the King from a pool of names provided by Parliament. Five persons only of the King's allies were to be excepted from pardon; the rest could make composition. The Army should be kept standing on a fixed establishment until two months into the first biennial parliament, at which point the needs of the realm would be determined by Parliament. The questions of the King's and Lords' negative voice in legislation and of the terms of the religious settlement were omitted. Very possibly it was felt that the powers accorded Parliament by the permanent constitutional arrangement would sort those matters out by effectively relegating the King to a titular and ceremonial role along the lines of that performed by the modern English monarchy. Charles in effect advised the Army that its proposals would be 'taken into consideration' if and when he was able to come to London to treat with the Parliament. While putting the Army firmly in its place, this response suggested the very slight significance the King attached to his current Newport negotiations.

On 18 November the Army Council of Officers voted to send the *Remonstrance* to the House of Commons. There were only two votes in dissent. It was presented in the name of the whole Army on 20 November, whereupon the Commons deferred consideration of it for a week and proceeded to treat with Charles. Being aware of the King's plans for effecting an escape, and that the projected dates for that escape were nigh, the Army tried to place the King in greater security. When correspondence with the governor of Carisbrooke proved unsatisfactory, Fairfax directed his officers to remove the King to Hurst Castle, a sombre fortification on the Hampshire Coast erected by Henry VIII to defend the Solent and cut off from land by tidal waters. The contrast with Carisbrooke suggests the shift that was taking place between negotiating with a king in detention and trying a king in remand.

The next step was to take control of Parliament, where there was a danger that the increasingly nervous Presbyterians might accept a settlement essentially on Charles's terms. Equally, there was no sign that the *Remonstrance* was seriously on the agenda. The Army had agreed with Lilburne that it would not use force against the Parliament until sufficient agreement on constitutional principles had been reached to prevent England coming under indefinite military rule. With only a loose agreement in place, to the effect that the constitutional arrangements should be worked out by a committee of 16 with a strong Independent and civilian majority, Lilburne gave intervention his blessing. He immediately assembled a committee and set to drafting a revised version of the *Agreement of the People.* On 30 November, the Army issued a declaration proclaiming the futility of further argument with the existing Parliament and suggesting the need for its immediate dissolution. In the interval before fresh elections created a new Parliament, members 'faithful to their trust' were urged to form a provisional government under the protection of the Army. This declaration was accompanied by news that the Army would march upon London to collect the substantial arrears owing to it from that city.

The Army's march into London coincided with Parliament's scheduled debate of the King's answers to their latest propositions and caused its deferral. On the next sitting day, with Fairfax quartered at Whitehall and effectively in command of the city, Parliament was advised of the King's removal to Hurst Castle. After a long debate which continued the following day (5 December), a motion to accept the King's answers was foreshadowed. The Independents were now keen to have such a motion put, to give a pretext to intervention, but the Presbyterians deferred putting the motion, discomfited by the implicit Army threat and also by the implications for the Covenant of accepting church government on Charles's terms.

On the afternoon of 5 December, a meeting of Army officers and Members of Parliament vigorously debated whether the Parliament should be wholly dissolved and new elections immediately called, or whether it should be purged and continue to act in the capacity stipulated in the *Declaration.* Ireton and Harrison were concerned that a purged Parliament would lack authority: it would be a 'mock Parliament and a mock power' and the Army had no 'law, warrant or commission to purge it'.[55] But the counter-argument (which is not recorded) prevailed. On the morning of 6 December, Colonel Pride took command of the lobby of Westminster Hall and barred the entrance to the House. This was done without Fairfax's instructions. Pride had a list of members to be excluded which had been drawn up the day before by three MPs and three Army officers. Lord Grey of Groby stood with him and identified those on the list as they arrived. There is some uncertainty about precisely how many members were excluded on the day,[56] but it appears that they numbered more than 100 and that some 40 who offered resistance were taken into custody and later released on a parole not to try to reenter or otherwise disturb the House. On 13 December, the vastly reduced House revoked the repeal of the vote of no addresses and the vote authorizing the Treaty of Newport.

The matter of bringing the King to justice was not expressly raised, but it was clear that this would be the major task of what became known as the Rump Parliament.

5

REGICIDE AND REPUBLIC, JANUARY–MARCH 1649

The Rump Parliament, in which those who supported the Army were in the majority, proceeded on two assumptions. The first was that the government of England could and should continue without its defeated and untrustworthy King. This followed the logic of the military victories which, in Puritan eyes, God had vouchsafed to Parliament and recognized that the King would never make peace on terms which conceded the things for which Parliament had successfully fought. The second was that Charles should be brought to trial. This was to satisfy outrage that the kingdom had been involved in a Second Civil War after God had delivered His verdict through the first, and to assert the principle of equality before the law by punishing the King along with his followers. Neither of these assumptions made regicide inevitable or pre-empted the final shape of things to come. Constitutional change might have taken the form proposed in the *Agreement of the People* or might simply have meant dispensing with the King's 'negative voice'. Putting the King on trial might have pressured him into accepting Parliament's terms,[1] or might have led to conviction and imprisonment rather than a death sentence. But what made these two assumptions so potent was their apparent coincidence with a biblical prophecy of a time when the righteous would take the place of kings who had corrupted their trust by yielding their kingdoms to 'the Beast'[2] – widely interpreted as the Antichrist, alias the Pope and other opponents of the true church.[3] The belief that a 'reign of the saints' would precede the imminent, earthly reign of Christ and the increasing conviction among Independents that the Army was the tool by which the

saints would come to power, gave an extraordinary impetus to the proceedings against the King. The dominance of those (such as Cromwell)
who held these beliefs also determined the shape of the constitutional
alternative, since the reign of the saints meant government by a spiritual
elite (oligarchy) rather than representative government as sought by the
more secular radicals (Leveller democracy).[4]

At the outset there were sharp differences of opinion as to the course
to be taken with the King. Among the Army leaders, Ireton was committed to putting him on trial, but Cromwell hesitated to do so – more for
political reasons than objection in principle[5] – while Fairfax was clearly
opposed to the trial, although 'as politically helpless as he was vigorous
in the field'.[6] The civilian Leveller Lilburne, who had consented to the
purging of the Long Parliament on the basis that constitutional arrangements for a democratized Parliament would swiftly be put into place, also
had no wish to put the King on trial, being concerned only that the King
be deposed. As to the constitutional arrangements, contrary to Lilburne's
expectations (but perhaps not surprisingly), the Army leadership
required the *Agreement of the People* as revised by Lilburne's committee to
be submitted first to the Council of Officers, where it underwent revi-
sion, and then to Parliament for its consideration.

After Pride's Purge, Parliament was virtually in the hands of the
Council of Officers. On 15 December 1648, in Cromwell's absence, the
Council voted 'that the King be forthwith sent for to be brought under
safe guards to Windsor Castle, and there to be secured in order to the
bringing of him speedily to justice'.[7] This pre-emptive action contained
the seeds of the later destruction of the Commonwealth, first by precipi-
tating Parliament into trying the King, contrary to the balance of public
opinion and through a judicial process that was unprecedented and
apparently without legal foundation, so that it became an immediate
source of disquiet and disaffection; and secondly, by so preoccupying all
parties with the trial of the King that the far more important question of
ongoing constitutional arrangements was pushed to the side. The unrepresentative Rump Parliament, which should have been a provisional
Parliament pending general elections, had the perfect rationale for
remaining in office, since elections were clearly not desirable while the
trial was taking place. Parliament could also be excused for being inat-
tentive to proposals for democratic reform when so much else of moment
was occurring. When the *Agreement* in its revised and amended form was
presented to it on 20 January 1649, Parliament resolved that it be considered when 'the necessity of the present weighty and urgent affairs
would permit'.[8] In the event, it was never properly considered.

Lilburne had quickly seen what would become of his constitutional plans. On 15 December 1648 – the same day as the order sending for the King – he published the *Agreement* in the original form proposed by his committee to make the true nature of their proposals known to the people. When the Army leadership resolved to let the Rump Parliament debate the wisdom of the proposals, rather than having the people sign the *Agreement* in such numbers that Parliament would be forced to adopt it, he broke away from these erstwhile allies. At the end of February 1649 he wrote a famous pamphlet, *England's New Chains Discovered* in which he attacked the Council of State of the newly proclaimed Commonwealth as preventing the people's voice from being properly represented, proposed a Parliamentary committee system supervised by a Parliament in permanent session, and called for a new Self-Denying Ordinance preventing senior military officers from occupying positions of political power. Cromwell was later to say of Lilburne, who with other Levellers was sent to the Tower in March for inciting the Army rank and file to mutiny against its officers and move politically against Cromwell, that the choice was 'to break them, or they will break you'.[9]

The pre-emptive action by the Council of Officers ensured that the Parliament was not democratized before the question of bringing the King to trial was debated. In the short term it achieved its end: power remained with the militia and with those in Parliament and the Army who were determined to bring the King to justice. But it meant that the critical moment for constitutional reform passed, allowing hard-line Independents to consolidate their power in the ensuing weeks through bonds formed by the extremities of the regicide. By the end of that process the King had been supplanted by an oligarchy so remote from its former power base that it savagely suppressed the Army mutineers who rose in May in support of Lilburne. The hour for the social revolution had come and gone. The political revolution took place without the altered social order that might have given it survival.

Between the resolution to fetch the King for trial and the commencement of proceedings, various parties sought to moderate the course being taken. Some Londoners produced an alternative *Agreement of the People*, contending for the reinstatement of the King on penalty that, if he should thereafter refuse his Royal assent to laws tendered by the Commons, he would be deposed. Pride himself (perhaps at Cromwell's instigation) is said to have cautioned the Council of War not to kill the King and thereby 'exchange a King in their power for a King out of their power [the Prince of Wales], potent in foreign allies and strong in the affections of the people'.[10] Presbyterians like William Prynne, who were committed by article three of the Solemn League and Covenant to protect 'the King's majesty, person and authority', may have been prepared to see the King deposed by a properly constituted Parliament, but certainly did not support the idea of his being condemned to death by an unrepresentative, Independent Rump. Even the Council of Officers hesitated to call for the taking of Charles's life;[11] and Cromwell, venturing one last approach to the King through the Earl of Denbigh, urged the Council at its meeting on 25 December 1648 to consider sparing the King if he accepted the terms then being offered.[12]

On 23 December, the House of Commons appointed a committee to consider means of proceeding against the King. As well as signalling that it was in earnest, the House thereby delayed resolving on the proceeding until the result of the further approach to the King was known. When Charles refused even to receive Denbigh, reaction followed swiftly, fuelled by Thomas Brooks's Fast Sermon to the House of Commons on 26 December, urging the Members to become 'a new sharp threshing instrument having teeth'.[13] At the Council of Officers on 27 December support for more moderate dealings with the King had evaporated. It was resolved that all ceremonial attendance upon the King should cease. He was on his way to becoming that 'Charles Stuart' whom the High Court of Justice would sentence to death for high treason and 'other high crimes'. On 28 December, an Ordinance creating a special court to try the King was introduced into the House of Commons. It was approved on 1 January 1649 in a momentous start to what the Puritans would later call 'the first year of freedom'.

The following day, the Ordinance was sent on to the House of Lords together with a resolution pronouncing that 'by the fundamental laws of this kingdom, it is treason in the King of England for the time being to levy war against the Parliament and the kingdom of England'.[14] This effectively created the crime in laying the charge. Under the Statute of Treasons (1352) it was treason for any subject to imagine or plot the death of the king (as the Rump Parliament was doing), but there was nothing by which a king could be incriminated as a traitor to his kingdom. The proposition was therefore a novelty, justified either by reference to unspecified 'fundamental laws' or 'natural law' or to biblical precedents or prophecies seen as generating imperatives superior to the law. The Lords rejected both the Ordinance and the resolution, on the moral ground that 'not one in twenty of the people in England are yet satisfied whether the King did levy war against the Houses first, or the Houses first against him' and on the legal ground that, even if the King levied war first 'we have no law extant that can be produced to make it treason in him to do'.[15] It declared that to define the crime upon the occasion without trial of fact upon a discernible law was (as it was) an abuse of process. Having made this stand, the Lords adjourned for a week, perhaps in the belief that a recess would inhibit the legislative progress of the matter, but at least to obtain some space for themselves and distance from what they sensed would occur with or without their consent.

On 3 January, the House of Commons passed a further Ordinance creating a High Court of Justice consisting of 135 commissioners who were to act conjointly as judges and jury. This varied the previous Ordinance, which had appointed three judges and a jury of 150 commissioners to the trial, and probably reflects the unwillingness of the legal profession to participate in a trial of dubious legality. The next day, the Commons dispensed with the Lords by passing three resolutions establishing the Commons as the exclusive law-making and judicial body in England, with authority deriving from the people. These resolutions provided 'That the people are, under God, the original of all just power: that the Commons in England, in Parliament assembled, being chosen by and representing the people, have the supreme power in this nation; [and] that whatsoever is enacted or declared for law by the Commons in Parliament assembled, hath the force of law, and all the people of this nation are concluded thereby, although the consent and concurrence of King or House of Peers be not had thereunto.'[16] They effected only so much constitutional reform as the unseemly rush and unpopular determination to indict the King made necessary.

Moreover, little attention was paid to the fact that this purged Parliament could not claim the 'just power' of a representative assembly. Although the Council of Officers had voted on 3 January that the Rump Parliament should be dissolved on 30 April 1649 (i.e. well after the trial) to make way for a properly representative body, Cromwell's own view was that the Parliament should be left to determine the date for itself. In the event, the Rump Parliament did not consent to disband and remained in office until 1653 when Cromwell ousted it by military force and began to govern in the capacity of Lord Protector.

On 6 January, what was now styled an Act of the Commons in exercise of its supreme power, appointed persons for the 'hearing, trying and adjudging the said Charles Stuart', against whom the preamble charged that he:

not content with those many encroachments which his predecessors had made upon the people in their rights and freedoms, hath had a wicked design totally to subvert the antient and fundamental laws and liberties of this nation, and in their place to introduce an arbitrary and tyrannical government; and that besides all other evil ways and means to bring this design to pass, he hath prosecuted it with fire and sword, levied and maintained a cruel war in the land, against the parliament and kingdom, whereby the country hath been miserably wasted, the public treasure exhausted, trade decayed, thousands of people murdered, and infinite other mischiefs committed: For all which high and treasonable offences, the said Charles Stuart might long since justly have been brought to exemplary and condign punishment.[17]

It went on to refer to Parliament's past forbearance in the hope that the King's imprisonment 'after it had pleased God to deliver him into their hands' would of itself quiet the distempers of the kingdom; but this having failed, the present measure was needed to prevent further commotion and to deter future officers of state from believing that they could with impunity 'enslav[e] or destroy . . . the English nation'.

As Gardiner points out,[18] this is a political rationale, not a legal one. According to precedent, it may have justified dispatching Charles by the sword as a dangerous war-prisoner, but it was not grounds for subjecting him to a judicial process. Cromwell had no use for a dispassionate trial. He reacted impatiently to criticisms of the legality of the Court by brutally stating the intention behind the process: 'I tell you, we will cut off his head with the crown upon it'.[19] A judicial process without a legal basis, authorized by an unrepresentative Parliament and conducted by non-judicial officers to a predetermined end was likely to strike even those who believed in the general case against the King as improper and unfair.

When the High Court of Justice assembled on 8 January, only 52 out of the 135 commissioners attended. Fairfax was among them, but thereafter absented himself. Lady Fairfax was more visible, attending later sessions as an observer and interjector, crying shame on the proceedings. On 9 January, the House of Lords resumed its sitting and attempted to rescue both the King and legal propriety by appointing a committee to draw up an Ordinance providing 'that whatsoever King of England shall hereafter levy war against the Parliament and Kingdom of England shall be guilty of high treason and be tried in Parliament'. This had the virtue of defining the crime before the event and might (or might not) have been sufficient to deter the King from further military adventure. But the House of Commons was no longer interested in the views of the Lords and did not bother answering matters referred to it. Its determination to exercise supreme and sole authority was encapsulated in the ordering of the new Great Seal which not only embodied the claim of the Commons to sovereignty but by proclaiming 'the first year of freedom' rejected as illegitimate the sovereign power it replaced.

The notable thing about the official formulation of the charge against Charles, apart from its political rather than legal nature, is its secular character. The allegation of 'arbitrary and tyrannical government' subverting 'antient and fundamental laws and liberties' might be expected from the Levellers rather than the religious Independents. Wastage of lands, disruption of trade, loss of Treasury reserves and even the murder of civilians appear from the charge to be at the heart of the matter, yet were not. For the driving force behind the trial of the King, the thing that gave it an unstoppable momentum, was the spiritual passion and militancy of the Independents, fed by their fundamentalist beliefs and the insistence of highly influential preachers that key prophecies from the Bible were about to be fulfilled and that justice upon the King was the only godly course. Without this dimension, the killing of Charles appears merely brutal and vindictive. While it did have those characteristics, it was spiritualized in the minds of the Independents by religious convictions which placed them under a compulsion to dispense Old Testament justice to the King and clear the way for the reign of the righteous and Christ's second coming.

Such is the importance of this framework to understanding the trial and execution of the King that some time must be spent examining it. It created a logic in which the King's death became necessary, but it was not a logic that would command broad public support and was not replicated in the Ordinance. Nevertheless, it was the iron fist within the glove of the seemingly defensible public charges.

As we have seen, especially before 1644 there was a general reluctance to nominate the King as the opposing party or lay blame directly upon him. Elizabethan and early Stuart Puritans preferred to maintain that they were loyal to the Crown and lay blame instead upon the bishops for failing to support reforms which would complete the English Reformation. As the Civil War approached, they blamed 'evil councillors' and 'malignants' for the course events were taking and, when opportunity arose, condemned and executed scapegoats such as the Earl of Strafford and Archbishop Laud rather than confront the King himself. The attainder on Strafford was made in the name of the King as well as Parliament and was – as the King himself recognized – a shameful example of the King's weakness and capacity to betray his allies to preserve his crown. But the terms of the charge against Strafford so parallel the terms of the later charge against Charles in 1649 as to make it clear that Strafford was executed as a surrogate. Even when Parliament went to war, it proclaimed that it was doing so to defend His Majesty and preserve his liberty and honour. In 1643, when Parliament after more than a year of fighting summed up its war aims in the Solemn League and Covenant, it claimed to be defending the King's person and authority against incendiaries, malignants and evil instruments who were hindering the Reformation and dividing the King from his people. To the question 'For whom do you fight?' the soldier in *The Souldiers' Catechisme* (1644) was expected to reply: 'To recover our King out of the hands of a Popish malignant company that have seduced his Majesty with their wicked counsels and have withdrawn him from his Parliament.'[20] As late as 1644, therefore, the official view of the King was still that he was passive and innocent of what was taking place, and that his person remained sacrosanct.

However, while this was the prevalent view and the one generally published, an alternative view began to be fostered within the Army. Clarendon recounts that in recruiting for the Eastern Association Cromwell 'would not deceive or cozen' his soldiers by commissioning them to fight for King and Parliament but 'told them, that if the King chanced to be in the body of the enemy that he was to charge, he would as soon discharge his pistol upon him as at any other private person'.[21] In Cromwell's eyes there was no divinity hedging a King at war with his people. This willingness to have the King take his chance in battle (or even to target him) is a far cry from executing the King after a judicial process, but it was the genesis of a change in the Puritan perception of the King, which became a metamorphosis after the Second Civil War. The veil which shielded Charles was lifted and he himself became the Grand Scapegoat. He was no longer God's vice-regent on earth, but Charles Stuart, on trial by his subjects. The accusation against him was so profound, and so conditioned by the culture of those who had won the war, that there was no defence open to him.

The war was not just a civil war: to the Puritans it was an extension of the spiritual warfare within the Christian soul. Parliament's soldiers were clothed in 'the whole armour of God'[22] and fought for 'the extirpation of Popery, prelacy . . . superstition, heresy, [and] . . . whatsoever shall be found to be contrary to sound doctrine and the power of godliness'.[23] If there were any ambiguity as to which was the godly party, that was dispelled by providence, which gave Parliament the victory – twice. Especially after the Second Civil War, it was common for Independents to count those who died in Parliament's holy war as saints, which made the Royalists and Charles as their figurehead persecutors with hands stained with saintly blood.

Thus the identification of Charles with the opponents of Christ (or positively with the Antichrist) was intensified by the concept of blood-guilt. The biblical *locus* of this idea is the Book of Numbers 35:33, where it is commanded 'Ye shall not pollute the land wherein ye are, for blood it defileth the land: and the land cannot be cleansed of the blood that is shed therein, but by the blood of him that shed it.' The Geneva Bible drew attention to this text by a marginal comment: 'That God is mindful of the blood wrongfully shed.' While based on an 'eye for an eye' mentality, this text is imbued with the notion of defilement. The shedding of innocent blood pollutes the land, and when the blood is that of the saints and is shed by the King appointed to protect the land and the innocent, the whole kingdom is polluted and cannot be restored to wholeness unless the saints are avenged.

The term 'man of blood' was applied to Charles at the Army's prayer meeting at Windsor on 1 May 1648 at the commencement of the Second Civil War. The Army vowed that, if it won, it would bring 'Charles Stuart, that man of blood' to account for the blood that was shed. The indictment of January 1649 included the charge that '[a]s a result of these cruel and unnatural wars, levied [First Civil War], continued and renewed [Second Civil War] by Charles Stuart much innocent blood of the free people of this nation hath been shed'. The King's defeat in the Second Civil War indicated not only that God was not with Charles, but that judgement should be exacted on him. Cromwell described Charles as 'that man against whom the Lord hath witnessed'.

Milton in *Eikonoklastes* cites the text from Numbers and employs it specifically to condemn Charles. In Milton's eyes the King's blood-guilt erases his sanctity, which is seen as dubious anyway. 'Were it true', he says, 'which is most false, that all kings are the Lord's anointed, it were yet absurd to think that the anointed of God should be, as it were, a charm against law and give them the king's privilege to punish others who sin themselves unpunishable.'[24] Through his blood-guilt, the King becomes mere 'Charles Stuart' who can be tried like any other man, but is more culpable than other men because his shedding of blood is a violation of his earthly office and his God-given trust.

Eikonoklastes, by its title, touches another keynote in this alternative perception of Charles, which is that of 'icon (or idol)-breaking'. Puritans took the Old Testament stipulations against idolatry very seriously and were encouraged by the Geneva Bible glosses to take violent action to eradicate it. Churchmen praised King Asa from II Chronicles for deposing Queen Maachah (his mother) 'who made an idol in a grove' and ridding the land of idolatry, but the Geneva Bible criticized him for not putting her to death:

> therein he shewed that he lacked zeale, for she ought to haue died both by the couenant, as verse 13, and by the law of God: but he gaue place to foolish pitie, and would also seeme after a sorte to satisfie the Law.[25]

The gloss on the Book of Jeremiah, 48:10 declared 'Cursed be he that doeth the work of the Lord with negligence and cursed be he who keepeth his sword from blood.'

The figure of appropriate zeal was Phinehas, who 'stood up . . . and executed judgment'[26] by killing adulterers with a spear. Churchmen sought to contain the threat Phinehas posed to civil order by framing him as the type of the zealous civil magistrate and not as licensing the individual to take the law into his own hands.[27] Bishop Bancroft made a scathing early attack on the use the Puritans made of Phinehas, which meant that

> when Princes grow to be tyrants, (whereof seditious spirites will bee the iudges, (and that the inferiour Magistrates will not do their duties: the people then, (if any *Ionathan* will step foorth, to be their captaine) are bound to ioyne themselues vnto him, and may vse the sword in their own right: or otherwise some priuate man, that is moued with zeale *extra ordinem*, may execute vengeance, vppon Prince or Potentate, Idolater, wicked persons, &c. euen as the spirit shal moue him.[28]

In 1641 a Suffolk Minister, Samuel Fairclough, called for the speedy execution of the Earl of Strafford by reference to Phinehas:

> So shal you by this worke of expedition . . . turne away the wrath of God from yourselves, and others, as *Phinehas* elsewhere.[29]

In October 1644, Edmund Staunton called for the death of Archbishop Laud in a sermon entitled *Phinehas's Zeal in Execution of Ivdgement*. While acknowledging that Phinehas's action had 'a blush of irregularitie in it' and finding in Phinehas an 'encouragement to all in authoritie, to burne with zeal for God against his enemies', Staunton believed Phinehas also stood for the proposition that 'when God hath work to do, he can finde out workmen, a Phinehas with zeale in his heart and a javelin in his hand'.[30]

In December 1641 the Puritan preacher Stephen Marshall had contrasted the upright figure of Phinehas with magistrates and ministers who had 'God, Conscience, their office, the lawes' on their side, but dared not act against idolatry and profanity. Applying the text from Ezekiel 22:30, he 'sought for a man among them, that is some Phinehas, to stand in the gap, to make up the hedge, some zealous ministers to stand up and mediate with God for them'.[31] Like the call to arms in the First World War poster – 'Your country needs *you*' – this was a personal call to Puritans to 'stand in the gap', not only for their own salvation but to save the kingdom from the scourge that would result if profanity and idolatry went unchecked. Initially this required action against the King's evil informants and the execution of scapegoats. But after the Second Civil War when Charles could be identified as a 'man of blood' as well as an idolator in that he supported popish practices in the English Church which the Puritans regarded as idolatrous, this was implicitly a call for a Phinehas prepared to save the kingdom by calling Charles to account with his life.

Thomas Brooks's Fast Sermon, *God's Delight in the Progress of the Upright*, delivered before Parliament two days before its formal resolution to try the King, draws all of these strands together. Brooks's opening text was from Psalm 44.18: 'Our heart is not turned back, neither have our steps declined from thy ways', which he meshed skilfully with the secular axiom 'Not to go forward is to go backward'. His theme was the determination of 'upright hearts' to persist in God's ways despite opposition and discouragement, and the need to resist the 'carnal reason and carnal counsel' of God's enemies. The core of the Sermon is the 'use' or application of the text, which Brooks says is 'the main thing I have my eye upon at this time', noting that the House has 'begun to fall upon the execution of justice, which is a way wherein God delights to walk'. In this context he recommends the 'glorious resolution of Jerome', who was prepared to 'throw down [his] father, break through [his] brethren and trample upon [his] mother, to cleave to Jesus Christ'. So, he exhorts, 'Let justice be done, though the world be ruined'.

Brooks advances five grounds upon which the pursuit of justice is necessary. First, justice performed turns away God's wrath and averts national calamities. See Phinehas, he says, who by his action stayed the plague. See, by contrast, Jerusalem, which was destroyed because, as recounted in Ezekiel 22:29–31, God 'sought for a man . . . "that should make up the hedge" . . . but he could not be found'. Second, God throws religious observances 'as dung in [the] faces' of those who neglect justice. See Isaiah 1:11–15, he says, where sacrifices and sabbaths were loathsome to God because the hands of those who performed them were 'full of blood', and Amos 5:21–4, where God rejected Israel's feast days and solemn assemblies because judgement and justice did not 'run down as waters'. Members must therefore see to it that 'justice and judgment run down as a mighty stream'.[32] Third, '[w]hen justice is not executed, a land is defiled' and those who permit such defilement partake of the blood-guilt. See Numbers 35:33 'the land cannot be cleansed of the blood that is shed therein, but by the blood of him that shed it'. The Lord forbid, he says, that Members should 'wrap [themselves] up in the treachery, and murder, and blood, and cruelty, and tyranny of others'. Though the King is not named, 'tyranny' has but one referent and defines 'him' by whom the blood was shed. Fourthly, 'those persons that have neglected the execution of justice upon their implacable enemies, when God hath given them into their hands, those God hath left to perish basely and miserably'. See Ahab in 1 Kings 20:42, whose life – as the prophet reveals – God resolved to take 'because thou hast let a man go that I had appointed to destruction'. And likewise Saul in 1 Samuel 15:26 whom God rejected as king because he did not utterly destroy the Amalekites as commanded, but spared Agag, and whom God also brought to misery and destruction (1 Samuel 31:4). Fifthly, neglect of justice encourages the wicked and discourages the godly from doing their duty: 'You were better a thousand times to set some of those grand malefactors a-mourning . . . by the execution of justice, than by the neglect of justice to keep a kingdom still mourning in garments of blood.'

Further telling notes are struck. Apostasy – the faithful abandoning the faith, like Satan in his fall from grace – is the unpardonable sin. 'As a soldier when he forsakes his colours and runs to the enemy, all his former good service is lost and buried in oblivion':

There shall be no more talk – This was a gallant man for God, and this man stood bravely up for his people and his ways, and for the liberty of the nation, suitable to the trust reposed in him. There shall be no mention of this if a man play the apostate.

Conversely, God will shelter those who protect the saints:

Right Honourable, God hath made you in some blessed measure instrumental to shelter his people; and certainly that hath been one great reason that God hath sheltered you, notwithstanding all the designs, plots and treacheries of men to destroy you.

Finally, they should not be surprised at the means God might use to achieve his purpose. See 'his delivering of his people and ruining their grand enemy, Haman, by Esther's attempting that which was directly against the law of the land' (Esther 4:10,16):

> Esther adventures and throws herself on God's providence, and comes to the court, directly cross to the law of the land, to the letter of the law; and by this untrodden way . . . , God delivered his poor people.

For, as Brooks had informed them moments earlier, 'God is now about a glorious design to exalt his Son, and the children unborn shall rise and call you blessed if you will be instrumental to further this design.' But if not, 'it were better that you had never been born'.[33]

This was the point at which the Old Testament case for justice fused with the New Testament prophecies of the reign of Christ, which radical religious thinkers in the 1640s felt to be imminent. Milton's case against Charles in *Eikonoklastes* taps this well of Puritan convictions which flowed from interpretations of the *Book of Revelation,* encouraged by the Geneva Bible annotations which identified the second of the two Beasts in Revelation 13 as the papacy, which was thus in partnership with the Antichrist. The ten horns of the beast were identified as the ten kingdoms of western Europe, and Revelation 17:17 prophesied that ten kings would yield their power to the beast before God's kingdom on earth was fulfilled. Some 20 years before the Civil War, during the reign of James I, Richard Sibbes delivered a powerful sermon entitled *The Beast's Dominion over Earthly Kings* in which he labelled the actions of these kings in giving their kingdoms over to God's enemies as 'treason against God':

> For commonly the idol of the people is their king, and, being led by sense and not by faith, they fear him more than they fear God, . . . and so they come to this damned [antichristian] religion by depending on him.[34]

For many later Puritans, it was not hard to see Charles in this light. In a sermon delivered before Parliament on 25 February 1645, Thomas Goodwin, an Independent preacher who later became a state chaplain to the Commonwealth, expressly identified England as one of the ten

kingdoms 'which set up the beast, or Antichristian Rome'[35] and by impli-
cation identified Charles as a king who had yielded his kingdom. He told
the Members of the Commons that 'we are in the last times of these [ten]
kingdoms, and we all here live in one of them'. A king who had yielded
his kingdom forfeited his authority from God and was to be seen as a
traitor and false idol. Milton in *Eikonoklastes* branded Charles as a 'brazen
serpent', diverting what was due to God into adulation of his own person
and worship of the Antichrist. Thus Charles became a target for those
Phinehases who might answer the call. Killing the King was iconoclasm
at the core of the state, answering that same duty that was urged even
upon the ordinary soldier in *The Souldiers' Catechisme* to use the 'sword of
reformation' God had placed in his hand to 'cancel and demolish . . .
monuments of superstition and idolatry, especially seeing the Magistrate
and Minister that should have done it hath neglected it'.

Revelation 20 spoke of a time when Satan would be bound and the
earth would become sinless. At Armageddon there would be a final
confrontation between Satan and Christ's true church in which the
latter would prevail. Both Presbyterians and Independents put store by
this prophecy, but as Noel Henning Mayfield has demonstrated[36] there
were significant differences in the way they interpreted it, which left the
Presbyterians conceptually on the side of monarchy and encouraged
anti-monarchism among Independents. Presbyterians were inclined to
take a historical and figurative view of the millennium, identifying it
historically with the golden age of Constantine and figuratively with
the spiritual awakening of Christ's true church. They looked to the past
and celebrated monarchs such as Elizabeth I as instruments of God in
promulgating a reformed church. But Independents took the view that
the millennium was still to come and that it referred to the literal realization of Christ's kingdom on earth, his 'second appearing in glory'
when the 'church militant' would be released from suffering and warfare
to become the 'church triumphant' in the reign of the saints.[37] Christ
would then take his rightful place as King and would be the 'fifth
monarch' after the four monarchies referred to in Daniel 2:45. Hence
the term 'fifth monarchists' which was applied to radical exponents of
this view.

Inevitably, this latter view implied a distinction between earthly monarchs and the perfection of Christ's kingship, especially in view of the ten
kings in Revelation 17:17. Christ would govern 'not by tyranny, oppression and sensually, but with honour, peace, . . . all nations and kingdoms
doing homage to him'.[38] He would not be waylaid by the Beast. It was a

small jump from the view that Christ would end the four monarchies to the view that he would destroy them. Milton, who must be counted among the Independents, believed the Messiah would 'put an end to all Earthly Tyrannies, proclaiming [a] universal and milde Monarchy through Heaven and Earth'.[39] He went on in *The Reason of Church Government* (1642) to warn that 'if it should happen that a tyrant . . . should come to grasp the scepter', such a king would be an instrument of Antichrist.[40]

John Goodwin looked forward to the imminent time 'when Christ will put down all rule, and all authority and power', which he identifies with 'the downfall of Antichrist'.[41] By 1646 Presbyterians and Independents were engaged directly in a battle of words over this anti-monarchism within Independent thinking: Presbyterians like William Prynne and Robert Baillie invoking Old Testament precedents to support a case for the sanctity in the monarchy, and Independents like Goodwin, Hugh Peters and John Cooke responding that the Old Testament kings were types (that is, foreshadowings) of Christ's unique kingship, and that the days of earthly kings were numbered. On 22 December 1648, Hugh Peters spoke before Parliament of the Army leading England out of bondage, and of a similar liberation occurring throughout Europe in advance of God's kingdom.

For Independents, therefore, God purposed the downfall of kings. To restore a king against whom God had given them victory was to stand 'in a direct opposition against Jesus Christ in the work that he is about'.[42] Rather, God had called forth his saints to 'execute vengeance upon the heathen . . . to bind their kings with chains and their nobles with fetters of iron . . . to fight with the beast, and overcome him and his followers':[43] all of them categories with which Independent reasoning identified Charles. Milton makes this explicit in *Eikonoklastes*, where he draws together images from each stage of this reasoning in describing the duty of the saints

> *To bind thir Kings in Chaines, and their Nobles with links of Iron* . . . not to build *Babel* . . . but destroy it . . . to overcome those European Kings which receive thir power . . . from the beast; and are counted no better than his ten hornes . . .[44]

Moreover, this king was not just a tyrant who had compacted with the Beast, but a 'man of blood'. The connection between the King's blood-guilt and his service of the Antichrist is made retrospectively in a declaration of the Army on 1 August 1650, which explains:

. . . we were then powerfully convinced that the Lord's purpose was to deal with the late King as a man of blood. And being persuaded in our consciences that he and his monarchy was one of the ten horns of the Beast (spoken of, Rev.17:12–15) and being witnesses to so much of the innocent blood of the Saints that he had shed in supporting the Beast . . . we were extraordinarily carried forth to desire justice upon the King, that man of blood.[45]

Presbyterians, by contrast, claimed to have warred against the King 'not to bring his majesty to Justice (as some now speak) but to put him into a better capacity to do Justice: to remove the wicked from before him, that his throne might be established in righteousness'.[46] They had done so with 'loyal hearts and affection toward the king', mindful of their obligations under the Solemn League and Covenant and 'not intending the least hurt to his person'. These alternative strands in Puritan thinking underlie the differences of view between various factions on the Parliamentarian side about what should be the fate of the King, and help explain the extraordinary and unbending determination of radical Independents to see him executed.

The logic of the Independent position might have meant putting the King to the sword in what was effectively both a military act and a religious act worthy of Phinehas. Cromwell's justification to his friend Lord Wharton – 'Be not offended at the manner, perhaps no other way was left. What if God accepted the zeal, as he did that of Phinehas, whose reason might have called for a jury?'[47] – seems to pretend to such a case. But Cromwell had two scruples which prevented this from being done. The first of these was spiritual. It concerned whether destruction of the King at that time was the 'mind of God'. That is, although he accepted that God would ultimately destroy Charles in accordance with biblical prophecy, he was concerned that 'some men are apt to be carried away' by an apprehension of God's will as reflecting their own. He was also concerned to see the saints 'abstain from all appearance of wrong, and for that purpose avoid the bringing of scandal to the name of God', because God would see to his own ends 'without necessitating us to do a thing which is scandalous, or sin'. This was the paradox for people exhorted to act in the name of the Lord, yet bound by prophecies which might or might not depend on their agency for fulfilment.

The second scruple was that of the lawyer whose 'reason . . . called for a jury', although his religion did not. Cromwell simply could not perform an act as momentous as regicide without at least the appearance of legal process and sanction. In fact, this was part of his undoing because the sham legal process attracted widespread criticism, while also giving Charles dramatic opportunity to appear in the role of sacrificial victim. It allowed Charles to develop that imagery of self which the *Eikon Basilike* immediately amplified and which dominates the public imagination to this day, supplanting the more complex history of Charles's behaviour over the preceding years. Instead of the 'man of blood', Charles became the sacrificial lamb, luminously spiritual in a hall filled with steel-clad butchers.

Henning Mayfield comments that '[m]ost members of the Long Parliament, the legal profession, and the Presbyterians could justify resistance to the King, even to the point of deposition and possibly tyrannicide; but not his public trial and execution'.[48] Under the 'contract' view of the relationship between monarch and subject, subjects had a right to depose and even execute a sovereign who had breached that contract. This doctrine had precedents in the depositions of Edward II in 1326 and Richard II in 1399. But there was no precedent for subjects to put their monarch *on trial* and, as previously noted, the Statute of Treasons did not provide for treason *by* a King. The King's Ministers might be put on trial for breaches of public duty, but it was not possible to try the person of the Crown. The proceeding was therefore viewed by many (almost certainly the majority) as contrary to both common law and statute law, and without legal or political precedent.

This issue of legality was raised by the King himself on the first day of his trial when he challenged the Court to say 'by what power I am called hither . . . by what authority, I mean *lawful*'. Those constituting the Court responded to Charles's challenge by affirming that they were 'satisfied with [their] authority, and it is upon God's authority and the kingdom's'.[49] That is, they appealed to principles beyond or behind the letter of the law. The Army Remonstrance of 16 November wanted the King called to account, whether or not there were 'particular laws' to support the process. It alleged that the concept that the King was sacrosanct was 'begot by the blasphemous arrogance of tyrants' and remained 'in our law books as heirlooms only of the Conquest'.[50] Milton followed this line in labelling the laws 'norman gibbrish'[51] and pointed to the irony if the King's 'arbitary voice' as manifest in laws made in exercise of his prerogative were able to stand in the way of justice.[52] Instead, the Independents appealed to the 'Spirit and soul of the Law'[53] and in particular to Genesis 9:6 which they alleged predated kingship and was 'a statute-law unto all flesh by that Great Law-Giver'.[54] Here again the Presbyterians and Independents parted company, with Presbyterians affirming the law of the land and condemning the trial process as illegal and Independents claiming to act in accordance with the intention of the law, or with fundamental laws superior to all written laws, which required those written laws to be, in Milton's phrase, 'mutable upon just occasion'.[55]

This dispute about the applicable law arose out of and paralleled the larger constitutional crisis. Prynne, as a prominent spokesman for the Presbyterians, attacked the Independents as 'lawless men without and against all precedent, law, and Justice'.[56] The Independents, on the other hand, regarded the Presbyterians as cowards and 'traitors to the cause of God', hiding under cover of legal formality.[57] After all, Roman law had been used to convict and execute Christ himself. The chief prosecutor in the trial, John Cooke, appealed to the concept of 'fundamental law' to oppose this legal formalism. While the Statute of Treasons might not provide for a king to be brought to trial, it was 'intended for the People's safety [and] never meant, to give liberty to the king to destroy the people'. If a king 'entrusted with the sword for the protection and preservation of the people . . . employ[s] it to their destruction', such action must be 'High Treason . . . more transcendent than in the former case' of a subject who contemplates the destruction of his king. This was a fundamental law which had 'a suspensive power over all human laws'.[58] While it was a stage more abstract than the 'fundamental rights and liberties' which the Levellers imputed to the ancient constitution, both appealed to an abstract moral justice superior to what they regarded as degenerated human laws reflecting the Conquest and its power relations. But for the Independents (unlike the Levellers) the object was spiritual justice: justice as meted out at Judgment Day, when 'no Murderer shall . . . plead Prerogative to exempt him from Trial'.[59] Even in an earthly court, they doubted whether the King could claim the prerogative since 'a King deposed is no longer a king, but a subject'.[60] This explains the insistent reference in the charges to 'Charles Stuart', rather than to the King by office.

The trial took place at Westminster Hall, commencing on 20 January 1649. When Charles was brought before the Court he refused to acknowledge its legal jurisdiction over him and would not plead to the charges. Again on 22 January and 23 January, Charles was called before the Court to plead and refused. He declared that his refusal was made not only on his own behalf but to preserve the liberties of the people, 'For, if Power without Law may make Laws, may alter the Fundamental Laws of the Kingdom, I do not know what subject he is in England that can be sure of his life, or any thing that he calls his own.'[61] Gardiner notes that 'Charles's reasoning was not unanswerable'[62] – especially by those who saw Charles's own power as descended from the Norman Conquest – but the polarization of the parties was such that argument could not fruitfully proceed. Charles was removed from the Court, which proceeded in private session in the Painted Chamber, Parliament having anticipated the King's refusal to plead by providing in the statute that such refusal would be regarded as a tacit admission of guilt. Nevertheless, by forcing the Court to proceed *ex parte* in private session Charles succeeded in dramatizing the martial rather than judicial nature of the proceedings and dealt his opponents a significant blow in public opinion.

Two days were spent taking depositions as to the King's past activities while Cromwell and Ireton worked behind the scenes to shore up support among the commissioners for a conviction in the face of mounting public opposition and pleas from many quarters for the King's life to be spared. In addition to the Presbyterians, the Scottish Parliament, the Assembly of Divines, two Netherlands ambassadors and, it is said, Fairfax, sought to intervene in Charles's favour. Of the 135 persons appointed as commissioners only 68 took part in the proceeding and only 46 were present when the conviction and sentence were first accepted in committee. This is significant, because the commissioners can be presumed to have had strong Parliamentarian sympathies, but covered a cross-section, being MPs from both Houses, Army officers, London aldermen, commanders from the Trained Bands, and some county gentlemen.[63] On 26 January, with 62 commissioners present, the conviction and sentence were ratified. Charles was condemned as a 'Tyrant, Traitor, Murderer, and public Enemy' (no reference to High Treason) and condemned to death by 'the severing of his head from his body'.[64] It was resolved to communicate this judgment to Charles in person in the Court on 27 January. This may have been to appease those who wished to give the King a last chance to plead for his life, but may equally have been to allow further time to gather signatures on the death warrant, since some of those who had been party to the verdict and sentence were loath to place their names on the warrant for carrying it out. Whereas it was originally intended that the execution should take place on 27 January, the day after the conviction, no more than 28 signatures on the death warrant were obtained on 26 January and the warrant was set aside and later amended. It has been suggested that the reason the warrant was amended rather than a new warrant issued was because of uncertainty whether some of those who had signed would agree to sign again.[65] (Ultimately, there were 59 signatures; some of those who had been party to the judgment never did sign.) Before the Court on 27 January, after the recital of the charges and announcement that a sentence had been determined subject to the prisoner's right to speak, the King sought leave to answer the charges before a combined sitting of the Lords and Commons in the Painted Chamber (rather than the Court). After an adjournment, this request was refused and Charles was denied further permission to speak. The sentence was read out and the commissioners stood in a unanimous show of approval. Charles again impugned the process by complaining 'I am not suffered to speak: expect what justice other people will have',[66] though he had in fact declined earlier opportunities to speak.

The death warrant provided for the execution of 'Charles Stuart, King of England' upon conviction for 'high treason and other high crimes'. He was condemned personally for breaching the trusts implied in his kingship, which in one view at least upheld the probity of the office. But in the early afternoon of 30 January 1649, just before the King was executed, Parliament passed an Act forbidding the nomination of any Royal successor, and Charles's execution before his own palace of Whitehall, built as a symbol of the Stuart monarchy, was itself potently symbolic. So, perhaps, was the fact that the crowds who had come to witness the event were thereafter quickly dispersed by horse troops to curb the display of public anger and the threat of disorder.

It has often been said that 'nothing became [Charles's] life like the leaving of it', and that his dignity before the Court and on the scaffold, in conjunction with his supposed state of mind as disclosed in the *Eikon Basilike*, sowed the seeds of the Restoration in 1660. While this is undoubtedly the case, his final days also afford glimpses of the real man behind Charles on the path to sainthood. First, there is his self-management at the trial, evincing his rhetorical and dramatic skills in casting himself as a victim, notwithstanding the contribution his own stubbornness had made to that process. Second, there is his confessional remark about the downfall of Strafford and his own complicity in it: 'An unjust sentence that I suffered to take effect is now punished by an unjust sentence upon me.' Third, there is his insistence to Bishop William Juxon and Colonel Tomlinson that the liberty and freedom of the people consisted in freeing them from the affairs of government: 'not their having a share in the government; that is nothing appertaining to them'. He died with his belief in divine kingship and the Royal prerogative intact, impervious to two civil wars, years of public debate and friction with Parliament, and the manifest desire of a significant percentage of his subjects for constitutional change.

John Cooke described the trial and execution of Charles as 'the most . . . glorious piece of justice, that ever was acted . . . upon the theatre of England, for the trying and judging of Charles Stuart, whom God in his

Wrath gave to be King of this nation'. He wished that Charles 'may look the saints in the face . . . ; for the saints must judge the world'. Consistent with this, the High Court was in his view 'a semblance and representation of the great Day of Judgement when the saints shall judge all worldly powers, and where this judgement will be confirmed and admired'.[67] For such as he, the government to follow was a transitional government by those whom God in His grace had 'elected' to Himself and assigned that task, pending Christ's assumption of His earthly kingship and the reign of the saints. Among Independents and Fifth Monarchists, the latter was expected to occur around about 1650.

Once the grim 'necessity' of the King's death was out of the way, the Rump Parliament reacted with relief and fervour, declaring on 6 February that 'the House of Peers in Parliament is useless and dangerous, and ought to be abolished' and on the following day that

> It hath been found by experience . . . that the office of a King in this nation . . . is unnecessary, burdensome, and dangerous to the liberty, safety and public interest of the people of this nation, and therefore ought to be abolished.[68]

Acts putting these resolutions into effect were later passed on 17 March and 19 March respectively. On 14 February, the Rump Parliament elected a Council of State of 41 members including Cromwell and Fairfax (but rejecting Ireton – perhaps, as Antonia Fraser suggests, because of his 'earlier efforts to secure a dissolution of Parliament'[69]). On 19 May, England became a 'Commonwealth and Free State'. The dispatching of the King and the compelling revolutionary imagery of the 'first year of freedom' as inscribed on the Great Seal suddenly made detailed public justification unnecessary. In the *élan* of the 'new order' it was enough to dismiss and dismantle constitutional arrangements by reference to 'past experience'. The confidence and vigour with which these steps were taken reflects the psychological, as well as political, relief of no longer having to contend with the King. But the constitutional changes were reactive, not creative. Parliament merely dismissed the Lords – whom it had disregarded in killing the King – and the office of a king whose execution it had already sponsored. The Republic followed the regicide; but the regicide was not undertaken for the sake of the Republic.

For this reason, the Republic was not the experiment it might have been. For all the rhetoric of freedom, the governance of England remained in the hands of an unrepresentative Rump. Although the statue of Charles had been taken from its pedestal and replaced with the words

Exit Tyrannus, Regum ultimas,[70] the tools of tyranny merely passed to new hands. This was virtually inevitable, given the opposition of Royalists, Presbyterians and Levellers alike to the regicide which gave birth to the Republic. A populace made to stomach the execution of the King was unlikely to accept change over and above that calamity. The task of the government ideologically in the minority was to reconcile people to the Commonwealth or to repress those who would not be reconciled. The return of the members of the Rump Parliament who had absented themselves during the King's trial and execution increased Parliament's own insecurity about the regicide, making it cautious of further change and defensive towards its many enemies. As Ronald Hutton notes, there was no tradition of republican thought in England to which it could appeal, with the result that the Republic's strongest argument for survival was the past military successes of its army and its continuing flexing of military muscle.[71] It must also be said that the 'righteous few' whom God had installed to power were impatient of compromise or power-sharing with an unrighteous majority and were conditioned not to seek or expect popular consensus for their rule.

But even if it had been ideologically open to democratic influence, the new government could not have survived without repression. It was beleaguered on all sides. The controversy of the King's trial and execution did not wane, but increased and continued to undermine the Republic's claim to legal and political legitimacy. The 'Royal Martyr' of the *Eikon Basilike* commanded more and more support, which Milton's *Eikonoklastes* failed to check. On 5 February, even before the English Republic was proclaimed, the Scottish Parliament proclaimed the Prince of Wales as their King, thus constituting Scotland as the alternative rejected by the regicides (a monarchy with an exclusively Presbyterian Church system), right at England's doorstep. The Presbyterian clergy in England preached against the regicide, which had put an end to the Presbyterian Church settlement their final negotiations with Charles had seemed to put in sight. They were openly hostile to the Republic and the religious toleration of the Independents who controlled it. Had they not been divided by their views of Church government and Royalist memory of the part the Presbyterians had played in the First Civil War, the Royalists and Presbyterians might have presented a formidable joint opposition to the Rump.

The Levellers were quickly disillusioned by increases in taxation introduced to pay army arrears and quell disquiet in that quarter, which were directly contrary to *The Agreement of the People*. They objected to the summary justice dispensed to leading Royalists, who were tried in the absence of juries, and the continuation of the Rump Parliament and the absence of elections implementing the widened franchise (which, in the political climate, would almost certainly have meant the defeat of the regicides). The Levellers' animosity to the regime as being centralist, unrepresentative, non-reformist and despotic is evident in Lilburne's pamphlet, *England's New Chains Discovered*, which has already been mentioned. For their part, the Fifth Monarchists were dissatisfied at the secular nature of the Council of State and pressed for government by the Church.

Thousands of seamen were conscripted into the Navy (also against the principles of *The Agreement of the People*), to meet the perceived threat from abroad, where the Prince of Wales (styling himself Charles II) was being harboured by the Dutch. The Army, too, was restive in the face of continuing arrears and the prospect of service in Ireland against the monarchist Confederacy there. When two regiments, including soldiers who had been Agitators before the regicide, mutinied, Fairfax and Cromwell marched on them, put down the mutiny and had the leaders shot. The Republic was nothing if the loyalty of the Army was not enforced. Even Milton, when asked to produce a reply to Lilburne's pamphlet, refused the request, though he later served in the Government of the Commonwealth as Foreign Secretary.

Thus besieged, on 17 July 1649 the government of the Commonwealth (alias the Rump) passed an Act creating new forms of the offence of treason, which mirror-imaged the case being mounted against it and the threats by which it was assailed. It became an offence to publish 'by writing, printing, or openly declaring' the government of the Commonwealth to be 'tyrannical, usurped, or unlawful; or that the Commons in Parliament assembled are not the supreme authority of this nation'. It was also an offence to 'plot, contrive, or endeavour to stir up, or raise force against the present Government, or for the subversion or alteration of the same' and for any person who was not a member of the Army to 'stir up any mutiny in the said army'.[72] In the minds of the authorities, allegations of illegitimacy and tyranny were obviously viewed as seriously as the threat of active subversion. These measures were followed by an Act imposing a blanket censorship on all pamphlets, books and newssheets[73] and, on 2 January 1650 an Act was passed requiring all men over the age of eighteen to take what was effectively an oath of allegiance to the Republic.

The Government of the Commonwealth tapped new skills and abilities from men experienced in legal, business, military and political affairs. But internal and external hostility prevented them from capitalizing on the opportunity the Republic represented. There was a 'strange distaste against them',[74] which had so increased by April 1653 that Cromwell abandoned even the semblance of democracy by intervening against the Rump Parliament and replacing it with a military-based 'Protectorate'.

Instead of restoring every Englishman to his 'ancient rights and liberties', the Commonwealth denied the protection of the law to any man who refused to engage to be 'true and faithful to the Commonwealth of England, as it is now established, without a King or House of Lords'.[75] Instead of securing peace, it invaded Scotland in June 1650, after Prince Charles landed there to assume his kingship, and sent troops to Ireland to put down a rising in support led by the Earl of Ormonde. In September 1651 it fought a major battle at Worcester against invading Scots and English Royalists. Though graced with military success, the Commonwealth could not escape the turbulence of a 'world turned upside down' where the old order refused to die or relinquish its claim to legitimacy. Nor did it succeed in exporting the revolution to its neighbouring kingdoms of Scotland and Ireland. It struggled to gain recognition from European countries, which remained opposed to and uncooperative with the Republic. Worst of all, the reign of the saints did not come to pass, leaving men who had acted in the firm conviction that they were part of an ordained grand plan wrestling both with disappointed expectations and the complexities of a secular situation in which the guiding hand of the Lord was less evident. The Army *Declaration* of August 1650 manifests that loss of certainty when it acknowledged that its members in 1648/9 were '*then* powerfully convinced that the Lord's purpose was to deal with the late King as a man of blood' (my italics). Defensiveness soon took the place of anticipation, culminating in the pitiful spectacle of the regicides, on trial for their own lives in 1660, explaining their actions by reference to religious ideologies and millenarian expectations which had become painful through non-fulfilment, although some continued to cling actively to them. Major-General Thomas Harrison acknowledged that the Lord appeared to have abandoned the regicides, but spoke of 'the terrors of that presence of God that was with his servants in those days', less in excuse of his actions than with a backward tremor of recall of the spiritual passion of that time.[76]

So while the reign of the saints failed to eventuate, the Republic failed, and the scars left by the trauma of the Civil War and the execution of the King are still visible today, English society remained an hourglass, with two counterweight halves of Royalist and Parliamentarian sympathies. Hubert Le Sueur's statue of Charles has been re-erected at Charing Cross facing down Whitehall, but Cromwell continues to stand heroically yet ambiguously beside the Palace of Westminster. Notwithstanding the demise of the Republic and the Restoration of the monarchy in 1660, the events of 1642–9 were critical in forcing the acknowledgement of interests independent of the monarchy which underlie the present constitutional checks and balances and the very concept of representative government. Equally, they populate the political imagination with a cast of characters as rich as anything in Shakespearean drama, by which the political spectrum can be calibrated and in whose interactions the drama of the political process and the march of ideas are compellingly demonstrated. While modern people may find the Puritan mentality repugnant for its fundamentalism and violence, the aspiration to moral rectitude in management of the state and the discipline and passion of Puritan religious logic and expectation give a fascinating texture to these events. The bliss Wordsworth felt in being alive at the dawn of the French Revolution has its antecedent in Milton's England 'casting farre from her the *rags* of her old *vices*' amidst 'the *Hymns,* and *Hallelujahs* of *Saints*'.[77] A part of that bliss survives the palpable horror and confusion of those years.

Notes

Introduction

1. J. P. Kenyon (ed.), *The Stuart Constitution 1603–1688*, 2nd ed. (Cambridge: Cambridge University Press, 1968), p. 71.
2. Ibid., p. 72.
3. See C. H. Firth, *Cromwell's Army: A History of the English Soldier during the Civil Wars, the Commonwealth and the Protectorate* (London: Methuen, 1962). Firth writes colourfully that 'The history of the Civil War is the history of the evolution of an efficient army out of a chaos' (p. 1).
4. Robert Ram, *The Souldiers' Catechisme, composed for the use of the Parliament's Army* (1644).
5. Ephesians 6:11. This was the main text of John Downame's book entitled *Christian Warfare* (London, 1604), which went through many editions and created a culture among Puritans which encouraged them both to expect spiritual assault and violently resist its earthly manifestations.
6. 'An Homily Against Disobedience and Wilful Rebellion', *Certain Sermons and Homilies Appointed to be Read in Churches in the Time of Queen Elizabeth of Famous Memory* (London: Society for Promoting Christian Knowledge, 1843), p. 587f. This homily was delivered regularly from church pulpits.
7. Roy Strong, *And when did you last see your father? The Victorian Painter and British History* (London: Thames and Hudson, 1978), pp. 136–45.
8. F. Guizot, *History of the English Revolution of 1640*, trans. W. Hazlitt (London, 1845), pp. xcvi–xvii.
9. 'An Act for the Abolishing of Kingly Office', 17 March 1649, in Kenyon, *The Stuart Constitution*, op. cit., p. 306.
10. Sir C. Grant Robertson, *Select Statutes Cases and Documents to Illustrate English Constitutional History, 1660–1832*, 6th ed. (London, 1931), p. 1.
11. For a fuller account of this political 'great divide' and its effect on the recasting of history see D. E. Kennedy (ed.), *Authorized Pasts. Essays in Official History* (Melbourne: University of Melbourne, 1995), pp. 113–44.
12. These words appeared on the Great Seal of the Commonwealth, 1649.
13. The 350th Anniversary was marked in London by an exhibition in the Queen's Gallery at Buckingham Palace titled 'Charles 1: King and Martyr'. A book published to coincide with the Anniversary, Graham Edwards' *The*

Last Days of Charles I (Stroud: Sutton Publishing Ltd, 1999), also adopts this typography. Although the commemorations were low-key, they generally accepted the 'martrydom' view of these events.

14. C. Hill, *The English Revolution 1640* (first published 1940); see also his 'A Bourgeois Revolution?', in *The Collected Essays of Christopher Hill*, vol. 3 (Brighton: Harvester Press, 1986).

15. Ronald Hutton, *The British Republic 1649–1660* (London: Macmillan 1990), p. 4.

16. John Milton, 'On the Lord Gen Fairfax at the Siege of Colchester', Cleanth Brooks, *Complete Poetry and Selected Prose of John Millon* (New York: Random House, 1950), p. 85.

17. Andrew Marvell, 'An Horatian Ode Upon Cromwel's Return from Ireland'. The text and context of this poem are discussed in John Dixon Hunt, *Andrew Marvell: His Life and Writings* (London: Paul Elek, 1978), pp. 69–80.

18. Donald Nicholas, *Mr. Secretary Nicholas (1593–1669). His Life and Letters* (London: Bodley Head, 1955), p. 229, cited from *Clarendon State Papers* I, folio 2628.

1   The War for King and Parliament, 1642–6

1. S. R. Gardiner, *The Constitutional Documents of the Puritan Revolution 1625–1660*, 3rd ed. revised ('*CD*') (Oxford: Clarendon, 1906), p. 203.

2. Gardiner, *CD*, pp. 206–7.

3. Ibid., p. 204.

4. Gardiner, *CD*, p. 233.

5. Ibid., p. 235.

6. Thomas May, *The History of the Parliament of England, which Began November the Third, M.DC.XL* (London: Wilks, 1812 reprint), p. 90.

7. Gardiner, *CD*, p. 245.

8. Ibid., p. 249.

9. Ibid., p. 257.

10. H. Hallam, *The Constitutional History of England*, 3 vol. (London:Murray, 1881), vol. II, p. 162. Edward Hyde, Earl of Clarendon, *The History of the Rebellion and Civil Wars in England*, W. D. Macray (ed.), 6 vol. (Oxford: Clarendon, 1888), vol. II, pp. 107–18.

11. John Rushworth, *Historical Collections*, pt. III, Vol. II (London: 1692), pp. 339–43. James F. Larkin, (ed.), *Stuart Royal Proclamations. Volume II. Royal Proclamations of King Charles I 1625–1646* (Oxford: Clarendon, 1983), pp. 974–6.

12. Andrew Sharp, (ed.), *Political Ideas of the English Civil Wars 1641–1649* (London: Longman, 1983), pp. 40–3. Sharp describes this Answer as 'the most-discussed single statement made during the civil wars', and prints part of the text not included in J. P. Kenyon, (ed.), *The Stuart Constitution 1603–1688*, 2nd ed. (Cambridge: Cambridge University Press, 1986), pp. 19–20.

13. Rushworth, *Historical Collections*, pt III, vol. I, p. 753.

14. Diary of the Rev. Ralph Josselin. Quoted in C. Hill and E. Dell, (eds), *The Good Old Cause, The English Revolution of 1640–60* (London: Lawrence and Wishart, 1949), pp. 237–8.

15. Thomas May, *A History of the Parliament of England*, op. cit., p. 140.
16. Rushworth, *Historical Collections*, pt. III, vol. I, p. 496.
17. Clarendon, *History of the Rebellion*, op. cit., vol. II, p. 215.
18. The *Seamans Protestation concerning Their Ebbing and Flowing to and from the Parliament House at Westminster: Upon Tuesday the II. day on Ianuary, 1642* (London:1642), and Rushworth, *Historical Collections*, pt. III, vol. I, p. 483. *A Letter sent from the Right Honorable Robert Earle of Warwick, Admirall of the Sea: to Mr. John Pim, Esquire*, 6 July (London:1642).
19. Clarendon, *History of the Rebellion*, op. cit., vol. II, p. 224.
20. Bulstrode Whitelock, *Memorials of the English Affairs from the beginning of the reign of Charles the First to the happy restoration of King Charles the Second*, 4 vol. (Oxford: Oxford University Press, 1853), vol. I, pp. 166–7.
21. Rushworth, *Historical Collections*, pt. III vol. I, p. 496.
22. Ibid., p. 586.
23. Ibid., pp. 579, 598.
24. Ibid., pp. 578, 591, 598.
25. J. F. Larkin, (ed.), *Stuart Royal Proclamations. Volume II.*, op. cit., pp. 786–90. It is 'given' from Beverley, which was the first place listed in the indictment of the King for levying war against Parliament and people. Rushworth, *Historical Collections*, pt. III vol. I, pp. 601f, 755. May, *A History of the Parliament of England*, op. cit., p. 138.
26. Rev. Daniel Parsons, (ed.), *The Diary of Sir Henry Slingsby, of Scriven, Bart.* (London: Longman, 1836), p. 76. Blinds or blindages are screens for protection against enemy fire. Slingsby was later executed for his loyalty to the King.
27. Gardiner, *CD*, p. 372.
28. Lt.-Colonel Alfred H. Burne, *The Battlefields of England* (London: Methuen, 1950), p. 197.
29. The encounter at Turnham Green is described by Austin Woolrych, *Battles of the English Civil War* (London: Batsford, 1961), pp. 15–20. Philip Tennant, *Edgehill and Beyond. The People's War in the South Midlands 1642–1645* (Sutton and The Banbury Historical Society, vol. 23, 1992), p. 77.
30. Siegeworks of Newark remain as impressive evidence of the Civil War: *Royal Commission on Historical Monuments [England]. Newark on Trent. The Civil War Siegeworks* (London: H.M. Stationery Office, 1964).
31. Brigadier Peter Young and Richard Holmes, *The English Civil War. A Military History of the Three Civil Wars 1642–1651* (London: Eyre Methuen, 1974), pp. 127–39.
32. May, *A History of the Parliament of England*, op. cit., pp. 193–4.
33. Ibid., p. 193.
34. Martyn Bennett, *Traveller's Guide to the Battlefields of the English Civil War* (Devon: Webb and Bower, 1990), pp. 70–7 gives a well-illustrated brief account of these events, which acknowledges the tactical skills of the Earl of Essex. So too does Richard Atkyns, a Gloucestershire Captain in Prince Maurice's Regiment of Horse, who provides personal recollections of the Newbury fight: *Military Memoirs. The Civil War. Richard Atkyns* (Peter Young, ed.) *John Gwyn* (Norman Tucker, ed.), (London: Longmans, 1967), pp. 52–3.
35. Allan Pritchard, (ed.), *Abraham Cowley. The Civil War* (University of Toronto Press, 1973), pp. 3–4,17,117–18,121.

36. Clarendon, *History of the Rebellion*, op. cit., vol. III, p. 179. See Hugh Trevor-Roper, *Catholics, Anglicans and Puritans. Seventeenth Century Essays* (London: Secker and Warburg, 1987), chap. 4, 'The Great Tew Circle'.

37. Joshua Sprigge, *Anglia Rediviva*, (1647), quoted in John Wilson, *Fairfax. A Life of Thomas, Lord Fairfax, Captain-General of all the Parliament's forces in the English Civil War, Creator and Commander of the New Model Army* (London: Murray, 1985), p. 56.

38. David Underdown describes how the Royalist's Western Association, embracing Devon, Dorset and Cornwall, came under the control of Prince Maurice, a professional soldier, in a reorganization which in many ways was 'a step towards centralization and military rule': developments which the local freeholders had resisted in the 1630s and in 1642. David Underdown, *Somerset in the Civil War and Interregnum* (Newton Abbot: David and Charles, 1973), pp. 72–3.

39. Text in Gardiner, *CD*, pp. 267–71.

40. Young and Holmes, *The English Civil War*, op. cit., chap. 13, 'The Oxford Campaign'.

41. Thomas Carlyle, *Oliver Cromwell's Letters and Speeches: With Elucidations*, 3 vol., 2nd ed., (London: Chapman and Hall, 1846), letter XVI. Woolrych, *Battles of the English Civil War*, op. cit., pp. 63–80.

42. For a clear account of the battle, see Bennett, *Traveller's Guide to the Battlefields*, op. cit., pp. 142–6.

43. Ian Gentles, *The New Model Army in England, Ireland and Scotland, 1645–1653* (Oxford: Blackwell, 1992), p. 4 f.; and Young and Holmes, *The English Civil War*, op. cit., p. 223. Rushworth, *Historical Collections*, pt. III, vol. II, prints a contemporary account of the second Battle of Newbury (pp. 724–9) and Manchester's defence of his conduct (pp. 733–6).

44. Gentles, *The New Model Army*, op. cit., p. 5.

45. Whitelock, *Memorials*, vol. I, pp. 343–7, gives an account of a meeting which he attended with Essex and others (including the Commissioners for Scotland) who were planning 'to rid Cromwell out of the way'. One of the Commissioners opened the matter with the words:

> You ken vary weele that lieutenant-general Cromwell is no friend of ours, and since the advance of our army into England he hath used all underhand and cunning means to take off from our honour and merit of this kingdom.

The text of the Ordinance can be found in Gardiner, *CD*, pp. 287–8.

46. Essex quoted in Gentles, *The New Model Army*, op. cit., p. 23.

47. Ibid., p. 24.

48. Wilson, *Fairfax*, op. cit., pp. 63, 66. John Lilburne was an officer who refused to take the Covenant.

49. Clarendon, *History of the Rebellion*, op. cit., vol. IV, p. 38.

50. Clarendon wrote that upon the surrender of the town, 'the conquerors pursued their advantage with the usual license of rapine and plunder, and miserably sacked the whole town, without any distinction of persons or places, churches and hospitals as well as other houses [being] made a prey to the enraged and greedy soldier'; ibid., p. 39.

51. See the accounts of Woolrych, *Battles of the English Civil War*, op. cit., pp. 111–39; and Bennett, *Traveller's Guide to the Battlefields*, op. cit., pp. 150–62.
52. Edmund Ludlow described the contents of the King's cabinet in a damning indictment. *The Memoirs of Edmund Ludlow Lieutenant-General of the Horse in the Army of the Commonwealth of England 1625–1672*, C. H. Firth (ed.), 2 vol. (Oxford:Clarendon,1894), vol. I, p. 122. One paper was found 'giving some account of the troubles in Ireland, wherein the Papists who had taken arms being qualified rebels, that term was struck out, and the word Irish added by the King himself'. In a letter to the Queen, the King referred to 'his mongrel Parliament at Oxford'.
53. The Secretary at War's opinion is quoted in Gentles, *The New Model Army*, op. cit., p. 75. For Jacob Astley, see Brigadier Peter Young and Wilfred Pemberton, *The Cavalier Army. Its Organisation and Everyday Life* (London: Allen and Unwin, 1974), pp. 99–100.
54. Robert Monteth of Salmonet, *The History of the Troubles of Great Britain* (London: Strahan, 1735), 3rd ed.; previously published in Paris in 1649 and 1661, p. 125.
55. Monteth, *History of the Troubles*, op. cit., p. 131.
56. Gardiner, *CD*, pp. 271–86.
57. Ibid., pp. 286–7.
58. Whitelock, *Memorials*, op. cit., vol. I, pp. 375–96 and Clarendon, *History of the Rebellion*, op. cit., vol. III, pp. 468–501.
59. The King to Lord Digby, 26 March 1646, printed in Sir Charles Petrie (ed.) *The Letters Speeches and Proclamations of King Charles I* (London: Cassell, 1935), p. 176.
60. Gardiner, *CD*, pp. 290–306 (Newcastle Propositions); pp. 306–7 (King's first reply); pp. 308–9 (King's second reply).
61. For the background and early developments of the rebellion, see Aidan Clarke, *The Old English in Ireland 1625–42* (London: Macgibbon and Kee, 1966), chaps IX–XI. A broader study from a decidedly Irish perspective can be found in Thomas L. Coonan, *The Irish Catholic Confederacy and the Puritan Revolution* (Dublin: Clonmore and Reynolds, 1954): see here chap. X 'The Confederation of Kilkenny'.
62. Petrie, *The Letters Speeches and Proclamations of King Charles I*, op. cit., pp. 132–6,150.
63. Ibid., pp. 153,155,159.
64. Whitelock, *Memorials*, op. cit., vol. II, pp. 35,45,59. James Heath, *A brief Chronicle of the Civil Wars of England, Scotland & Ireland* (London: 1663), p. 225. Heath concluded his chronicle of the year 1646 with this 'indignity'.

2 Interregnum, 1646–7

1. Monroe described the disaster in a letter to the Scots Commissioners in London: printed in Rushworth, *Historical Collections*, pt. IV, vol. I, pp. 399–400. He wrote that 'the Lord of Hosts had a controversie with us to rub shame on our Faces, as on other Armies, till once we shall be humbled'.
2. The handover exposed tensions in the alliance during September 1646. To

the Scots Commissioners the discharge of the King into English custody 'with Honour, Safety, and Freedom', and the settlement thereafter, remained a matter for joint advice and agreement between the two kingdoms. Thomas Chaloner, a recent recruit to Parliament and later a regicide, warned the Commons to beware that 'in bringing [the King] home with Freedom you do not thereby lead the People of England into Thraldom'. If he were to be brought home, however, the terms on which this occurred were exclusively a matter for the English: Rushworth, *Historical Collections*, pt. IV, vol. I, pp. 336–40.

3. *Eikon Basilike. The Povrtraictvre of His Sacred Majestie in His Solitudes and Sufferings* (M.DC.XLVIII. i.e. 1649), p. 151, pagination erratic.
4. Rushworth recorded that a Privy Signet 'and another little Signet' escaped the hammer: *Historical Collections*, pt. IV, vol. I, p. 285: Gardiner, *CD*, pp. 308–9.
5. *Eikon Basilike*, op. cit., p. 216.
6. Ibid., p. 192.
7. Gardiner, *CD*, p. 314.
8. Cromwell's Naseby and Bristol letters are numbers XXIV and XXVI in Carlyle, *Letters and Speeches*, vol. I; the later reflection of January 1655 is in speech IV, vol. III, p. 103.
9. A copy of the *Apology* had been acquired by the London bookseller, George Thomason, on 26 March; see A. S. P. Woodhouse, *Puritanism and Liberty. Being the Army Debates (1647–9) from the Clarke manuscripts, with Supplementary Documents* (London: J. M. Dent, 1974), p. [21], fn. 2. S. R. Gardiner, *History of the Great Civil War 1642–1649* ('*CW*') (London: Longmans, Green, 1911), vol. III, pp. 223–5.
10. Wilson, *Fairfax* op. cit., p. 99.
11. Henry Cary, *Memorials of the Great Civil War in England From 1646–1652*, 2 vols. (London: Colburn, 1842), vol. I, pp. 187–8.
12. Rushworth, *Historical Collections*, pt. IV, vol. I, pp. 444–5.
13. Kenyon, *The Stuart Constitution*, op. cit., p. 248, notes that the modern connotations of the term 'Agitator' are misleading and that the term should be read neutrally to mean 'agent', or perhaps 'shop steward'. The phrase, 'rights and desires' is from *A Solemn Engagement of the Army* (5 June), Woodhouse, *Puritanism and Liberty*, op. cit., p. 401.
14. Woodhouse, *Puritanism and Liberty*, op. cit., pp. 396–7.
15. Ludlow, *Memoirs*, op. cit., vol. I, p. 151. Woodhouse, *Puritanism and Liberty*, op. cit., p. 399.
16. G. E. Aylmer (ed.), *The Levellers in the English Revolution* (London: Thames and Hudson, 1975), p. 9.
17. *Apology of the Soldiers to their Officers*, 3 May 1647, cited Woodhouse, *Puritanism and Liberty*, op. cit., p. 397.
18. Joyce informed the Parliamentary Commissioners with the King that he had come with authority from the soldiers to seize the commander of the Holmby garrison, who was a known Presbyterian. When asked by the King for his commission, Joyce indicated the horsemen behind him. Joyce's own account of the seizure of the King is printed in Rushworth, *Historical Collections*, pt. IV, vol. 1, pp. 513–17.
19. Woodhouse, *Puritanism and Liberty*, op. cit., pp. 402–4.

20. John Morrill, 'Mutiny and Discontent in English Provincial Armies, 1645–1647' in his *The Nature of the English Revolution* (London: Longman, 1993), p. 333.
21. Gardiner, *CW*, vol. III, p. 341; Gentles, *The New Model Army*, op. cit., p. 184.
22. Ludlow wrote that 'the King finding himself courted on all hands became so confident of his own interest, as to think himself able to turn the scale to what side soever he pleased': *Memoirs*, op. cit., vol. I, pp. 155–6.
23. The King's answer was sent on 9 September: Gardiner, *CD*, p. 326.
24. Gardiner, *CW*, vol. III, p. 365.
25. Gardiner, *CD*, pp. 316–26.
26. John Wildman, *Putney Projects* (December, 1647), cited in Woodhouse, *Puritanism and Liberty*, op. cit., pp. 426–9.
27. Rushworth, *Historical Collections*, pt. IV, vol. II, p. 856; Aylmer, *The Levellers in the English Revolution*, op. cit., p. 29.
28. Woodhouse, *Puritanism and Liberty*, op. cit., pp. 429–32.
29. Rushworth, *Historical Collections*, pt. IV, vol. II. p. 838.
30. Ibid., p. 845.
31. Ireton's own account of the events, delivered at Putney on 28 October: Woodhouse, *Puritanism and Liberty*, op. cit., pp. 5–6.

3   The Army in Debate

1. The manuscript source for the debates is in the Clarke MSS, vol. 67, Worcester College, Oxford. C. H. Firth edited the *Clarke Papers* for the Camden society (4 vol., 1891–1901): see vol. 1. Firth took great liberties with the text. Woodhouse, too, has interpolated text to make the debates more readable. The interpolations are indicated in square brackets. For convenience, textual references in this chapter are to Woodhouse's *Puritanism and Liberty*, op. cit. and are cited as '*PL*'. The quotation here is from *PL*, p. 2.
2. *PL*, pp. 2–4.
3. *PL*, pp. 437–8.
4. *PL*, p. 439.
5. Compare, for example, C. Hill and E. Dell, *The Good Old Cause*, op. cit., p. 352, which acclaims the debates as giving 'a brilliant picture of a spontaneous discussion on the foundations of the state', with J. P. Kenyon, *The Stuart Constitution* (2nd ed.), op. cit., which omitted extracts included in the previous edition, in part because the debates were 'confused and inconclusive' and focused on issues of 'little practical contemporary relevance', p. 250 and fn. 28. A comprehensive study of the Army Council and its activities can be found in Austin Woolrych, *Soldiers and Statesmen. The General Council of the Army and its Debates, 1647–1648* (Oxford: Clarendon, 1987).
6. Firth suggests that the fair copy may have been made soon after the Restoration. Woodhouse follows him, neither giving an explanation of this late date. Aylmer thinks it just as plausible that Clarke made his fair copy to 'while away the time in Scotland, where he was stationed as Secretary to successive Commanders-in-Chief from 1651–1659', (*PL*, p. [12]): Aylmer, *The*

Levellers, op. cit., p. 97). In the absence of any explanation from these editors as to why they believe the fair copy was produced some years after the short-hand copy, the present author suggests that the fair copy may have been made very quickly after the event and for official rather than private pur-poses. Given the import of the debates and the intense interest of parties not present, it is highly likely that a fair copy would be promptly made as a basis for report and reference, the shorthand transcript being ineffective for such a purpose.

7.　Rushworth, *Historical Collections*, pt. IV, vol. II, pp. 856–7.
8.　Gardiner, *CW*, vol. I, p. ix; *PL*, p. [11].
9.　*PL*, p. 1.
10.　*PL*, p. 2.
11.　*PL*, pp. 4–5.
12.　*PL*, p. 6.
13.　*PL*, pp. 7–8.
14.　*PL*, p. 9.
15.　*PL*, p. 10.
16.　*PL*, p. 25.
17.　*PL*, p. 11.
18.　*PL*, pp. 13–14.
19.　*PL*, p. 14.
20.　*PL*, pp. 433–4.
21.　*PL* p. 434.
22.　*PL*, pp. 15–17.
23.　*PL*, p. 24.
24.　*PL*, p. 25.
25.　*PL*, pp. 26–7.
26.　Aylmer, *The Levellers in the English Revolution*, op. cit., p. 90.
27.　*PL*, p. 52–3.
28.　*PL*, p. 53.
29.　*PL*, p. 54.
30.　*PL*, p. 57.
31.　*PL*, p. 57.
32.　*PL*, p. 72.
33.　*PL*, p. 66.
34.　*PL*, pp. 118–19.
35.　*PL*, p. 52.
36.　*PL*, p. 120.
37.　*PL*, p. 69.
38.　*PL*, p. 61.
39.　*PL*, p. 67.
40.　*PL*, p. 69.
41.　*PL*, p. 71.
42.　*PL*, p. 74.
43.　*PL*, p. 82.
44.　*PL*, p. 78.
45.　*PL*, p. 83.
46.　*PL*, p. 87.
47.　*PL*, p. 86.

48. *PL*, p. 88.
49. *PL*, p. 87.
50. *PL*, p. 88.
51. *PL*, p. 89.
52. *PL*, p. 92.
53. *PL*, p. 93.
54. *PL*, p. 94.
55. *PL*, p. 95.
56. *PL*, p. 96.
57. *PL*, p. 97.
58. *PL*, p. 98.
59. *PL*, p. 98.
60. *PL*, p. 103.
61. *PL*, p. 103.
62. *PL*, p. 105.
63. Ibid.
64. *PL*, p. 107.
65. Ibid.
66. *PL*, p. 108.
67. See *PL*, pp. 108–9.
68. *PL*, p. 109.
69. See *PL*, p. 449. These principles are derived from the report of the meeting on 30 October, but do not appear to have been substantially amended except as in particulars subsequently recorded in the chapter.
70. *PL*, p. 114.
71. *PL*, p. 123.
72. *PL*, p. 124.
73. See Rushworth, *Historical Collections*, pt. IV, vol. II, P. 861, and *PL*, p. 452. 'Proceedings in the General Council, 4th–9th November', derived from *A Letter from Several Agitators to their Regiments* (11th Nov.).
74. *PL*, p. 452.
75. *PL*, p. 453.
76. *PL*, p. 453.
77. *PL*, p. 454.
78. *PL*, p. 455.
79. Gentles, *The New Model Army*, op. cit., p. 218.
80. *PL*, p. 454.
81. Carlyle, *Letters and Speeches*, op. cit., vol. I, letter XLV.
82. See Fairfax's Letter to Parliament about the Ware rendezvous in Rushworth, *Historical Collections*, pt. IV, vol. II, pp. 875–6.
83. Gentles, *The New Model Army*, op. cit., p. 233.

4 The Second Civil War

1. Gardiner, *CD*, p. 332.
2. Ibid.
3. Ibid., p. 346.
4. Ibid., p. 347.

5.   Ibid., pp. 353 6.
6.   Ibid., p. 349.
7.   Ibid., p. 351.
8.   Ibid., pp. 349–50.
9.   Ibid., p. 351.
10. Clement Walker, *The Compleat History of Independency. Upon the Parliament Begun 1640* (London: Royston, 1661), pp. 69–70, prints brief accounts of speeches attributed to them.
11. Clarendon, *History of the Rebellion*, op. cit., vol. IV, p. 281.
12. Philip J. Haythornthwaite, *The English Civil War 1642–1651. An Illustrated Military History* (London: Blandford, 1985), p. 116.
13. Gentles, *The New Model Army*, op. cit., p. 233.
14. Quoted in Gardiner, *CW*, vol. IV, p. 85.
15. Gardiner, *CW*, vol. IV, p. 84.
16. Ibid., p. 87.
17. Rushworth, *Historical Collections*, pt. IV, vol. II, p. 1062.
18. These are the recollections of William Allen, Agitator and subsequently Adjutant-General of the Horse in the Irish Army: quoted in Carlyle, *Letters and Speeches*, op. cit., vol. I, p. 338.
19. Carlyle, *Letters and Speeches*, op. cit., p. 339.
20. Ibid., p. 340.
21. Gentles, *The New Model Army*, op. cit., p. 243 and note 43 to Ch. 8; Ludlow, *Memoirs*, op. cit., vol. I, p. 192.
22. Rushworth, *Historical Collections*, pt. IV, vol. II, p. 1110.
23. Gardiner, *CW*, vol. IV, p. 132.
24. *Derby House Committee for English Affairs. Letters sent 1648*, State Papers Domestic, [Public Record Office] 21/24, 56.
25. Walker, *The Compleat History of Independency*, op. cit., p. 93.
26. *Derby House Committee for English Affairs Day Book 1648*, State Papers Domestic 21/9, 76 [Public Record Office]; *Derby House Committee for English Affairs. Letters Sent 1648*, State Papers Domestic, 21/24, 58, 59, 65–6 [Public Record Office].
27. Carey's *Memorials*, op. cit., I, pp. 237–40.
28. Gardiner, *CW*, vol. III, p. 349.
29. George Bate, *Elenchi motum nuperorum in Anglia: OR, A short Historical ACCOUNT of The Rise and Progress of the Late Troubles in England* (London, 1685), p. 86.
30. *Mercurius Pragmaticus*, No.5, October 12–20 (1647).
31. *The Independent's Loyalty. OR The most Barbarous Plot (to Murther his sacred Majestie) very fully Discovered* (1648), pp. 14, 16. [Cambridge University Library].
32. D. Gardiner (ed.), *The Oxinden and Peyton Letters 1642–1670* (London, 1937), p. 138.
33. *Historical Manuscript Commission Reports*, Portland I, p. 460.
34. *Clarendon Papers*, vol. 31, 2790 [Bodleian Library].
35. *A Letter from Kent: Of the Rising at Rochester* (1648) Thomason Tracts E.443,26.
36. *Sad News out of Kent* (1648) Thomason Tracts E.443,41.
37. *Clarendon Papers*, vol. 31, 2792.

38. *Newes from Kent* (1648), Thomason Tracts E.448,5, p. 5.
39. Rushworth, *Historical Collections*, pt. IV, vol. 11, p. 1131. M[atthew] C[arter] A Loyal Actor in that Engagement . . . , *A Most Trve And exact Relation of That as Honourable as Unfortunate Expedition of Kent, Essex, and Colchester* (1650), p. 77.
40. Whitelock, *Memorials*, op. cit., vol. II, pp. 320–1.
41. Gentles, *The New Model Army*, op. cit., p. 248.
42. Whitelock, *Memorials*, op. cit., vol. II, p. 324.
43. Gentles, *The New Model Army*, op. cit., p. 255.
44. Ibid., p. 256.
45. Ibid., pp. 259–60.
46. *Memoirs of Sir James Turner* (Edinburgh, 1829), cited in Carlyle, *Letters and Speeches*, op. cit., vol. I, p. 360.
47. Quoted in Gentles, *The New Model Army*, op. cit., p. 256.
48. Gardiner, *CW*, vol. IV, p. 208.
49. Ibid., p. 215.
50. Ibid., p. 219.
51. Rushworth, *Historical Collections*, pt. IV, vol. 11, p. 1298.
52. Ibid., pp. 1308–9, and Gardiner, *CW*, vol. IV, p. 225.
53. Gardiner, *CW*, vol. IV, p. 226.
54. Lilburne's *Legal, Fundamental Liberties* (1649), extracted in *PL*, at p. 343.
55. Gardiner, *CW*, vol. IV, p. 269.
56. Gardiner, *CW*, vol. IV, p. 273 sets the total number affected by Pride's purge at 143. Peter Young (in *The English Civil War*, op. cit., p. 292) puts the number excluded on 6 December at 240, 39 of whom were detained. Blair Worden in his specialist study, *The Rump Parliament 1648–1653* (Cambridge: Cambridge University Press, 1974) at pp. 23–5, says that only 110 were excluded on the day, but that many withdrew on their own initiative from distaste at the purge or did not attempt to claim seats from which they had been absent over previous weeks. Worden says that the purge permanently removed about 270 members out of a House of 470, but that a further 100 were absent between the purge and the King's execution. It appears therefore that the Rump Parliament was a parliament of between a half and a third of the official number of MPs in the Commons.

5 Regicide and Republic, January–March 1649

1. Although the King did not yield, the Prince of Wales responded to the death sentence on his father by sending Parliament a blank sheet of paper bearing his signature and seal for Parliament to subscribe any terms it pleased (Gardiner, *CW*, vol. IV, p. 316). By then, however, the judicial process in which Parliament had engaged made an alternative political resolution impossible.
2. Rev. 17:17.
3. See B. S. Capp, *The Fifth Monarchy Men* (Totowa: Rowan and Littlefield, 1972); and Christopher Hill, *Antichrist in Seventeenth-Century England* (London: Oxford University Press, 1971). Although mentioned only briefly

in the Bible (I John 2:18, 22; 2 John 7), Antichrist engendered an extensive literature in sixteenth- and seventeenth-century England as a central expression of the conflict between Rome and the reformed churches.

4. This irreconcilable conflict between the secular ambitions of the Levellers and the millenarian beliefs of the Independents is one of the central theses of Noel Henning Mayfield's book, *Puritans and Regicide: Presbyterian–Independent Differences Over the Trial and Execution of Charles (I) Stuart* (Lanham: University Press of America, 1988), to which this chapter is in part indebted.

5. Henning Mayfield, *Puritans and Regicide*, op. cit. at pp. 16–21 disputes the account of Cromwell's position given in Gardiner *CW*, vol. IV, pp. 281–2 and argues persuasively that Cromwell was not opposed in principle to the execution of the King and had no residual reverence for monarchy, but believed that the time was not yet ripe.

6. Gardiner, *CW*, vol. IV, p. 304.

7. Ibid., p. 278.

8. *Journals of the House of Commons ('CJ')* vol. VI, p. 122.

9. Firth, *Cromwell*, op. cit., p. 248.

10. Royalist agent's letter (*Clarendon MSS*, 2,968), cited in Gardiner, *CW*, vol. IV, p. 282.

11. Gardiner (*CW*, vol. IV, pp. 281–2) refers to their rejection on or before 21 December of a proposition 'the actual tenor of which is unknown, but of which the general sense aimed at the taking away of Charles' life'.

12. Ibid., p. 285.

13. Thomas Brooks, *God's Delight in the Progresse of the Upright* (printed 1649), in Alexander Balloch Grosart (ed.), *The Complete Works of Thomas Brooks* (Edinburgh: James Nichol, 1867), vol. VI, p. 362.

14. *CJ*, vol. VI, p. 107.

15. Gardiner, *CW*, vol. IV, p. 289.

16. *CJ*, vol. VI, pp. 110, 111.

17. T. B. Howell (compiler), *A Complete collection of State Trials and Proceedings for High Treason and Other Crimes and Misdemeanours ('State Trials')* (London: Longman, 1809) vol. IV, pp. 1046–7.

18. Gardiner, *CW*, vol. IV, p. 291.

19. Firth, *Cromwell*, op. cit., p. 218.

20. Robert Ram, Rector of Spalding, *The Souldiers' Catechisme* (London, 1644). By 1645 this catechism, written 'especially for the common soldier' had reached its seventh edition. Ram's personal experience conditioned his view of Royalists as 'inhuman . . . the enemies of God' (pp. 1–2). In March 1643 he had been arrested as a supporter of Parliament and taken to the Royalist garrison at Crowland. During a Parliamentarian assault upon the place, Ram was tied up and placed in the line of fire 'above the North Bulwark in plain view, where he remained for three hours until he was recognized and the firing stopped'. See Charles Carlton, *Going to the Wars. The Experience of the British Civil Wars 1638–1651* (London, New York: Routledge, 1992), p. 257.

21. Clarendon, *History of the Rebellion*, op. cit., vol. IV, p. 305.

22. Eph. 6:11. Quoted in John Downame's *Christian Warfare* (1604), a highly influential Puritan text which went through four editions in thirty years.

23. The Solemn League and Covenant: Gardiner, *CD*, pp. 268–9.

24. Christopher Hill in *Milton and the English Revolution* (London: Faber and Faber, 1977) wrote that 'in *Eikonoklastes* [Milton] had an opportunity to defend a rational cultural revolution against the Royalist appeal to the primitive magic of kingship' (p. 170). See also chapter 12, '*Eikonoklastes* and Idolatry'.

25. *The [Geneva] Bible* (London: Robert Barker, 1607) II Chronicles 15:16. The 'Christian Reader' is advised that the Annotations serve 'for the declaration of the text, as for the application of the same, as may most appertain to God's glory and the edification of his Church'. The Geneva notes on I Kings 15:13, in a cross-reference to the Chronicles text, stated that 'Neither kindred nor authority ought to be regarded, when they blaspheme God & become idolaters, but must be punished'.

26. Ps. 106:30.

27. Like the Puritan appeal to Phinehas, the Church counter-view was well rehearsed even before Charles came to the throne. Lancelot Andrewes in *A Sermon preached at Cheswick in the time of Pestilence, 21 August 1603*, on the text of Psalm 106: 29,30, attacked Puritan 'inventions' in scripture reading and incorporated Phinehas within the institutional framework by casting him as a priest and prince: not a private individual, but a magistrate (i.e. an office-bearer in the administration of justice). He claimed that Phinehas's action against idolatry was legitimate within the framework of Mosaic law, and was not zealous beyond or outside the established law. See Lancelot Andrewes, *XCVI Sermons . . .* , (London: published by His Majestie's special command, 1629), pp. 166–7.

28. Richard Bancroft, *Dangerovs Positions and Proceedings, published and practised within this Iland . . . vnder pretence of Reformation and for the Presbiteriall Discipline* (London, 1593), pp. 141–2.

29. Samuel Fairclough, *The Trovblers Trovbled, Or Achan Condemned and Execvted . . .* , preached before the House of Commons 4 April 1641, (London, 1641), p. 51.

30. Edmund Staunton, *Phinehas's Zeal in Execvtion of Judgement . . .* , preached before the House of Lords 30 October 1644 on the text of Psalm 106:30, (London, 1641), pp. 5–6, 9, 23. Staunton conceded that Phinehas, in respect of the administration of justice, was 'a private man, one among the people, so that this act of his might seeme not to be *zeal*, but *murther* rather . . .' (p. 6). Reprinted in Robin Jeffs (ed.), *The English Revolution I. Fast Sermons to Parliament*, ('*Fast Sermons*') (London: Cornmarket Press, 1971), vol. 13.

31. Stephen Marshall, *Reformation and Desolation: or, A Sermon tending to the Discovery of the Symptomes of a People to whom God will by no meanes be reconciled*, preached before the House of Commons, 22 December 1641, (London, 1642), pp. 38–40. Reprinted in *Fast Sermons*, vol. 2.

32. The text in Amos actually refers to *judgment* running down as waters and *righteousness* flowing down in a mighty stream. The emphasis on 'justice' is Brooks's own variation, reflecting the strong political undercurrent in the sermon.

33. Grosart, *The Complete Works of Thomas Brooks*, op. cit., pp. 335–63. A facsimile of the Sermon appears in *Fast Sermons*, vol. 32. The Commons ordered that Sir John Bourchier thank Brooks 'for the great pains he took in his sermon'. Bourchier, a Yorkshire MP with a grievance against the King,

attended the Trial and was the eighth signatory to the death warrant, Ireton being the ninth.

34. Alexander Grosart (ed.), *The Works of Richard Sibbes DD* (Edinburgh: James Nichol, 1862–4), vol. VII, p. 527. This was an anniversary sermon commemorating the Gunpowder Plot, which took as its text Revelation 17:17. Two other anniversary sermons on the same theme, both called *The Saints Safety in Evill Times*, appeared in a major collection of Sibbes's sermons titled *The Saints Cordialls . . .* , (London, 1637). Sibbes laments the evil of the times and the divisions among the people. Judgment, he wrote, 'is not far from us' (p. 222).

35. *The Great Interest of States and Kingdoms*, in Thomas Smith (ed.), *The Works of Thomas Goodwin DD* (Edinburgh: James Nichol, 1861–6), vol. XII, pp. 55–6. The sermon cited Joseph Mede (see note 37 below) with approval and discussed the fall of the monarchies (the ten horns of the Beast [p. 51]), telling the members of the Commons 'you are one of these ten kingdoms' (p. 56). The sermon was delivered on 25 February 1645, when the debate between Lords and Commons over the creation of the New Model Army was at its height.

36. *Puritans and Regicide*, op. cit. See especially chapters 2 and 3.

37. See, for example, Joseph Mede's *The Key of the Revelation, Searched and demonstrated out of the Naturall and Proper Characters of the Visions . . .* (London, Stephens, 1650 ed.), which defined the essence of the millennium: '*Saints* with [Christ] to judge the earth; Antichrist to be abolished' (p. 125).

38. John Archer, *Personal Reign of Christ upon the Earth* (1642), quoted in Henning Mayfield, *Puritans and Regicide*, op. cit., p. 62.

39. John Milton, *Of Reformation* (1641), in Don M. Wolfe (ed.), *The Complete Prose Works of John Milton* ('*Complete Prose of John Milton*') (New Haven: Yale University Press, 1953–82), vol. I, p. 616.

40. Ibid., p. 852.

41. John Goodwin, *Anti-Cavalierisme* (1642), quoted in Henning Mayfield, *Puritans and Regicide*, op. cit., p. 69.

42. Lt-Col. William Goffe at the Putney Debates: Woodhouse, *PL*, p. 40. Goffe was one of the commissioners of the High Court of Justice appointed to try the King and was the thirteenth signatory to the death warrant.

43. John Owen, *Ebenezer: A Memorial of the Deliverance of Essex County and Committee*, dedicated to Fairfax and preached before the Army at a thanksgiving on the fall of Colchester in 1648, in Willliam H. Goold (ed.), *The Works of John Owen DD* (Edinburgh: Clark, 1862), vol. VIII, pp. 114–15.

44. Wolfe (ed.), *Complete Prose of John Milton*, op. cit., vol. III, p. 598.

45. *A Declaration of the English Army Touching the Justness and Necessity of their Proceedings* (London 1650), in Woodhouse, *PL*, pp. 474–8.

46. A Statement by the London Provincial Synod of Presbyterians, meeting at Sion College. Quoted in Henning Mayfield, *Puritans and Regicide*, op. cit., p. 135. A vigorous defence of Sion College and its political and religious integrity was made in *Sion-College Vindicated* (London, 1648). The anonymous author took pains to clear the Presbyterian ministers from any desire to offend the Army.

47. G. F. Trevallyn Jones, *Saw-Pit Wharton. The Political Career from 1640 to 1691 of Philip, fourth Lord Wharton* (Sydney: Sydney University Press, 1967), p. 134.

48. *Puritans and Regicide*, op. cit., p. 37.
49. *State Trials*, op. cit., IV, pp. 995–7. See C. V. Wedgwood, *The Trial of Charles I* (London, Collins, 1964), chapter VI.
50. Kenyon, *The Stuart Constitution*, op. cit., pp. 287–8.
51. Wolfe (ed.), *Complete Prose of John Milton*, op. cit., vol. III, p. 424. This was a private reflection recorded in Milton's 'Commonplace Book'.
52. *Eikonoklastes*, ibid., vol. III, p. 573.
53. John Goodwin, *The Obstructors of Justice, Or, a defense of the honourable sentence passed upon the late King . . .* (London, 1649), pp. 58–9, cited in Henning Mayfield, *Puritans and Regicide*, op. cit., p. 171.
54. Ibid.
55. Wolfe (ed.), *Complete Prose of John Milton*, op. cit., vol. III, p. 573.
56. William Prynne, cited in Henning Mayfield, *Puritans and Regicide*, op. cit., p. 133.
57. William Dell, *The City Ministers Unmasked* (London: 1649), ibid., p. 99.
58. *State Trials*, vol. IV, pp. 1033, 1035. This is the case Cooke prepared to answer a challenge as to the law upon which the King was charged, which was not used because the King refused to plead.
59. George Cokayne, *Flesh Expiring, and the Spirit Inspiring in the New Earth . . .* (29 November 1648), (p. 16) in *Fast Sermons*, op. cit., vol. 32, p. [32].
60. John Goodwin, *Right and Might Well Met* (London, 1648) (p. 13), quoted in Henning Mayfield, *Puritans and Regicide*, op. cit., p. 172.
61. *State Trials*, vol. IV, p. 1082.
62. Gardiner, *CW*, vol. IV, p. 301.
63. Whitelock, *Memorials*, op. cit., vol. II, p. 387.
64. *State Trials*, vol. IV, p. 1121.
65. Gardiner, *CW*, vol. IV, p. 316.
66. *State Trials*, vol. IV, pp. 1121, 1128.
67. *King Charles's Case*, reprinted in *State Trials*, vol. IV, pp. 1018, 1044.
68. *CJ*, vol. VI, p. 132.
69. Antonia Fraser, *Cromwell our Chief of Men* (London: Weidenfeld and Nicolson, 1973), p. 302.
70. Tanner, *English Constitutional Conflicts*, op. cit., p. 155.
71. Ronald Hutton, *The British Republic 1649–1660*, (London: Macmillan, 1990), pp. 21–2.
72. Gardiner, *CD*, pp. 389–90.
73. *CJ*, vol. VI, p. 298.
74. Tanner, *English Constitutional Conflicts*, op. cit., p. 164.
75. Gardiner, *CD*, p. 388.
76. J. W. Willis-Bund (ed.), *A Selection of Cases from the State Trials. Vol. II Part I Trials for Treason (1660–1678)* (Cambridge: Cambridge University Press, 1882), p. 133.
77. *Of Reformation*, in Wolfe (ed.), *Complete Prose of John Milton*, op. cit., vol. I, p. 616.

FURTHER READING

Introduction

The causes of the English Civil War remain matters of contention. The following books provide a good introduction to the issues and the divergent views of historians:

1. Conrad Russell, *The Causes of the English Civil War. The Ford Lectures Delivered in the University of Oxford 1987–1988* (Oxford: Clarendon Press, 1991 reprint).

2. Ann Hughes, *The Causes of the English Civil War* (London: Macmillan, 1991 reprint). See pp. 19–29 for her critical commentary on Conrad Russell's assessment of the pre-war problems of the monarchy.

3. Conrad Russell, *The Fall of the British Monarchies 1637–1642* (Oxford: Clarendon Press, 1991). See especially chapter 6, 'The Projected Settlement of 1641'; chapter 10, 'The Origins of the Irish Rebellion'; and chapter 11, 'The Grand Remonstrance and the Five Members'.

4. Conrad Russell (ed.), *The Origins of the English Civil War* (London: Macmillan, 1973). These essays, especially Conrad Russell's own, have been criticized for over-emphasizing the 'inevitability' of the war (see, for example, *Times Literary Supplement*, 10 August 1973).

5. Kevin Sharpe, *Politics and Ideas in Early Stuart England. Essays and Studies* (London: Pinters, 1989). His Chapter, 'The Personal Rule of Charles I', questions the 'eleven years' tyranny' view of the personal rule, claiming that Parliament in 1629 was 'an event, not an institution'. He suggests that the personal rule was a time of co-operation between the Monarchy and local government and takes a defensive view of the levy of 'ship money'.

6. Brian Manning, *The English People and the English Revolution* (Harmondsworth: Penguin Books, 1978). This book focuses on the economic causes of the war, its class basis, and the attempt by 'the middle sort of people' to achieve a social revolution.

7. Brian Manning, *Aristocrats, Plebeians and Revolution in England 1640–1660* (London: Pluto Press, 1996). Follows a similar approach to the above, but is structured more chronologically, commencing with an analysis of English society on the eve of the revolution.

Specifically on the 'personal rule':
8. Kevin Sharpe, *The Personal Rule of Charles I* (New Haven: Yale University Press, 1992).
9. Esther S. Cope, *Politics Without Parliaments 1629–1640* (London: Allen & Unwin, 1987).
10. An earlier account, accepting the 'eleven years' tyranny' view of the personal rule, is to be found in J. R. Tanner, *English Constitutional Conflicts of the Seventeenth Century 1603–1689* (Cambridge: Cambridge University Press, 1952), chapter V, 'The Eleven Years of Non-Parliamentary Government'.

Specifically on the Scottish Rebellion:
11. Mark Charles Fissel, *The Bishops Wars. Charles I's campaigns against Scotland, 1637–1640* (Cambridge: Cambridge University Press, 1994).
12. Martyn Bennett, *The Civil Wars in Britain and Ireland, 1638–1651* (Oxford: Blackwell, 1997), chapter 2.

For a biographically oriented account of Charles's 'personal rule', his views on kingship and the role of Parliament, and his reaction to particular events:
13. Charles Carlton, *Charles I. The Personal Monarch*, 2nd ed. (London: Routledge, 1995).

On the first histories of the period, historical 'propaganda' and the 'great divide' in historiographical approaches to the Civil War and revolution:
14. D. E. Kennedy (ed.), *Authorized Pasts. Essays in Official History* (Melbourne: University of Melbourne, 1995), Part 1, 'History and Authority in Early Modern England: Official History and the Great Divide'.

I The War for King and Parliament, 1642–6

On the lead-up to the outbreak of war:
15. Anthony Fletcher, *The Outbreak of the English Civil War* (London: Edward Arnold, 1981). Includes a detailed discussion of political developments, November 1640–October 1642.
16. Anthony Fletcher, 'The Coming of War', in John Morrill (ed.), *Reactions to the English Civil War* (London: Macmillan, 1982).
17. Brian Manning, 'The Outbreak of the English Civil War' and D. H. Pennington, 'The Rebels of 1642' in R. H. Parry (ed.), *The English Civil War and after, 1642–1658* (London: Macmillan, 1970).

On the Royalist war effort:
18. Ronald Hutton, *The Royalist War Effort, 1642–46* (London: Macmillan, 1983).
19. Ronald Hutton, 'The Royalist War Effort', in John Morrill (ed.), *Reactions to the English Civil War* (London: Macmillan, 1982).
20. Peter Young and Wilfrid Emberton, *The Cavalier Army. Its Organisation and Everyday Life* (London: George Allen & Unwin, 1974).

On political alignments:
21. Martyn Bennett, 'The Agony of Choosing Sides', in his *The Civil*

Wars in Britain and Ireland, 1638–1651 (Oxford: Blackwell, 1997), pp. 113–41.

22. Roger Howell, 'Neutralism, Conservatism and Political Alignment in the English Revolution: the case of the Towns, 1642–9', in John Morrill (ed.), *Reactions to the English Civil War, 1642–1649* (London, Macmillan, 1982).

23. Brian Manning, *The English People and the English Revolution* (Harmondsworth: Penguin Books, 1978), pp. 215–83. The section 'Resistance of the Industrial Districts' (pp. 215–35) gives a fascinating account of parliamentarian support in the large cities, especially London, and the importance of the London Trained Bands.

24. David Underdown, 'The Civil War and the People' and 'The Distribution of Allegiance', in his *Revel, Riot & Rebellion* (Oxford: Oxford University Press, 1985), pp. 162–207.

On the Civil War experience:

25. Charles Carlton, *Going to the Wars. The Experience of the British Civil Wars, 1638–1651* (London: Routledge, 1992).

26. Martyn Bennett, *The Civil Wars in Britain and Ireland, 1683–1651* (Oxford: Blackwell, 1997), Part II.

On military operations and major battles:

27. Peter Young and Richard Holmes, *The English Civil War. A Military History of the Three Civil Wars, 1642–1651* (London: Eyre Methuen, 1974).

28. Austin Woolrych, *Battles of the English Civil War. Marston Moor, Naseby, Preston* (London: Batsford, 1961).

29. Philip J. Haythornthwaite, *The English Civil War 1642–1651*, 2nd ed. (London, Guild Publishing, 1983), chapters 4–6.

30. Martyn Bennett, *Traveller's Guide to the Battlefields of the English Civil War* (Exeter: Webb & Bower, 1990).

31. David Smurthwaite, *The Ordinance Survey Complete Guide to the Battlefields of Britain* (Exeter: Webb & Bower, 1984), pp. 131–77.

On the New Model Army:

32. Mark A. Kishlansky, *The Rise of the New Model Army* (Chicago: University of Chicago Press, 1979).

33. Ian Gentles, *The New Model Army in England, Ireland and Scotland, 1645–1653* (Oxford: Blackwell, 1994).

On the impact of the Civil War:

34. Donald Pennington, 'The War and the People', in John Morrill (ed.), *Reactions to the English Civil War, 1642–1649* (London, Macmillan, 1982), pp. 115–35.

35. Charles Carlton, 'The Impact of the Fighting' and David L. Smith, 'The Impact on Government', in John Morrill (ed.), *The Impact of the English Civil War* (London: Collins & Brown, 1991).

36. David Underdown, 'The Civil War and the People', in his *Revel, Riot & Rebellion* (Oxford: Oxford University Press, 1985), pp. 146–82, especially pp. 148–62.

Some useful studies of the Civil War in particular counties and regions are:

37. R. Warmington, *Civil War, Interregnum and Restoration in Gloucestershire 1640–1672* (Woodbridge, Suffolk: The Boydell Press, 1997).

38. Malcolm Atkin and Wayne Laughlin, *Gloucester and the Civil War. A City under Siege* (Stroud: Alan Sutton, 1992).

39. Philip Tennant, *Edgehill and Beyond. The People's War in the South Midlands 1642–1645* (Stroud: Alan Sutton, 1992).

40. Roy Sherwood, *The Civil War in the Midlands 1642–1651* (Stroud: Alan Sutton, 1992).

41. David Underdown, *Somerset in the Civil War and Interregnum* (Newton Abbot: David & Charles, 1973).

42. Eugene A. Andriette, *Devon and Exeter in the Civil War* (Newton Abbot: David & Charles, 1971).

43. Roger Howell, *Newcastle upon Tyne and the Puritan Revolution. A Study of the Civil War in North England* (Oxford: Clarendon Press, 1967).

44. Arthur Leonard Leach, *The History of the Civil War (1642–1649) in Pembrokeshire and on its Borders* (London: Witherby, 1937).

45. Charles Thomas-Stanford, *Sussex in the Great Civil War and the Interregnum, 1642–1660* (London: Chiswick Press, 1910).

On the generals:

46. F. T. R. Edgar, *Sir Ralph Hopton. The King's Man in the West (1642–1652). A Study in Character and Command* (Oxford: Clarendon Press: 1968).

47. John Adair, *Roundhead General. A Military Biography of Sir William Waller* (London: Macdonald, 1969).

48. John Wilson, *Fairfax. A Life of Thomas, Lord Fairfax, Captain-General of all the Parliament's forces in the English Civil War, Creator & Commander of the New Model Army* (London: John Murray, 1985).

49. Maurice Ashley, *The Greatness of Oliver Cromwell* (London: Hodder and Stoughton, 1957), chapters 7, 8 and 10.

50. Austin Woolrych, 'Cromwell as a Soldier', in John Morrill (ed.), *Oliver Cromwell and the English Revolution* (London: Longman, 1990), pp. 93–118.

On the Irish rebellion and the use of Irish troops in England:

51. John Reeve, 'Secret alliance and Protestant agitation in two kingdoms: the early Caroline background to the Irish Rebellion of 1641', in Ian Gentles, John Morrill and Blair Worden, *Soldiers, Writers and Statesmen of the English Revolution* (Cambridge: Cambridge University Press, 1998), pp. 19–35.

52. Martyn Bennett, 'Rebellion in Ireland', in his *The Civil Wars in Britain and Ireland 1638–1651*, (Oxford: Blackwell, 1997), pp. 82–109.

53. Joyce L. Malcolm, 'All the King's Men: the impact of the Crown's Irish soldiers on the English civil war', *Irish Historical Studies*, XXI (1979).

A recent general study:

54. John Kenyon and Jane Ohlmeyer, *The Civil Wars. A Military History of England, Scotland and Ireland 1638–1660* (Oxford: Oxford University Press, 1998). Part I, 'Civil Wars in the Stuart Kingdom', has chapters on Scotland, Ireland and England. Chapter 5 discusses the war at sea: see the useful map on p. 163.

2   Interregnum, 1646–7

Two general and contrasting accounts of the period following the First Civil War are:

55.   Derek Hirst, 'Reaction and Revolution 1646–1649' in his book *Authority and Conflict. England 1603–1658* (London: Edward Arnold, 1986), pp. 265–87.
56.   Mark Kishlansky, 'Civil War and Revolution 1645–1649' in his book *A Monarchy Transformed. Britain 1603–1714* (London: Allan Lane, 1996), chapter 7.

On the peace negotiations:
57.   Robert Ashton, 'The Failure of Settlement, June 1646–February 1648', in his book *Counter-Revolution. The Second Civil War and its Origins, 1646–8*, (New Haven: Yale University Press, 1994), especially pp. 7–17.
58.   David Smith, 'The Impact on Government' in John Morrill (ed.), *The Impact of the English Civil War* (London: Collins & Brown, 1991), pp. 32–49, especially pp. 40–4 dealing with the Newcastle Propositions.

On Army radicalism, dissension and the role of the Agitators:
59.   Mark Kishlansky, 'Ideology and Politics in the Parliamentary Armies 1645–9', in John Morrill (ed.), *Reactions to the English Civil War 1642–1649* (London: Macmillan, 1982), pp. 163–83. This article gives little weight to the role of religious ideology.
60.   Ian Gentles, *The New Model Army in England, Ireland and Scotland, 1645–1653* (Oxford: Blackwell, 1992), pp. 150–89.

On Puritan ideology and conflict between Presbyterians and Independents:
61.   J. T. Cliffe, *Puritans in Conflict. The Puritan Gentry During and After the Civil Wars* (London: Routledge, 1988). See especially chapters 8–13, which examine the development of divisions between Presbyterians and Independents.
62.   George Yule, *Puritans in Politics. The Religious Legislation of the Long Parliament 1640–1647* (Appleford: Sutton Courtenay Press, 1981).
63.   David Underdown, 'Conflict and Revolution, 1646–9' in his *Somerset in the Civil War and Interregnum* (Newton Abbot: David & Charles, 1973), pp. 138–54. A good county-based account of the conflict between Presbyterians and Independents.

On the conflict between the Army and the City of London and Parliament:
64.   Stephen Porter (ed.), *London and the Civil War* (London: Macmillan, 1996).
65.   Keith Lindley, *Popular Politics and Religion in Civil War London* (Aldershot, Hants: Scolar Press, 1997), especially chapter 7 'War and Peace' and chapter 8 'Presbyterians and Independents'.
66.   Brian Manning, 'The Revolt of the New Model Army, 1647', in his *Aristocrats, Plebeians and Revolution in England 1640–1660* (London: Pluto Press, 1996), pp. 89–97.
67.   Ian Gentles, *The New Model Army in England, Ireland and Scotland, 1645–1653* (Oxford: Blackwell, 1992), pp. 150–202.
68.   Valerie Pearl, 'London's Counter-Revolution', in G. E. Aylmer (ed.), *The Interregnum: the Quest for Settlement 1646–1660* (London: Macmillan, 1972), pp. 29–56.

69.   Brian Manning, 'Counter-Revolution in London', in his *Aristocrats, Plebeians and Revolution in England 1640–1660* (London, Pluto Press, 1996), pp. 97–102.

3   The Army in Debate

See footnote 1 to chapter 3 for the MSS source of the Debates and details of C.H. Firth's printed version of 1891.

The main printed text used in this chapter is A. S. P. Woodhouse, *Puritanism and Liberty. Being the Army Debates (1647–9) from the Clarke Manuscripts with Supplementary Documents* (London: J. M. Dent, 2nd ed. 1974).

Selections from the Debates are printed in:

(a)   Christopher Hill and Edmond Dell, *The Good Old Cause. The English Revolution of 1640–1660: its Causes, Course and Consequences* (London: Laurence and Wishart, 1949), Part Ten, pp. 352–8.

(b)   Charles Blitzer (ed.), *The Commonwealth of England. Documents of the English Civil Wars, the Commonwealth and Protectorate, 1641–1660* (New York: Capricorn Books, 1963), pp. 44–79.

(c)   G. E. Aylmer (ed.), *The Levellers in the English Revolution* (London: Thames and Hudson, 1975), pp. 97–130.

Modern commentaries on the Debates:

70.   Austin Woolrych, *Soldiers and Statesmen. The General Council of the Army and its Debates, 1647–1648* (Oxford: Clarendon Press, 1987), especially chapters VIII–X.

71.   Ian Gentles, *The New Model Army in England, Ireland and Scotland, 1645–1653* (Oxford: Blackwell, 1992), pp. 202–19.

72.   Mark A. Kishlansky, 'Consensus Politics and the Structure of Debate at Putney', *Journal of British Studies*, 20 (Spring 1981), pp. 50–69.

On the ambiguities of Cromwell's position as General and MP:

73.   J. S. A. Adamson, 'Oliver Cromwell and the Long Parliament', in John Morrill (ed.), *Oliver Cromwell and the English Revolution* (London: Longman, 1990), pp. 49–92.

On the 'Norman Yoke':

74.   Christopher Hill, 'The Norman Yoke', in his *Puritanism and Revolution. Studies in Interpretation of the English Revolution of the 17th Century* (London: Secker & Warburg, 1958), pp. 50–122.

On the Levellers:

75.   H. N. Brailsford (ed. Christopher Hill), *The Levellers and the English Revolution* (Stanford: Stanford University Press, 1951).

76.   Howard Shaw, *The Levellers* (London: Longman, 1968), especially chapters 4 and 5.

77.   Brian Manning, 'The Levellers', in E. W. Ives (ed.), *The English Revolution 1600–1660* (London: Edward Arnold, 1968), pp. 144–57.

78.   Keith Thomas, 'The Levellers and the Franchise', in G. E. Aylmer (ed.), *The Interregnum: The Quest for Settlement 1646–1660* (London: Macmillan, 1972), pp. 57–78.

79. G. E. Aylmer (ed.), *The Levellers and the English Revolution* (London: Thames and Hudson, 1975).
80. Mark Kishlansky, 'The Army and the Levellers: The Roads to Putney', *Historical Journal,* xxii (1979), pp. 795–824.

4 The Second Civil War

Some useful general studies of the Second Civil War period are:
81. Robert Ashton, *Counter-Revolution. The Second Civil War and its Origins, 1646–8* (New Haven: Yale University Press, 1994), especially chapter XII, 'The Second Civil War in Perspective', pp. 423–75.
82. Ian Gentles, *The New Model Army in England, Ireland and Scotland, 1645–1653* (Oxford: Blackwell, 1992), chapter 8, 'The Second Civil War', pp. 235–65.
83. Martyn Bennett, *The Civil Wars in Britain and Ireland, 1638–1651* (Oxford: Blackwell, 1997), chapter 11, 'Engagement to Execution', pp. 284–314.
84. Maurice Ashley, *The English Civil War. A Concise History* (London: Thames and Hudson, 1980), chapter 7, 'The Second Civil War, 1648', pp. 137–60.
85. Charles Carlton, *Going to the Wars. The Experience of the British Civil Wars, 1638–1651* (London: Routledge, 1994), chapter 13, 'Then we Started All Over Again', pp. 310–38.

Military histories:
86. Peter Young, *An Illustrated History of the Great Civil War* (Bucks: Spurbooks Ltd., undated), chapter 8, 'The Second Civil War', pp. 119–32.
87. Austin Woolrych, *Battles of the English Civil War. Marston Moor, Naseby, Preston* (London, Batsford, 1961), chapter 8, 'Preston', pp. 152–82.
88. Peter Young and Richard Holmes, *The English Civil War. A Military History of the Three Civil Wars, 1642–1651* (London: Eyre Methuen, 1974), Part III, pp. 269–92.
89. Philip J. Haythornthwaite, *The English Civil War 1642–1651. An Illustrated Military History* (London: Guild Publishing, 1985), chapter 8, 'The Second Civil War', pp. 117–23.

Battlefield guides:
90. David Smurthwaite, *The Ordinance Survey Complete Guide to the Battlefields of Britain* (Exeter: Webb & Bower, 1984), pp. 170–1.
91. Martyn Bennett, *Travellers' Guide to the Battlefields of the English Civil War* (Exeter: Webb & Bower, 1990), pp. 172–81.

On the naval revolt:
92. D. E. Kennedy, 'The English Naval Revolt of 1648', *The English Historical Review,* lxxvii (1962), pp. 247–56.
93. J. R. Powell, *The Navy in the English Civil War* (London: Archon Books, 1962), especially chapters X, XI and XII.
94. Bernard Capp, *Cromwell's Navy. The Fleet and the English Revolution 1648–1660* (Oxford: Clarendon Press, 1989) especially chapter 1 'The Revolt of 1648'.
95. Bernard Capp, 'Naval Operations', in John Kenyon and Jane Ohlmeyer

(eds), *The Civil Wars. A Military History of England, Scotland and Ireland 1630–1660* (Oxford: Oxford University Press, 1998), especially pp. 177–87.

On Pride's Purge and the Rump Parliament:
96. Blair Worden, *The Rump Parliament 1648–1653* (Cambridge: Cambridge University Press, 1974), especially Introduction and Part One.
97. D. E. Underdown, *Pride's Purge. Politics in the Puritan Revolution* (Oxford: Oxford University Press, 1971).

5 Regicide and Republic, January–March 1649

The regicide:
98. Noel Henning Mayfield, *Puritans and Regicide. Presbyterian–Independent differences over the Trial and Execution of Charles (I) Stuart* (New York: University Press of America, 1988).
99. C. V. Wedgwood, *The Trial of Charles I* (London: Collins, 1964).
100. Jane Roberts, *The King's Head. Charles I: King and Martyr* (London: Royal Collection Enterprises, 1999). A selection of portraits of Charles to mark the 350th anniversary of his execution and a good compendium of the visual iconography of the King's life and death.

Charles as man of blood:
101. Patricia Crawford, 'Charles Stuart, That Man of Blood', *Journal of British Studies*, xvi (1977).
102. Stephen Baskerville, *Not Peace But a Sword. The political theology of the English revolution* (London, Routledge, 1993), chapter 3, especially pp. 126–30.

Revolutionary Puritanism, millenarianism and the reign of the saints:
103. Noel Henning Mayfield, *Puritans and Regicide. Presbyterian–Independent differences over the Trial and Execution of Charles (I) Stuart* (New York: University Press of America, 1988).
104. Stephen Baskerville, *Not Peace But A Sword. The political theology of the English revolution* (London: Routledge, 1993).
105. Murray Tolmie, *The Triumph of the Saints. The separate churches of London 1616–49* (Cambridge: Cambridge University Press, 1977), section 8.
106. Christopher Hill, *Milton and the English Revolution* (London: Faber and Faber, 1977), especially Part III, Milton and the Commonwealth.
107. Michael Fixler, *Milton and the Kingdoms of God* (London: Faber and Faber, 1964), especially chapter IV, 'The Sword of Justice'.
108. Michael Walzer, *The Revolution of the Saints. A Study in the Origins of Radical politics* (London: Weidenfeld and Nicolson, 1966).

The Republic:
109. Brian Manning, 'Displacement of the Ruling Class from Political Power' and 'Success and Failure of the Left' in *Aristocrats, Plebeians and Revolution in England 1640–1660* (London: Pluto Press, 1996), pp. 111–18.
110. Brian Manning, *1649: The Crisis of the English Revolution* (London: Bookmarks, 1992).

111. David Underdown, *Revel, Riot & Rebellion* (Oxford: Oxford University Press, 1985), chapters 8 and 9.

112. Robert Ashton, 'From Cavalier to Roundhead Tyranny, 1642–9', in John Morrill (ed.), *Reactions to the English Civil War 1642–1649* (London: Macmillan, 1982), pp. 185–208.

113. J. S. A. Adamson, 'Oliver Cromwell and the Long Parliament', Part VI, in John Morrill (ed.), *Oliver Cromwell and the English Revolution* (London: Longman, 1990), pp. 81–92, explores the tensions in Cromwell's attitudes to parliamentary democracy.

114. Robert S. Paul, 'The Beginnings of the Commonwealth: military and political problems' in *The Lord Protector. Religion and Politics in the Life of Oliver Cromwell* (London: Lutterworth Press, 1955), pp. 196–206.

115. Ronald Hutton, *The British Republic 1649–1660* (London: Macmillan, 1990), Part 1.

The defeat of the Levellers:

116. Howard Shaw, *The Levellers* (London: Longman, 1968), chapter 5 'Death of the Party' and chapter 6 'Why did the Levellers fail?'

117. Henry Holorenshaw, *The Levellers and the English Revolution* (London: Victor Gollancz, 1939), chapters V and VI.

The Revolution in perspective:

118. Brian Manning, *Aristocrats, Plebeians and Revolution in England 1640–1660* (London: Pluto Press, 1996), chapter 8, 'Conclusion: the Unfinished Revolution'.

119. R. C. Richardson, *The Debate on the English Revolution* (Manchester: Manchester University Press, 3rd ed., 1998), especially chapters 1, 2 and 12.

120. Geoff Eley and William Hunt, *Reviving the English Revolution. Reflections and Elaborations on the Work of Christopher Hill* (London: Verso, 1988), Part IV, 'Christopher Hill and the Future of the English Revolution'.

121. Roger Hainsworth, *The Swordsmen in Power. War and Politics under the English Republic 1649–1660* (Stroud: Sutton Publishing, 1997).

122. Sean Kelsey, *Inventing a Republic. The Political Culture of the English Commonwealth 1649–1653* (Manchester: Manchester University Press, 1997).

Dictionary of the Period

Readers are also referred to Ronald H. Fritze and William B. Robison (eds), *Historical Dictionary of Stuart England 1603–1689* (Westport, Conn.: Greenwood Press, 1996). Events and documents are listed alphabetically for ease of reference and the entries are useful and often quite detailed.

INDEX